The World News Prism

D0873655

The World News Prism

Digital, Social and Interactive

Ninth Edition

William A. Hachten
and James F. Scotton

WILEY Blackwell

This ninth edition first published 2016
© 2016 John Wiley & Sons, Inc

Edition History: Iowa State University Press (1e, 1981; 2e, 1987; 3e, 1992; 4e, 1996; 5e, 1999; 6e, 2002); Blackwell Publishing Ltd. (7e, 2007); John Wiley & Sons, Ltd (8e, 2012)

Registered Office
John Wiley & Sons Ltd, The Atrium, Southern Gate, Chichester, West Sussex, PO19 8SQ, UK

Editorial Offices
350 Main Street, Malden, MA 02148-5020, USA
9600 Garsington Road, Oxford, OX4 2DQ, UK
The Atrium, Southern Gate, Chichester, West Sussex, PO19 8SQ, UK

For details of our global editorial offices, for customer services, and for information about how to apply for permission to reuse the copyright material in this book please see our website at www.wiley.com/wiley-blackwell.

The right of William A. Hachten, James F. Scotton to be identified as the authors of this work has been asserted in accordance with the UK Copyright, Designs and Patents Act 1988.

All rights reserved. No part of this publication may be reproduced, stored in a retrieval system, or transmitted, in any form or by any means, electronic, mechanical, photocopying, recording or otherwise, except as permitted by the UK Copyright, Designs and Patents Act 1988, without the prior permission of the publisher.

Wiley also publishes its books in a variety of electronic formats. Some content that appears in print may not be available in electronic books.

Designations used by companies to distinguish their products are often claimed as trademarks. All brand names and product names used in this book are trade names, service marks, trademarks or registered trademarks of their respective owners. The publisher is not associated with any product or vendor mentioned in this book.

Limit of Liability/Disclaimer of Warranty: While the publisher and authors have used their best efforts in preparing this book, they make no representations or warranties with respect to the accuracy or completeness of the contents of this book and specifically disclaim any implied warranties of merchantability or fitness for a particular purpose. It is sold on the understanding that the publisher is not engaged in rendering professional services and neither the publisher nor the author shall be liable for damages arising herefrom. If professional advice or other expert assistance is required, the services of a competent professional should be sought.

Library of Congress Cataloging-in-Publication Data

Hachten, William A.
   The world news prism : digital, social and interactive / William A. Hachten, James F. Scotton. – Ninth edition.
      pages cm
   Summary: "Fully revised new edition of a well-respected treatise on the changing role of transnational news media in the 21st-century"– Provided by publisher.
   Includes bibliographical references and index.
   ISBN 978-1-118-80904-4 (paperback)
   1. Foreign news.   2. Communication, International.   3. Digital media.   4. Mass media and globalization.   I. Scotton, James Francis, 1932–   II. Title.
   PN4784.F6H3 2015
   070.4'332–dc23

                                                                                        2015015812

A catalogue record for this book is available from the British Library.

Cover image: Original reference map taken from NASA © Vertigo3d / iStockphoto

Set in 10.5/13pt Minion by Aptara Inc., New Delhi, India

1   2016

To the many journalists around the world who have been killed, kidnapped, or jailed for reporting the news

Contents

Notes on Contributors

Rasha Abdulla is Associate Professor and former Chair of the Department of Journalism and Mass Communication at The American University in Cairo (AUC). She has a Ph.D. in Communication from the University of Miami in Coral Gables, Florida. She is the recipient of the AUC Excellence in Research Award for her research on social media and political activism leading to and during Egypt's revolution. She is the author of three books and numerous articles and book chapters. She tweets regularly at @RashaAbdulla.

Natalia Bubnova is an Associate at the Institute of World Economy and International Relations at the Russian Academy of Sciences in Moscow. She was formerly Deputy Director of the Carnegie Moscow Center and Associate Director of the Center for International Studies at Marquette University in Milwaukee, Wisconsin.

William A. Hachten is Professor Emeritus of Journalism and Mass Communication at the University of Wisconsin-Madison, where he taught for thirty years. His publications include *The Troubles of Journalism*, 3rd edition (2005), *The Growth of Media in the Third World* (1993), and *The Press and Apartheid* (with C. A. Giffard, 1984).

Heloiza Golbspan Herscovitz is Associate Professor at the Journalism and Mass Communication Department of California State University, Long Beach, where she teaches Global News Media and other courses. She is a veteran journalist with extensive experience as a reporter and editor in Brazil and has transnational academic experience.

Sandhya Rao is Professor of Journalism and Mass Communication and Honorary Professor of International Studies at Texas State University. She taught in India as a Fulbright Scholar and has edited *Cyberpath to*

Development in Asia – Issues and Challenges and *Critical Issues in Communication: Looking for Answers.*

James. F. Scotton is Associate Professor of Journalism at Marquette University, Milwaukee. He has taught in Lebanon, China, Egypt, Uganda, Kenya, and Nigeria. He has worked as a correspondent in Washington DC, as a reporter and editor with the Associated Press, and with newspapers in California, Wisconsin, North Carolina, and China.

Together James Scotton and William Hachten are the authors of *New Media for a New China* (Wiley-Blackwell, 2010).

Preface to the Ninth Edition

Why another edition of *The World News Prism*? The answer is pretty much the same as before. The phenomenon of international news continues to evolve and change in many ways – mostly because of the ongoing digital revolution in communication media.

The Internet, which has spawned the digital age, was not predicted. Just over twenty-five years ago the net caught the world by surprise and further surprises keep tumbling out. Now, in the second decade of the twenty-first century, the number of earthlings connected to the Internet has increased from 350 million to more than 2 billion worldwide. During this same decade, the number of mobile phone users rose from 750 million to well over 5 billion in the world. (It is now estimated at about 6 billion.)

Eric Schmidt and Jared Cohen, both with Google, have predicted that by 2025 the majority of the world's population will have gone from virtually no access to information to unfiltered access to almost all the information in the world. If the current pace of growth is maintained, they say, most of the nearly 8 billion people on earth will be online by 2025.

In this ninth edition we will describe and analyze how the ways of gathering and disseminating global news and information have been expanded (and complicated) by the increasing role of the so-called social media. Twitter, Facebook and other platforms that provide photos, videos and other "posts" will be looked at, and also the "blogosphere" that supports and enhances the flow of news.

This ninth edition includes new or revised chapters on media systems in regions outside the orbits of the United States and western Europe. We have recruited media specialists for appraisal of media in Brazil, India, Russia and the Middle East. The world's media look different from Rio de Janeiro, New Delhi, Moscow and Cairo than they do from New York or London. But no matter where people live in the world, most "news" or public information is local. People care about what happens in their community, their country, their part of the world. Yet in today's interconnected and globalized world people everywhere easily learn about and are affected by news – about civil wars, civil strife, terrorist attacks, economic upheavals and great catastrophes, even tsunamis and epidemics, that occur far from home. More than ever before in history, more people are both informed and have opinions – whether about globalization, terrorist warfare, nuclear proliferation or the ominous threat of climate change. The onrush of digital communication – the Internet, social media, cellphones, computers – has made this possible.

In early 2011 international news media made a dramatic comeback fueled by a series of unexpected political revolutions – first in Tunisia and then in Egypt, where President Hosni Mubarak was ousted. The revolutionary upheavals spread rapidly throughout the Arab world to Bahrain, Libya, Yemen, Jordan, Syria and elsewhere during this "Arab Spring." The streets of long-standing authoritarian Arab capitals were filled with angry, mostly young, protestors demanding freedom, democracy, human rights and jobs. The new communication media had clearly facilitated the uprisings. Protestors were mobilized and kept informed by cellphones and the social media of Facebook and Twitter. And news of these startling events was transmitted by Al Jazeera, the satellite TV channel that had broken the Middle East government news monopolies. Al Jazeera also provided news about the deadly and protracted civil war in Syria, where over 200,000 civilians, including journalists, have been killed. But much of the news of that conflict came from Syrians themselves with small communication devices in their hands.

Unrest, protests and brutal repressions continued, including warfare with Libya against NATO forces and rebels. The reporting of these horrific events and the world's response were reminders of how much we have become a global society. Not just in trade and economic affairs but in social and political ways, we are increasingly coming together. But the acts of terrorism also were grim reminders that deep divisions between rich and poor countries remain. Democratic societies with their open borders and individual freedoms were vulnerable to stealth attacks. Radical terrorism was termed the dark underside of globalization.

As the first decade of the twenty-first century ended, the world was still an unstable and dangerous place. War receded in Afghanistan, but terrorism threats emerged in the failing states of Mali, Somalia and Yemen. During the summer of 2014 global journalism was roiled by several regional wars and crises:

- The invasion of Ukraine by Russia as President Putin challenged America and the NATO nations and brought back memories of the Cold War.
- In the Holy Land, Hamas rockets targeted Israel, which retaliated with aerial bombings that killed hundreds in Gaza.
- Several jihadist militias clashed in the anarchy of Libya.
- In the border region of Iraq and Syria the Islamic State or ISIS launched a series of brutal terror attacks against various religious and ethnic populations. The US response was to declare war on ISIS and attempt to rally allies.
- Finally, in West Africa a deadly Ebola epidemic spread rapidly in Liberia, Guinea and Sierra Leone, killing hundreds and threatening thousands more.

Yet another less apparent series of technological changes in communication has both facilitated and disrupted the traditional news media and the many publics or audiences for serious news and commentary throughout the world. The digital media – the Internet, personal computers, email, cellphones, bloggers and social websites such as Twitter and Facebook – have all encroached on or modified the journalism long practiced by the traditional newspapers, magazines, news agencies and TV and radio organizations that historically reported what was happening in the world. The audiences for traditional media have diminished but for digital media they have greatly expanded.

In this revised edition we will show how the news media have responded to great crises as well as to technological changes. Only history will determine how significant were the events before 2014. But there is no doubt that 1989 was important. That year the world watched in dazzled amazement as communist regimes were toppled in Poland, East Germany, Hungary, Czechoslovakia, Bulgaria and Romania. Two years later the Soviet Union itself, after a failed right-wing coup, went through a convulsive revolution of its own, outlawing the Communist Party and its media and breaking up the Soviet Union itself. These historic events also heralded the end of the Cold War and of the "information wars" that had enlivened international communication for nearly fifty years. However, new propaganda wars, now focused on terrorism and the relations of Muslim nations with the West, have gained momentum in recent years.

The post-Cold War world of the 1990s proved to be a harsh and forbidding place. The forces of intense nationalism and unleashed ethnic animosities led to civil wars, genocide, terrorism, political instability and economic and social chaos starkly evident in the prolonged and agonizing strife engaging the Bosnian and Kosovo Muslims, Croatians and Serbs of the former Yugoslavia. Elsewhere, various experiments in democracy and market economies sputtered and failed.

The decade of the 1990s was one of great global economic expansion. In China and throughout East and South Asia economies grew at spectacular rates and world trade expanded in a new phenomenon known as "globalization." Globalization is an inexact expression for a wide array of worldwide changes in politics, business and trade, lifestyles and culture, and above all communication. International communication in general has been affected by world events as it has continued to expand its reach. International broadcasting has become less propagandistic and more informative and entertainment-minded. New independent and outspoken publications and broadcast outlets have sprouted like mushrooms in spring, Communication satellites transmitting news and pop culture have proliferated and media audiences have greatly expanded, especially in China and India. In most countries the public has enjoyed greater access to news.

Personalized digital media have proved to be a many-headed hydra that has greatly increased the ability of people everywhere to receive news and commentary about the day's events AND to then communicate it onward. But the old model of global communication based on a few large news organizations has been undermined. This downsizing of print and broadcast media has great significance for global news communication. But the future is unclear – just as it was when Gutenberg's printing press shook up the Middle Ages.

The ongoing rush of technological innovations in foreign reporting has accelerated. Direct broadcasting from portable transmitters to satellites and then back to dish antennas – bypassing complicated and expensive ground installations – has become commonplace. Small, portable earth terminals, for example, have enabled broadcast journalists reporting remote events to send their video stories directly to satellites and thus to the whole world. With a cellphone or videophone, a news event in almost any faraway area can instantly become a global news event. In just a few years the Internet has become a player of great and ominous potential in international communication for journalism and as a means of letting people share ideas freely on a global network. Bloggers and even hackers have joined the fray as controversial conveyers of news and comment that critique and challenge traditional news media.

In this age of information, communication systems are at the leading edge of social, economic and political change. With the unprecedented growth in global telecommunications, an informed public has developed a more immediate concern with both world news and the symbolic relationship between events and those who report them.

For this ninth edition the text has been thoroughly revised with new material added to every chapter. More attention has been given to significant media developments in developing nations, some of which have been producing many more media users who respond in different ways to the world news prism. Kappa Tau Alpha contributed support for Professor Scotton's Middle East research.

– W.A.H. and J.F.S.

Introduction:
Fall and Rise of the Media

As the twentieth century (and the old millennium) came to an end, we were reminded both of the changes as well as continuities that have marked journalism and international communications in our times. In 1900, all the elements were in place in Western nations – great metropolitan newspapers, rotary presses and linotypes, the typewriter, the telephone, the telegraph and the underseas cable, the Associated Press, Reuters, and other cooperative news gatherers – as building blocks for the changes to come. News was recognized as a valued and useful commodity in itself and as an essential means of comprehending and coping with a strange and distant world. At the same time, sensationalism and trivia had long been standard fare in the press and entertainment media.

But few would understand the importance of what was to come – the personal computer, the Internet, digital communication – that would lead to the rapid decline of print on paper. For well over a century, the press has reported news from abroad, but it has been only in the past three decades that we have seen how great events abroad vividly illustrate the digital age, that melding of technology and electronics, that planet Earth has entered. It is a new era of information whose potential we but dimly perceive; whose complicated gadgetry only few of us totally grasp; whose social, political, and economic consequences are accelerating change and cleavages among the nations of the world.

For the world we live in today is changing rapidly, in no small part because worldwide television, communication satellites, high-speed transmission of news and data, and other computer and electronic hardware and

The World News Prism: Digital, Social and Interactive, Ninth Edition.
William A. Hachten and James F. Scotton.
© 2016 John Wiley & Sons, Inc. Published 2016 by John Wiley & Sons, Inc.

software (including the Internet) have transformed the ways that nations and peoples communicate with one another. The fact that a news event can be transmitted almost instantaneously to newsrooms and onto television and computer screens (and now into cellphones) around the world can be as important as the event itself. Long-distance mass communication has become a rudimentary central nervous system for our fragile, shrinking, and increasingly interdependent, yet fractious, world.

Journalism has been undergoing rapid changes. In what journalist and biographer Walter Isaacson has called a "glorious disruption" the traditional journalism of print on paper is rapidly giving way to journalism by digital technology. As a result, newspapers, news services, broadcast stations and networks, and news and commentary magazines have been sustaining great losses in circulations, audiences, and advertising revenues. These financial setbacks make it difficult for traditional media to fully report global news and commentary. Basically, there is more information and news than ever before circulating the globe but there are fewer serious professional journalists reporting and verifying it. The Internet, with its proliferating blogs, emails, websites, etc., spews out vast amounts of information and data but much of it is unverified, inaccurate, biased, propagandistic, opinionated or just downright wrong.

People everywhere have more access to much more information than ever and also have an enhanced ability to communicate themselves through the Internet, cellphones, and other social media like Twitter, Flickr, YouTube, etc. But what the public is not getting is sufficient hard news that is verified, confirmed, and reliable.

The Western press, found mainly in North America and western Europe, is struggling to find a new business model that will enable the "old media" to survive economically. The Gutenberg model of printed words on paper (newspapers, magazines, journals, and books) still survives and even flourishes all over the world. Yet more and more the print-on-paper model is having an abrasive relationship with the new digital forms of communication, which are cheaper to produce.

The accelerating speed and efficiency of news media transmission have often created severe strains on the standards and ethics of responsible journalism. The same system can and does report much trivia, sensation, and misinformation. The news eruptions that followed the death of Michael Jackson illustrated how news now breaks twenty-four hours a day, around the clock, instead of at the more leisurely pace that prevailed before the rise of twenty-four-hour cable television news and interactive news on the Internet. As fierce competitors such as MSNBC, the Fox Channel, and CNN with their talk and opinion shows have proliferated on cable as well as with online blogs, some news organizations have relaxed their rules on checking and verifying sources. There is a growing sense that getting it first is more important than getting it right. One result is journalism that is sometimes shaky, inaccurate, or worse, and with it has come a serious loss of public trust in news media.

This book analyzes the changing role of transnational news media in our evolving globalization and its impact on rapidly changing news events. In the ongoing concern about terrorism, global news media have played a major role both in informing the world and in organizing and facilitating responses. (The media are also an unwilling accomplice of terrorism by publicizing the atrocities and carrying the email messages of terrorists.) Throughout this book, the emphasis is often on the role of US news organizations, yet we acknowledge that news media of many other nations – East and West – contribute to this cooperative activity of reporting the world to itself. And as the world modernizes, journalists of more and more nations are contributing to the flow of international news and popular culture.

Foreign news has increasingly become a powerful political and diplomatic force. For example, when US television shows stark pictures of starving Somali mothers and children, American public opinion becomes concerned, and the White House watches, hesitates, and then sends in the military to help feed the starving and keep the peace. A few months later, a dozen American soldiers are killed in an ambush in Somalia. The US public is outraged at seeing on television the body of an American soldier dragged through the streets of Mogadishu. Soon, the White House announces that troops will be withdrawn.

News, instantaneous and vivid, speeds up history as it directly influences diplomacy and government policies. At the same time, in this age of satellites, the Internet, and social media, autocratic regimes find it impossible to keep unflattering news about their regimes from reaching their own people. Technological and operational changes taking place in the international news media, with their enhanced capability for global communication, are reshaping "spaceship Earth." This wider communication often seems to exacerbate political and cultural conflicts between the West and Islam, between rich and poor nations. Also, there are the frictions and the problems these changes have wrought, including conflicts over transnational news gathering and the impact of television programming, motion pictures, videos, radio broadcasting, and other aspects of mass culture, most of it coming out of the United States and Europe.

Another area of concern is that, when no crisis intrudes, serious international news seems often to be shunted aside for more profitable content. "Infotainment" – scandal, sensation, celebrities – has become more and more the staple of news media in many countries.

This book is intended to provide some insights into how and why international news communication is evolving. We may not be aware of how our perceptions of the world are being changed by the transformed news system, but we quickly learn to take that system for granted. If there is another terror attack on a major city or another major earthquake in Haiti or Chile, we expect to see live television reports the same day or on a twenty-four-hour news channel, such as BBC World or CNN, within the hour via satellite. We are fascinated but not surprised to see detailed, computer-refined pictures of the exploration of planet Mars or the dramatic saga of the space shuttle as well as the grim daily war stories from the Middle East.

In a broader context, the fact that information of all kinds, including urgent news, can now be communicated almost instantly to almost anywhere has profound implications for international organization and interaction. News of Iraq's invasion of Kuwait, for example, had an almost immediate impact on the price of gas at the pump and initiated an international diplomatic reaction resulting in mass deployment of US military forces. And the world's subsequent perceptions of the crisis and war were certainly shaped and, at times, distorted by the flickering images on television screens. Instant information is often not the whole truth or a complete picture and, on occasion, does sharply distort images that people receive.

Still, global news has many uses. The global financial media's day-to-day reporting of financial crises in Asian stock markets and currencies, and their effects on the financial markets and economies of Asia, Europe, and America, illustrates how many millions around the world, including small stockholders, rely on fast, accurate information in their daily lives. The global economy simply could not function without the fast flow of reliable information provided by the growing global business media – both print and electronic.

A new global society of sorts is emerging rapidly and inexorably, though experts disagree about its extent and nature. (Many nations, especially in the Middle East and Africa, do not feel a part of it.) The media of mass communication, along with global telecommunications, air transportation, and growing interdependence of national economies, are providing the essential linkages that make interaction and cooperation – and stealth terrorist attacks – possible.

Full understanding of the nature of this new society requires that today's students of international communication be conversant with world politics and economics, including recent history, and be quick to recognize significant trends as they occur. Further, they must understand national and cultural differences and keep up with technological innovations in communication media, such as the Internet and social media, and with changing journalistic practices.

Communication satellites are just one example of the truly revolutionary impact that communication technology has had on the modern world. The earlier role of transistor radios in the Third World was another; today the small hand-held video camcorder is having news effects previously undreamed of. As we will see, the Internet is beginning to be perceived as yet another technological marvel that may dramatically alter international communication. FM radio, cellphones, and cable television are each having unexpected impacts in developing nations.

The interplay of these elements makes the study of international communication fascinating and important. The major emphasis throughout this book is on the journalistic aspects of international communication – the new challenges and perils of reporting the news, the important but imperfect and controversial ways that journalists and mass communicators keep the world informed. Further, the cultural and entertainment facets of media are often significant as well.

Several chapters concern the changing media – the ways that international journalism is adapting to altered global conditions, changing concepts of news, and utilizing the new hardware of our information age.

Currently, for the first time in history, all nations, however remote, have stepped onto the stage of the modern world. What happens in Rwanda, or Indonesia, or Afghanistan can have global significance and often has repercussions around the world, in part because events happening there are reported. More importantly, a much greater degree of interdependence among all peoples and nations has developed.

The world has been evolving an international news system that moves information and mass culture ever faster and in greater volume to any place on Earth where an antenna can be put on a shortwave radio receiver, where dish antennas can receive television programs from a communication satellite, or, increasingly, where there is a personal computer with a modem hooked onto the Internet. The cellphone with connections to the Internet is becoming a potent player in global communication. Although politics, economic disparities, cultural and linguistic differences, and ideology keep us apart on many issues, the international news system has on occasion made us one community, if only briefly – as when Neil Armstrong took that "one giant leap for mankind" in 1969. An estimated 600 million people throughout the world watched that first walk on the moon, and they sat before their television sets not as Chinese, French, Africans, or Japanese, but as earthlings watching in awe as one of their kind first stepped onto another sphere far away in space.

Actually, the reporting of Armstrong's moon walk has further relevance for this book because the new information age is partly an outgrowth of the exploration of space. The communication satellite, high-speed data transmission, and miniaturized computer technology are by-products of space technology and all are playing integral roles in the transformation of international communication and transnational journalism.

The modern practices of globally collecting and distributing news are only about 100 years old and were initiated by news agencies of Britain, the United States, and France. Today, the world agencies – the Associated Press (United States), Reuters (Britain), and Agence France-Presse (France) – are still important but far from the only conduits of transnational news, although they and other media have been transformed by digital technology. Change has been coming so quickly that it is often difficult to stay current with the ways in which news is being moved. And to understand the future potential of say, the Internet, is like trying to perceive in 1905 what the absurd horseless carriage or the telephone would do in time to the cities and lifestyles of the twentieth century.

Furthermore, technology and global reach are modifying some of the institutions of transnational communication. Subtly and almost imperceptibly, various media, including the news agencies, are evolving from national to increasingly international or, better, to supranational institutions of mass communication. Concomitantly, English is clearly the world's leading media language.

The international news media, furthermore, are unevenly distributed among nations, creating serious frictions between the haves and have-nots in mass communication. The explosion of communication technology has coincided with the post-World War II decolonization of the Third World, and the penetration of Western news and mass culture into the newly independent nations, as well as into the former communist bloc. This has been perceived by some as a new attempt to reassert the domination of the former colonial powers.

Part of this book focuses on the differences that frustrate and at times inhibit the flow of international news and divide journalists and mass communicators: political and ideological differences, economic disparities, geographic and ethnic divisions. The media of all nations, it can be argued, reveal biases imposed by the constraints of nationalism and parochialism. When US soldiers are engaged in a military clash in Afghanistan, the subsequent news report on NBC television will differ from that carried on Al Jazeera, the Arabic broadcaster. There is no "true" news report of any event, only a variety of conflicting views out of which hopefully a consensus of sorts can be reached about what exactly happened.

The conflicts and frictions in international communication arise in part from divergent concepts of mass communication. In the concept of the press that has evolved in Western democratic nations, journalists are relatively independent of government, free to report directly to the public that uses the information to understand the world and to assess its governors. This view is unacceptable to authoritarian nations, which control and manipulate their media to serve better the goals of the state and its, often unelected, leaders. In numerous, mostly impoverished nations, a similar theory – the developmental concept – has emerged, which holds that mass media must be mobilized to serve the goals of nation building and economic development.

The deep differences between the media-rich and media-poor nations reflect closely other differences between rich and poor nations. Despite the impressive gains in the technical ability to communicate more widely and quickly, the disturbing evidence is that in some ways the world may be growing further apart rather than closer together. Most of the benefits of the communication and information revolution have accrued to the industrialized nations of the West, and to Japan and the Pacific Rim nations. For an individual to benefit fully from the news media, he or she ideally should be literate, educated, and affluent enough to have access to a variety of news sources. Unfortunately, in our unfair world, the largest share of such individuals is found, for now, in the few industrialized democracies. Yet the world's two most populous nations, China and India, have greatly increased the audiences and readership of their media.

The world's system of distributing news can be likened to a crystal prism. What in one place is considered the straight white light of truth travels through the prism and is refracted and bent into a variety of colors and shades. One person's truth becomes, to another, biased reporting or propaganda – depending on where the light strikes the prism and where it emerges. As we understand the optics of a prism for measuring the spectrum of light, so must we understand and accept the transecting planes of different cultural and political traditions that refract divergent perceptions of our world. Obviously, Islamic terrorists have a radically different view of the world than most Europeans have.

We must acknowledge how the light refracts for us. In considering the problems of international communication, we have tried to be sympathetic to the views and frustrations of people in non-Western nations and the enormous difficulties they face. Journalism is a highly subjective pursuit, tempered and shaped by the political conditions and cultural traditions of the particular society where it is practiced; the news and the world do look different from Shanghai, Lagos, or Baghdad than they do from Chicago.

As products of the Western press tradition, we believe journalists in their pursuit of the news should be suspicious of, and disagree at times with, other political leaders and other journalists as well as the owners of the media. For the essence of journalism is diversity of ideas and the freedom to express them. We agree with Albert Camus, who wrote:

> A free press can of course be good or bad, but certainly without freedom, it will never be anything but bad. . . . Freedom is nothing else but a chance to be better, whereas enslavement is a certainty of the worst.

And in the dangerous, strife-ridden world of the twenty-first century, we believe that the billions of people inhabiting this planet deserve to know more about the events and trends that affect their lives and well-being. Only journalists who are free and independent of authoritarian controls and other constraints can begin the difficult task of gathering and reporting the news and information we all have a right and need to know.

1

Information for a Global System

The rapid integration of the world's economy, loosely called globalization, has been facilitated by an information revolution driven by communication technologies that provide a nervous system for our world today. Globalization is a broad and inexact term for a wide array of worldwide changes in politics, economics, trade, finance, lifestyles, and cultures. To its critics, globalization is trendy and controversial; they see the world becoming a consumer colony of the United States, led by Coke, McDonald's, Nike, and the vast pop-culture output of Hollywood. How people feel about globalization often depends a lot on where they live and what they do. With just a visit to a mall, one is struck by the plethora of products and services from many distant lands. In the past thirty years, much of the world's economy has become increasingly integrated; direct foreign investment has grown three times as fast as total domestic investment. But globalization is more than buying and selling; some see it as a profound interchange of cultures – a communication revolution that is dissolving our sense of boundaries, our national identities, and how we perceive the world. Deregulation of telecommunications systems and computerization have been called the parents of globalization. Three technologies in particular – computers, satellites, and digitalization – have converged to produce a global communications network that covers the Earth as completely as the atmosphere. Today's era of globalization is characterized by falling telecommunications costs, thanks to microchips, satellites, fiber optics, and the Internet. The popular culture of the West – movies, television shows, music CDs, video- and audio-cassettes, books, magazines, newspapers – has been increasingly flowing

The World News Prism: Digital, Social and Interactive, Ninth Edition.
William A. Hachten and James F. Scotton.
© 2016 John Wiley & Sons, Inc. Published 2016 by John Wiley & Sons, Inc.

about the world. It can be argued that the world is beginning to share a popular culture, based only in part on that of the West. Critics differ about what happens when cultures meet. Rather than fight, cultures often blend. Frederick Tipson noted, "More like a thin but sticky coating than a powerful acid, this cosmopolitan culture of communication networks and the information media seems to overlay rather than supplant the cultures it interacts with."[1] When cultures receive outside influences, it is said, they ignore some and adopt others, and soon begin to transform them. An example can be something called *bhangra pop* in India – music that sounds like Jamaican reggae but is played on Indian instruments and then amplified.

Critics of this global media market castigate globalization for several reasons: the centralization of media power, and heavy commercialism, which is linked to declines in public broadcasting and public service standards for media performance. Media are seen as a threat to democracy because of lessened public participation and concern with public affairs. Press critics have other concerns about these corporate giants. The news media, they argue, risk becoming submerged and neglected inside vast entertainment conglomerates that are primarily concerned with entertainment profits.

Most of these criticisms are leveled at Western media, and these critics neglect to consider how globalization has spurred the growth of media and their audiences in the developing non-Western nations.

Others see globalization in more positive terms. It is argued that many millions more people than ever before now have access to news and information, especially in such countries as China and India and much of Southeast Asia. Globalization means that multitudes now have many newfound choices: how they will spend their leisure time; what they will watch or read; what to buy with newly acquired personal income from rapidly rising standards of living. Anthropologist James Watson wrote, "The lives of Chinese villagers I know are infinitely better off now than they were 30 years ago. China has become more open because of the demands of ordinary people. They *want* to become part of the world – I would say that globalism is the major force for democracy in China. People want refrigerators, stereos, CD players."[2]

Journalist Thomas Friedman wrote that globalization is essentially about change, which is a reality and not a choice: "Thanks to the combination of computers and cheap telecommunications, people can now offer and trade services globally – from medical advice to software writing to data processing – services that could never be traded before. And why not? A three-minute call (in 1996 dollars) between New York and London cost $300 in 1930. Today it is almost free through the Internet."[3]

The primacy of the issue of globalization reminds us of the extent to which most of us now think and act globally – as a matter of course. In his book *The World Is Flat: A Brief History of the 21st Century*, Friedman expands his earlier views and sees dramatic changes in the forces for global leveling from the fall of the Berlin Wall, which eliminated the ideological divide in the world, to the rise of the Internet and technological changes that have led to new economic models of production and collaboration, including outsourcing and offshore manufacturing. Now nations such as China and India, as well as others in South Asia, have prospered in dramatic ways. The integration of some 3 billion people into the global economy is of major importance. Just one facet of this global flattening is that the media of communications have become increasingly pervasive in these rapidly modernizing places. Literally many millions are now, through the Internet, cellphones, satellite television, and publications, "in touch" with the greater world. But while the new technologies are closing gaps between parts of India and China and the advanced industrial nations, the gaps between those countries and Africa have been widened. The world's nations may not have a level playing field, but the world is changing in critical ways. And for many millions in those nations considered to be "developing," their standards of living have improved rapidly.

Perhaps one of the most significant photographs of modern times was taken during the Apollo 11 mission to the moon. The astronauts photographed the earthrise as seen from the moon, and there was our planet, like a big, cloudy, blue, agate marble. The widely reprinted picture illuminated the fragility and cosmic insignificance of our spaceship Earth.

That stunning image coincided with the worldwide concern about ecology, climate change, and global pollution; even more, it made it easy to grasp why many scientists already treated that cloudy, blue marble as a complete biological system, in which change in one part will inevitably affect other parts.

Certainly in the years since, concerned persons around the world have become more aware of our global interdependence. Although some experts disagree, an important trend of our times is that the world is becoming a single, rudimentary community. Today's world must grapple with an agenda of urgent and complex problems, most of them interrelated: overpopulation; poverty; famine; depletion of natural resources (especially energy); pollution of the biosphere; regional political disputes; continuing arms buildup, including the nuclear threat; global warming, and the widening gap between rich and poor nations, which seems exacerbated by economic integration. Recent events have pushed terrorism high on the agenda. Terrorist acts are somber reminders of how much hate and anger divide our diverse societies.

These and other global crises ebb and flow on the world's news agendas, but they are truly international in scope; the amelioration – much less solution – of any of them requires cooperation and goodwill among nations. To achieve that, there first must be information and understanding of these challenges, for these are crises of interdependence. No one nation or even combination of nations can deal effectively with such global concerns as international monetary crises, pollution of the air and oceans, population control, terrorism, regional warfare, and widespread famine and food shortages, yet the blinders of nationalism and modern tribalism continue to influence political leaders everywhere to react to international problems with narrow and parochial responses. The news media in all nations will reflect the national views and prejudices of their own societies on these pressing global concerns. It's not necessary that all nations agree on how to respond – and here is where the news media come in – but there should be general agreement about what the problems are.

Westerners and some leaders of developing countries are becoming aware that population growth is putting intolerable pressures on the Earth's land, water, and energy resources as well as its economies.

The world's population in 2008 was 6.8 billion, with 37 percent of its population living in China and India. The US Census Bureau has projected that in 2025 India will surpass China. The other most populous countries are, in order, the United States, Indonesia, Brazil, Pakistan, Bangladesh, Nigeria, Russia, and Japan.[4] By the end of this century another 3 billion people are expected to be added.

Africa is currently gripped by one of the greatest population explosions ever recorded. Over the past sixty years Africa's population has quadrupled to 1 billion people, an epic baby boom that threatens to trap a generation of children in poverty and strangle economic progress on the world's poorest continent. With low rates of contraception and high social pressures to have large families, African women bear 5.3 children each on average, compared with 2.1 in the United States. By 2050, Africa's population will reach 2 billion.[5] Nigeria's population alone, in a quarter-century, at the rate it is growing, will reach 300 million people (about the population of the present-day United States) living in a country the size of Arizona and New Mexico.

Scientists and development experts have been racing to increase food production by 50 percent in the next two decades to feed this growing population. The global number of hungry people increased to 1.02 billion in 2009, or nearly one in seven, according to the UN Food and Agriculture Organization. A central problem is whether food can be grown in the developing world where the hungry can actually get it at prices they can afford to pay. Poverty and difficult growing conditions plague the places that need new food production most – in sub-Saharan Africa and South Asia.[6] Finally, global warming makes this more difficult.

Paradoxically, even with greatly enhanced capability of involvement in world affairs, comparatively few people are well informed or even care much about what happens beyond their borders. Many who follow the news on television or other media have only a superficial knowledge of events such as a cancellation of an election in Nigeria or a stock-market crash in Indonesia. But for those comparative few who do follow public affairs closely (and they are found in every nation), perceptions of the world are being formed and reshaped by this revolution in long-distance instant communications.

Our ability, or lack of it, to use the fruits of this technological revolution is directly related to our success or failure to act decisively and in concert as a world community. International experts worry whether the world can organize itself and deal effectively with what have been called the seven major interrelated world problems: mass poverty, population, food, climate change, energy, military expenditure, and the world monetary system. To organize, though, we must communicate, since communication is the neural system of any organization. The extent of its ability to communicate determines the boundaries of any community – be it a primitive tribe in Papua New Guinea or a global society – and only expanded and more effective communication can make possible a viable global community.

The technology to circulate that information exists, but the barriers of illiteracy, parochialism and nationalism, poverty, and political constraints keep too many people in the world from receiving it.

The illiteracy situation is particularly vexing. Here are some facts and figures:

- There are about 1 billion non-literate adults (persons 15 years and above).
- 98 percent of all non-literate adults are in developing nations.
- Two-thirds of all non-literates are women.
- One-half of all non-literates are in China and India.

- It has been estimated that 30 to 50 million people are added each year to the numbers of non-literates due to population increases.
- So, worldwide the percentage of adult illiteracy is declining, but the absolute number of non-literates is increasing.

Over the long run, worldwide illiteracy dropped from 38.5 percent in 1970 to about 18 percent in 2010. Yet there is much room for improvement: currently about 670 million school-age children are not in school.

One hopeful trend to counter the dilemma of illiteracy is the global spread of cellphones and personal computers in the non-Western world. More communication, whether between sophisticated media or two illiterate peasants, can only be a positive thing.

The Importance of Foreign Information

Much of the essential information we need for our personal lives comes from the news media. Our economy, our society, and our government would have difficulty functioning without the flow of reliable news and information. An open, democratic society without independent news media is impossible to imagine.

Foreign news is a special genre of news. It's not just from afar but also news of widespread significance. The earthquake/tsunami of late 2004 in South Asia was major news everywhere. Even more thoroughly reported were the devastating earthquakes in Haiti and Chile in January 2010 and Japan in 2011. During 2014, foreign news was dominated by upheavals in Syria and Ukraine.

Serious journalists and editors have long held that important information from overseas should be reported capably and thoroughly, even though most people are primarily concerned about what happens in their own community or to themselves personally. Yet foreign news is perceived through the distorting prisms of culture and personal choice.

Many people rely on television for their news, yet anyone regularly watching network news is aware that foreign news has been typically reduced to several short items ("And now the news from abroad . . .") unless some video with violent footage is available (50 percent of television's foreign coverage does portray violence). Critics say that serious foreign news on television has been pushed aside in favor of scandal, celebrity, or the so-called "you news" – self-help and advice stories.

The public apparently does not mind. A recent survey of the US public by the Pew Research Center found that among regular users of the news media, the topics of most interest were, in this order, crime, local news about people and events, and health news. International news ranked ninth, well behind sports, local government, science, religion, and political news. Another 2001 poll (before 9/11), by Andrew Kohut, found that fewer than one in five Americans were strongly interested in serious news programs and publications – international, financial, government, and politics. Gender, generation, and education are keys: college-educated men over 40 years of age and older have the most interest; lesser-educated, younger women have decidedly the least.[7]

Other surveys conducted by the Pew Research Center in 1997 found that the percentage of people following foreign news dropped from 80 percent in the 1980s to 20 percent in 1990. The decline was most precipitous among young people, who were turned off by such traditional categories as international politics, security, war, and peace. The relatively few serious news stories that attract the attention of adult Americans are those that deal with national calamities or the use of American military force. The obverse is that readers in the affluent West show little interest in tragic and harsh news stories coming out of developing nations.

We agree with Stephen Hess of the Brookings Institution, who argued that we have become a nation with a two-media system, especially in regard to foreign news. Hess wrote, "Our society is awash in specialized information (including foreign news) available to those who have the time, interest, money, and education to take advantage of it. The other society encompasses the vast majority of Americans, who devote limited attention to subjects far removed from their necessary concerns (again, foreign news). They are content to turn to the top stories of television networks' evening news programs and their community's daily newspapers for the information."[8] We would argue that this happens in other affluent nations as well.

Yet perhaps this diminished interest in international events is not as significant as it would seem. Recent polls show that although the public is turned off by some foreign news, the public does crave engagement in the world's crises, but not in ways defined by government, academics, and the media. For example, a University of Maryland poll found that 74 percent of people wanted a sharing of power internationally, whereas only 13 percent wanted the United States to assert itself as the only superpower. Also, although Congress held up $1.5 billion in overdue assessments for the United Nations, a Pew Center survey found that Americans hold the organization in high regard. The Pew survey found broad support for cooperative action to halt global warming, even if it meant applying fuel consumption standards leading to higher US gasoline prices.

In short, publics everywhere seem highly concerned about issues they see as directly affecting their own lives. The British clearly felt their lives threatened by the July 7, 2005 terrorist attacks. They are also concerned about immigration and trade negotiations that could have an impact on their jobs and taxes, as well as environmental issues such as global warming, resource depletion, health threats, drug trafficking, and other cross-border crime.[9]

Whether the problem is pollution of the seas or proliferation of nuclear weapons, the fact remains that international society is marked by the absence of effective collective procedures, by competition rather than cooperation, and by the lack of a commitment to a common goal. The world is ruled by nation-states, not by an effective international organization, and each state will usually act according to its own interests and needs. In several African nations, such as Somalia, Liberia, and Congo, an even more discouraging trend has emerged: the complete breakdown of a nation into warring camps without a coherent central government. Some academics argue that the apparent thrust toward global unity and globalization is actually misleading. Political scientist Steven Krasner of Stanford believes that the idea that the world has fundamentally changed lacks historical perspective. The international transfer of ideas, trade, and capital has been going on for four or five centuries, he says. Others agree that the idea of global integration has been overblown and that we are not yet up to the late-nineteenth-century standard of integration. They argue that the current globalization is a return to a process interrupted by two world wars.[10] From the mid-1880s to the Great Depression, the world experienced a similar age of globalization. The volumes of trade and capital flows across borders and the flow of labor across borders, relative to populations, in the pre-World War I era of globalization was similar to what we are living through today. But today, powerful communications, including the Internet and the traditional media, drive our current globalization.

Others feel that the world is both converging and diverging at the same time. In 1993, *The New York Times* listed forty-eight nations where long-suppressed ethnic, religious, and sectional conflicts had surfaced. Policymakers say the ethnic conflicts are actually the third wave of the twentieth century, with the first having taken place after World War I and the second with the explosion of anti-colonial movements in Africa and Asia after World War II. Most of these nations' ancient rivalries and bigotry have remained largely unaffected by communication technology. The rise of international terrorism to the top of the world's agenda is further strong evidence of global divisiveness. Also, the sharp opposition of many Western nations to the US invasion of Iraq certainly indicated a shattering of political consensus.

On the other hand, powerful communication forces are binding the world together – circulating news, ideas, and information faster and in greater volume than ever before. These technologies are transforming many economic enterprises into truly global businesses. Further, countless more individuals are, through education and media participation, joining the modern world. So, although global integration may seem both real and illusory, there may be encouragement in the futuristic views that science fiction writer Arthur C. Clarke expressed nearly fifty years ago regarding the communication satellite:

> What we are now doing – whether we like it or not – indeed, whether we wish it or not – is laying the foundation of the first global society. Whether the final planetary authority will be an analogue of the federal systems now existing in the United States or the USSR I do not know. I suspect that, without any deliberate planning, such organizations as the world meteorological and earth resources satellite system and the world communications satellite system (of which INTELSAT is the precursor) will eventually transcend their individual components. At some time during the next century they will discover, to their great surprise, that they are really running the world.
>
> There are many who will regard these possibilities with alarm or distaste and may even attempt to prevent their fulfillment. I would remind them of the story of the wise English king, Canute, who had his throne set upon the seashore so he could demonstrate to his foolish courtiers that even the king could not command the incoming tide.
>
> The wave of the future is now rising before us. Gentlemen, do not attempt to hold it back. Wisdom lies in recognizing the inevitable – and cooperating with it. In the world that is coming, the great powers are not great enough.[11]

Some signs of this trend are visible; a slow but perceptible movement toward internationalization of the world's news media is taking place. The world's news agencies, a few newspapers and magazines, and both radio and television broadcasting (CNN and BBC World in particular) are transcending the national states from which they arose and are serving international audiences. With this has come, from the West, a pervasive popular culture. Such a transition will be welcomed by some as a contribution to better world understanding or resented by others as efforts by some nations to impose their models of mass communication and pop culture on everyone.

The technological capability for worldwide communication has never been greater, but then never have truly global problems and challenges seemed more urgent. Not enough people anywhere understand these problems or are in a position to cooperate with others in resolving them. Serious questions can be posed about the quality and adequacy of today's system of global news communication, but little doubt exists about the importance to the world of the newspapers, news agencies, and broadcasters that report the world's news to itself.

The audience that receives global news has vastly expanded because so much news is carried on digital platforms – the Internet, personal computers, cellphones and smartphones. And to more and more millions of people all over globe, especially young people, global news only reaches them through the social media rather than the traditional media that served their parents and grandparents.

Notes

1. Erla Zwingle, "Goods Move. People Move. Ideas Move. And Cultures Change," *National Geographic*, August 1999, 12.
2. Zwingle, "Goods Move," 13.
3. Thomas Friedman, *The Lexus and the Olive Tree* (New York: Anchor Books, 2000), xviii.
4. Sam Roberts, "In 2025 India to Pass China in Population Estimates," *The New York Times*, December 16, 2009, A16.
5. Shashank Bengali, "Population Boom in Land of Bust," *Wisconsin State Journal*, December 14, 2009, 1.
6. Neil MacFarquhar, "Experts Worry about Feeding the World as Its Population Grows," *New York Times*, October 22, 2009, A5.
7. Andrew Kohut, "Balancing News Interests," *Columbia Journalism Review*, July/August 2001, 58.
8. Stephen Hess, *International News & Foreign Correspondents* (Washington, DC: Brookings Institution, 1996), 8.
9. Barbara Crossette, "US Likes Its Foreign Affairs in Non-Traditional Terms, Polls Say", *The New York Times*, December 28, 1997, 8.
10. Susan Wels, "Global Integration: The Apparent and the Real," *Stanford Magazine*, September 1990, 46.
11. Arthur C. Clarke, "Beyond Babel: The Century of the Communication Satellite," in *Process and Effects of Mass Communication*, W. Schramm and D. Roberts, eds. (Urbana: University of Illinois Press, 1971), 963.

2

Game Changers:
Twitters, Videos, Blogs

Social media have markedly changed journalism, including international news and information. The process of reporting a foreign news event in the "old media" was sending a story that moved in one direction from a news source to a reporter to the newsroom of a newspaper, TV or radio station and from there to readers, viewers or listeners. That was it – completed. But was it? Of course not.

News is not a discrete event (man bites dog) but a process that continues, changes, evolves and, after leading to other news stories, like a many-headed hydra may just roll over and die. But now with the "new media" via the Internet, computers, cellphones, iPads, and other devices, the consumer or receiver of news often becomes an active participant in the news process by adding to or changing the original message and extending it in a new form to other audiences. A simple example – I listened on National Public Radio (NPR) to a reporter reciting a brief story and then he added five tweets (of 140 characters or less) that enhanced and certainly modified the original message.

Just what is the role of "social media"? The Internet itself as a massive global network was only about twenty-five years old in 2005 when Facebook emerged to send messages or videos between two parties anywhere or anytime. Twitter, with its 140-character "tweets," quickly followed. Twitter's IPO (initial public stock offering) in 2013 amazed the world. The company's valuation was $24 billion and its annual revenue was $535 million a year. Within a decade of its founding Twitter had 235 million active users who sent and received half a billion "tweets" a day. Facebook at the same time

The World News Prism: Digital, Social and Interactive, Ninth Edition.
William A. Hachten and James F. Scotton.
© 2016 John Wiley & Sons, Inc. Published 2016 by John Wiley & Sons, Inc.

had 1.28 billion adherents with two out of three using it every day. When Americans were using their omnipresent smartphones, about one-fifth of the time they were on Facebook.

But the most important number in all this social media explosion was probably ZERO. That's the amount Twitter charges people to use its services while rapidly building a company worth many billions.

How did this all happen so quickly? It happened because vast audiences want information of all kinds – from the personal to the broadly social and even international information. And much of this vast amount of activity involves what has long been defined as journalism – bringing important news and information to a large audience. Social media do this in new forms and often rely on the old media for the content. Twitter has become essential for journalists because its core function has become passing along pieces of information as a news story develops. Journalists often prefer to rely on Twitter because when a story emerges several staffers may be working on it. To stay on top of developments, these journalists keep on the alert for the latest Twitter feeds. Tweeting your story ensures that the story is seen, discussed, corrected, and added to. So Twitter has often been involved in the entire news gathering, editing, and finally publishing process. YouTube, currently owned by Google, often plays its own essential role by providing live video about the ongoing news.

A Pew survey found that nearly one in ten of US adults get their news through Twitter while one in three get their news via Facebook. Another study found 64 percent who use tablets (like iPads) and 62 percent of smartphone users received their news via social media in 2012. YouTube videos have drawn television viewers for a first look at such calamities as the 2011 Japanese earthquake and tsunami. Another Pew snapshot examining news across social media platforms showed the percentage of each social media website receiving information from the news and commentary source: Reddit 6%, Facebook 47%, Google Plus 30%, Tumblr's microblogs 29%.

Reporting the Bloody Syrian Civil War

All of the social media have been involved in reporting the civil war that began in Syria in 2011, one of the deadliest conflicts of the century. The United Nations set the death toll at 190,000 in 2014. The war proved so deadly for professional journalists (twenty-eight killed In 2012, eighteen more in 2013) that anyone with a smartphone, Internet access, and a desire to get a message out of Syria could and often did become a crucial source of video and eyewitness reports to the outside world. This phenomenon of amateur chronicling of war is changing the rules of war reporting and requires more astute editing to validate and authenticate the accuracy of these amateur reports and videos.

US Secretary of State John Kerry noted the significance of the social media when he stated, in a 2013 report on gas attacks and chemical weapons in Syria, that within 90 minutes of an attack "all hell broke loose in the social media," offering updates and videos from Syria. In the past, if professional journalists were not there to cover an event, it was likely that it had not happened as far as the rest of the world was concerned. The proliferation of amateur or "citizen" videos is more striking because Syria has been for long a closed society. When President Bashar Assad's father Hafez crushed a 1981–82 uprising in Hama, killing thousands of civilians, he was able to keep it almost completely hidden from the outside world.

Social media have been effective in overcoming official silence and secrecy throughout the Middle East:

- In Saudi Arabia and the Arab Gulf, Facebook, Twitter, and YouTube are providing vast, uncontrolled space for men and women to talk to each other and talk back to their rulers, something that has never happened before. A young Saudi techie, in a country where the government has almost complete control of the traditional media, told Tom Friedman of the *New York Times*, "I get all my news from Twitter." So much for government control! In Saudi Arabia over 4 million, mostly young, people have iPhones – the most in the Middle East – and Saudis produce half of the tweets in the Arab world.

- In Turkey in 2014, Prime Minister Recep Erdoğan planned to "eradicate" Twitter, as he put it, after reports of corruption within his government and family. Erdoğan instantly became the target of worldwide protests and mockery. It was a sign of the difficulty of banning Twitter in the age of Twitter that, within hours of the government efforts to block the social media site, Turkish president Abdullah Gül was one of the thousands who protested the ban – using Twitter to do it. In March 2014 a court in Istanbul ruled that the government could not ban Twitter.

Outside of the Middle East social activists using Twitter and Facebook also overcame bureaucratic and communication barriers that had baffled governments. For years Uganda, with the help of other governments, tried to expose and curb the elusive rebel band known as the Lord's Resistance Army, led by Joseph Kony. The group killed thousands of civilians in northern Uganda and kidnapped hundreds of children, forcing them to become child soldiers or sex slaves within the army. Jason Russell, a young American freelance journalist, exposed Kony and his army to the world in a matter of days, astounding diplomats, academicians, and Ugandans who had been trying to draw world attention to the tragedy for years. In March 2012, in a testament to the explosive power of social media, Russell and a small group of activists blitzed the world about the problem. Within a year of being posted, their video, "Kony 2012," attracted more than 50 million views on YouTube and Vimeo, a video-sharing website. On the first day alone "Kony 2012" rocketed across Twitter and Facebook to attract hundreds of thousands of dollars in contributions for the fight against Kony and his Lord's Resistance Army. The viral pace of the message had rarely been seen for any video, let alone an hour-long film about a remote conflict in East Africa. Russell had tapped into a vein of idealistic youths, many living in the United States.

But in the melding of traditional news gathering with social media platforms, it is important to remember that there is still a role for the "old media." With the rise of social media, "amateur" reporters have vastly increased in number. But the traditional media, including the Associated Press and Reuters news agencies and broadcasters such as the BBC, CBS, and the growing Al Jazeera network, plus the major world newspapers including the *New York Times*, London's *Guardian*, and others continue to collect, shape, and distribute much of the reliable world news after it has been verified, authenticated, and vetted.

"Glorious Disruption"

Like other institutions and organizations, the traditional news media – newspapers, news services, radio stations, television, cable channels and networks, and news magazines – are being strikingly altered by the information revolution. News communication is being dramatically affected by ongoing revolutionary changes in communication satellites, computers, digitalization, miniaturization, and the Internet.

The Internet has been playing a facilitating and supplementary role in the rapid dissemination of a fast-breaking story – either a trivial Hollywood scandal or the ominous events of the latest terrorist attacks. Online news junkies have quick access not only to more news but also to a heady mix of unconfirmed rumor, conjecture, commentary, discussion, and conspiracy theories. Sometimes, rumor and conjecture find their way into the legitimate news media. Further, the Internet and the twenty-four-hour cable news cycle can greatly accelerate a story, often to the detriment of traditional journalistic practices such as verifying sources and creating context. More and more people are getting their news from cable, the Internet, and social media.

The "glorious disruption" of international journalism is being deeply influenced by two basic trends: first, how the news is received and to whom it goes (the audience and readers of news), and second, the changing ways that news and commentary are gathered and communicated. Most of the traditional journalism practices persist, but much is changing as well.

The audience for online news tends not to stick with a single site; further, research has shown that with a vast array of digital sources, "promiscuous" news consumption goes only so far. Only 35 percent of people who go online for news have a favorite site, and just 21 percent are more or less "monogamous," relying primarily on a single Internet source, according to the Pew Research Center. But 57 percent of that audience relies on just two to five sites.[1]

Google vs. Old Media

Digital news has been infiltrating and changing the news media for many years, but many recent changes seem associated with the spectacular success of Google, the leading Internet search company. Directly competing with print news media, Google has in twelve years utterly transformed the media landscape. Google directly challenges news media because it provides so much "free news," has usurped a large share of print advertising revenue, and has beguiled or bewitched many young people, who no longer read newspapers. As a result news media based on print and paper are experiencing severe financial difficulties and finding it hard to gather news, especially news from distant places.

An estimated 1.6 billion people worldwide were connected to the Internet in 2009 – with less than 25 percent of them in America. While digital firms like Yahoo and Google boomed between 2000 and 2009, numerous printed papers faced huge financial losses. And some have shut down. During that period, 167,000 US newspaper jobs were lost. Potential buyers are leery of buying properties with doubtful profitable futures.

The print media were hardest hit; less so radio and television; book publishing's fate is currently being decided, and the music business has been turned upside down.

For newspapers, the trends were clear; circulation and advertising have been falling, newspaper readers are aging, debt service and production costs are rising, and stock prices are way down. Giving away online newspapers did not help print editions.

Amazingly, the traditional media did not see this upheaval coming. For example, they did not recognize that Craigslist, which carries free local classified advertising in many cities on the Internet, was a serious threat to newspapers' classified ads, a major source of revenue for daily newspapers. The same news available on so-called "dead tree" papers was available free on digital news sites. Google has eliminated barriers to finding information and knowledge – and news. The Internet, it has been said, makes information available. Google has made news accessible. Newspapers and other print publications are scrambling to find a new business model that will make ink journalism profitable again.

Driving this trend are the steeply declining prices of three essential technologies: computing power, digital storage, and transmission capacity. Digital content (including news) has become, as was once predicted about electricity, too cheap to meter. Whatever it costs to deliver a video today will cost half as much a year later, say experts. Perhaps leading this charge for inexpensive information is Google, called "the poster child of free." Its millions of daily users have come to expect no charges for access to an enormous and growing body of information.

Social Media and the Key Role of Satellites

In the past thirty-five years, global telecommunications by satellite have achieved remarkable results. In our concern with how international news moves about the globe, the significant changes initiated by communication satellites, a major by-product of the space age, must be recognized. Recently, there has been a quantum jump in the ability of people to talk to and see one another almost anywhere. Marshall McLuhan once wrote that we were experiencing a "global electronic village" being created by television. John Naisbitt countered that it is in fact the communication satellite that is "creating a super tribal community unlike any environment previously known to mankind since the Tower of Babel."[2]

In the past half-century global communication by satellite has achieved remarkable results. Joseph Pelton pointed out that "trillions of dollars of electronic funds transfers and hundreds of millions of dollars of airline reservations flow through global networks each year. Billions of conversations carry on international business, diplomacy, finance, culture, and recreation as a matter of routine."[3] Included in these vast communication flows are, of course, the world's news in pictures, sounds, data, and words.

Our interest is in the impact of telecommunications on international news flow. And the most immediate short-term effect of Comsats (that is, communication satellites) is a reduction in the cost of long-distance communications and a corresponding increase in the amount of words, data, and images exchanged. In other words, more news is flowing at less expense. We have seen dramatic changes in long-distance telephone calls, which form the bulk of traffic on the INTELSAT system; that system is operated by a multinational consortium controlling long-distance point-to-point Comsat communications.

Arthur C. Clarke dismissed the notion that Comsats are merely an extension of existing communication devices and do not engender much change. He placed Comsats in the same class as the atomic bomb and automobile, "which represent a kind of quantum jump which causes a major restructuring of society." Clarke recalled a parliamentary commission in England over 100 years ago, when the chief engineer of the Post Office was asked to comment on the need for the latest American invention, the telephone. The engineer made this remarkable reply: "No Sir. The Americans may have need of the telephone – but we do not. We have plenty of messenger boys."[4]

That telephone, in time, came to have its own revolutionary impact on modern life, and now the personal letter has been replaced by the long-distance call as well as by fax and email. And telephone services, as has been noted, constitute the primary activity today of communication satellites and are the major source of revenue for INTELSAT. (The telephone and its wireless version, it should be noted, are major tools as well in news gathering – formerly local tools but now used globally.)

At the end of the 1970s, the traffic of INTELSAT still consisted mostly of people talking to people, but since the mid-1980s, at least half the information volume has consisted of machines communicating with other machines. The mind-boggling information-carrying capacity of INTELSAT VI is driving this trend, and INTELSAT VII, launched in 1993, followed by INTELSAT VII-A, in 1995, have continued it. Pelton developed a term, TIUPIL, to show the relationship between human capabilities of processing information and the speed of the information machines – present and future. A "TIUPIL" represents the "Typical Information Use Per Individual Lifetime" and was defined as 20 billion bits of information: the total information received by a person who lives seventy years and processes some 27,000 written or spoken words a day. A TIUPIL can be transmitted on INTELSAT VII in a matter of just seven seconds, or about nine times a minute. "Soon we will have networks of satellites capable of sending up to 100 billion bits of information in a second. This means we will have machines capable of processing information thousands or even millions of times faster than the human brain," Pelton wrote. "If one asks why we need such high-speed machines, the answer is clearly for machine-to-machine communication. Once we have communication satellites and fiber optic cables capable of handling super high-definition, 3-D television, the meeting of telephone or human data requirements will be small potatoes indeed."[5]

Although they have been called microwave relay towers in the sky, Comsats do have broader, unique properties. They do not link just two points, but many. They can simultaneously receive and transmit to many places, sending a panoply of message forms – television, telephone, telex, photo facsimile, fax, and high-speed computer data. For example, an increased mobility of money is a result of the computer revolution.

Today, satellite systems are operational at the international (intercontinental) level, the regional (continental) level, and the domestic (national) level. Satellites extend the range of over-the-air broadcasting systems, but they have a much greater impact on satellite-cable networks. CNN and various other cable services extend their reach dramatically by being tied in with cable services. In addition, numerous specialized satellite systems are functioning, such as those designed for military, data relay, and maritime and aeronautical purposes.

INTELSAT is the largest and oldest system, with fifteen satellites (plus backups) over the Pacific, Atlantic, and Indian Oceans. Some 120 nations, each with its own earth segment, belong to the consortium, and any two member countries can communicate directly without going through former colonial capitals. User countries, territories, and possessions total about 170, operating internationally on almost 1,500 pre-assigned pathways. INTEL-SAT also functions as the carrier for national domestic services in about thirty countries.

Comsats have greatly expanded the capacity of news media to move international news around the globe, but the ability of the satellites to relay color television signals, giving that medium a global impact, is what has made Comsat technology such a significant mass communication development. This is true even though television use accounts for a comparatively small proportion of the monthly revenue of INTELSAT.

When Early Bird, the first commercial Comsat, was launched in 1965, the principal television use was expected to be for occasional live events such as sports, state funerals, space missions, and the coverage of disasters and wars. Although reportage of such major events still accounts for much television traffic on INTELSAT, the most extensive and consistent use of the global system is for daily television news "packages" sent from one country to another. The US networks – NBC, CBS, and ABC – plus CNN, daily incorporate satellite news feeds from their correspondents in various parts of the world or, for special coverage, sporadically purchased from foreign broadcast news services, such as Reuters Television or APTN.

Innovations in communication technology are changing both the ways that global news is gathered and disseminated and the ways that individuals receive the news. The speed and scope of foreign news reporting is constantly expanding as the use of laptop computers is increasing. Foreign correspondents have long said that their worst problems are not censorship or other authoritarian restraints, but logistics – getting to the remote news scene, such as an earthquake in Chile or a civil war in Congo, and then getting the story out. The technology to solve part of that problem has been developed and increasingly utilized: especially portable devices that can transmit stories over phone lines (or by wireless) directly to newsroom systems. Initially, these portables were used to cover golf matches, auto races, football and basketball games, and court trials, but now journalists covering the whole range of news carry them.

A major technological advance for television reporting was the development of new, highly portable "satellite uplinks," which can be disassembled, checked as baggage, and flown to the site of a breaking story in order to feed back live reports. A "flyaway" dish can become a temporary CNN or ABC bureau in just the time it takes to get one on the scene. Other innovations useful to reporters in the field (as well as to individual citizens) are the portable wireless telephone and the video telephone.

Personalized Media

Innovations in information media – personal computers with Internet connections, printers, fax capabilities, modems, videocassettes, cordless and smartphones, interactive television, databases, cable, and satellite connections – all often considered "personalized media," are having profound effects on the audience or recipients of international news. In fact, the term *audience* is itself becoming a bit obsolete, because it implies a mass of passive receivers of communication. Increasingly, personalized media are supplementing traditional media in the affluent West, but less so in developing countries.

In today's information societies, an individual is no longer a passive recipient of news or entertainment, but now is an "information seeker" who can select or choose his or her news or information from a widening variety of sources, many of which governments are unable or unwilling to control. Further, individuals themselves, such as those involved in computer networking, become sources of information; that is, communicators. Autocratic governments find it difficult to control personalized communications.

With a personal computer and a modem connected to a telephone or wireless, a person can tap into the fast-growing Internet system, providing access to many thousands of websites databases, including news publications and other current information from home and abroad. Further, that receiver can become a sender by freely communicating with other computers through the websites or Internet, email, and various networks and bulletin boards.

Digital recorders, both video and audio, have greatly enhanced the ability of individuals to choose what they will hear or see and, as a result, have expanded rapidly in recent years even to remote corners of the southern hemisphere.

The Internet and International News Flow

The potential of the Internet for international news communication is being realized, but is still a work in progress. In 2009, the Internet carried more news each day than 1,600 daily newspapers can provide, to a worldwide audience of 1.6 billion Internet users. More and more Internet users are getting their news online and from media in far-off places.

An Internet user in Pakistan, Paris, or Pretoria can read the online edition of *The New York Times, The Times* of London, or *Die Zeit* of Hamburg. Major newspapers and other news media, such as magazines, radio and television broadcasters, and cablecasters, from a variety of mostly Western nations – what was formerly called the "foreign press" – are available in ways never before possible for those with the means and inclination to log on. The impact on journalism education is obvious: instead of going to a university library to peruse back copies of several dozen foreign newspapers, a journalism student today using his or her computer can read, study, and compare hundreds of publications and broadcasting outlets of many countries. Many other related sources are available as well. For example, by calling up www.memri.org, the website of the Mideast Media and Research Institute, a student can read translations from Arabic of what the Arab press and broadcasters are reporting and proclaiming about the war on terrorism.

The BBC's impressive utilization of the Internet has placed the broadcast giant in direct competition with British newspapers. Starting its online operations in 1998, the BBC now has 525 sites. It spends $27 million on its news website and this is backed by the BBC's vast news-gathering resources, including 5,000 reporters scattered around the world, all of which is funded by its annual £2.8 million subsidy from the British government. The success of the BBC's news website clearly troubles British newspapers. Its audience increased from 1.6 million unique weekly users in 2000 to 7.8 million in 2005. The news website has a breadth and depth that newspapers have difficulty keeping up with.[6]

The Associated Press has adopted the Internet to distribute its articles and photographs over the global Internet. In so doing, it has followed other mainline news organizations into uncharted journalistic territory. The AP's great rival, Reuters, announced in 2000 similar plans to reposition itself as a high-flying Internet player. Reuters plans to spend $802 million to shift its delivery systems to the Internet.

The Internet incorporates many elements of various print and electronic media that have preceded it. Computers can be used to send and receive text, sound, still images, and video clips. Yet for all its versatility, the Internet is not expected to replace its predecessors, but to take its place alongside them as a social, cultural, and economic force in its own right. No longer a curiosity, the Internet has become another way for to people find out what is happening in the world.

Much news or information on the Internet is of dubious value and may be deliberately wrong or misleading. During the weeks after the September

11 attacks, the Internet was overwhelmed with wild rumors, deliberate misinformation, and conspiracy theories. But the discriminating and critical viewer could still find solid, reliable information because the world's best news organizations – newspapers, news magazines, television, and radio services – were reporting the real news daily. (An important role for professional online news media is to act as a check on unreliable and unsubstantiated reports.)

Cyber news so far is complementing the traditional news media, but may soon become a new kind of journalism. John V. Pavlik wrote, "Since networked news can be interactive, on-demand, and customizable; since it can incorporate new combinations of text, images, moving images, and sound; since it can build new communities based on shared interests and concerns; since it has the almost unlimited space to offer levels of reportorial depth, texture, and context that are impossible in any other medium – new media can transform journalism."

Perhaps the single most significant characteristic of the Internet is that it is a communication device that lets people share ideas (including news) on a global network. This feature suggests that international news communication has made tremendous strides in the past twenty-five or so years, which is the age of the personal computer. A PC with a modem, either hooked up to a telephone line or wireless, means that the world – literally the world – is more available than ever before. Not only individuals but professional news media now can reach and hold not just audiences or readers, but also communities of people with shared concerns literally anywhere in the world.

Bloggers Join the Fray

Internet journalism and international news have been influenced by the rapidly growing army of bloggers. A "blog" (web and log) is technically someone's record of the websites he or she visits. Bloggers have been called one-person Internet blabbermouths, who pop off to anyone who will listen. They criticize each other but, more importantly, they take on the mainline media. Sometimes right and often wrong, they provide a kind of instant feedback loop for media corrections. They often write personal diaries and commentaries, with the best of them weighing in on the pressing issues of the world. They report news items that the traditional media ignore or suppress, and they provide links to other bloggers with something to say. Anyone can be a blogger and no one is in charge.

Their sheer numbers are mind-boggling: in mid-2005, a website, Technorati, reported an astonishing growth: nearly 80,000 new blogs are created every day and there are some 14.2 million in existence: of these, 55 percent remain active. In December 2009, one online source, Netcraft Net Services, reported a total of 233,848,493 websites on the World Wide Web. There had been an increase of 47 million names and 7 million active websites over the previous seven months. News-related websites were a tiny fraction of this vast total. The influence of blogs on news flow is increasing. Some are quoted on regular media and some media have their own blogs – and being on the Internet, their reach and influence can and do become global.

Social media are, of course, an aspect of the blogosphere and contribute to its vast pervasiveness. Richard Posner wrote that "in effect, the blogosphere is a collective enterprise – not 12 million separate enterprises but one enterprise with 12 million reporters, feature writers, and editorialists with very little costs. It's as if Reuters or the AP had millions of reporters, many of them experts, all working for no salary for free newspapers that carried no advertising." If Posner is correct, the influence of the bloggers on international news media may be considerable, even if far flung and almost impossible to measure.[7]

Communications over the Internet have greatly multiplied and amplified the voices, information, exhortations, and diatribes passing through the world news prism. More people than ever before are getting information, tuning in, tuning out, and forming opinions. This is what freedom of expression is all about.

Thoughtful persons in mainstream journalism – the "news business" – are well aware of the importance, as well as the many pitfalls for journalism, of the Internet. Publishers, broadcasters, and journalists believe that the news media must be involved with the Internet, but neither they nor anyone else seems to know where this brave new world of communication is headed.

Journalism by bloggers stresses the importance and primacy of "citizen journalists," but print journalists say news bloggers lack the skills of professional reporters, who ask powerful people, at home and abroad, blunt and impertinent questions, and report back reliably and in plain language to a general audience. Moreover, bloggers lack the resources of a professional newsroom which can edit, critique, and supplement a story with further verified information. Global news is a process – not a single report. Such journalism, the old pros say, is better able to serve as a watchdog overseer on powerful authority, whether local, national or global. Media coverage of the extensive oil disaster in the Gulf of Mexico is a good example. All these consideration are part of the basics of the US/UK model of serious journalism which is spreading around the world and needs to be more widely emulated in online journalism.

Internet journalism is still in its infancy and is continuing to expand as readers, especially younger ones, turn to the Internet for a fast take on the news. The beneficiaries of this continued audience growth continue to be the largest and best-known national news organizations – those that stress national and international news.

The Internet is still an ancillary news source for most people, after broadcasting and newspapers, yet the audience for news and information sites is growing. Some of the most frequently used US news websites are www.msnbc.msn.com, www.cnn.com, www.nytimes.com, www.abcnews.go.com, www.usatoday.com, www.washingtonpost.com, www.time.com, www.latimes.com, www.foxnews.com, and www.wsj.com.

Implications of Rapid Change

To summarize, innovations in communication technology suggest certain broad trends for transnational journalism:

1   The unit cost of the international communication of news will continue to drop as usage of the world news systems increases, and as the efficiency, speed, and reach of the hardware become greater. But "free" digital media pose serious threats to the viability of ink-on-paper media.
2   Technology is making it possible to send and receive news and other essential information from almost anywhere in the world and with increasing speed. The continuing integration of computers with telecommunication means much more interactive, or two-way, communication.
3   The two-way capability of cablevision, tied in with Comsats and personal computers on the Internet, means that information users can seek out or request specific kinds of information or news and not remain a passive mass audience. The two-way capability of telecommunications means that there will be more two-way flows of information, with consumers having more choice about what they receive. The trend toward such interactive communications systems is clear, as is shown by the rapid increase in the numbers of bloggers and social media.

4 Because of continuing technical improvements, the potential numbers of channels and sources of information are virtually unlimited, and the possible varieties and kinds of future "content" stagger the imagination.

5 These personalized communications, typified by bloggers, the Internet, email, fax, social media, and cablevision, present a challenge to authoritarian governments, which traditionally control their newspapers and broadcasting. How does Big Brother stop someone from watching a pirated videocassette, or from calling up distant information on the Internet, or picking up news off a satellite, or receiving email from a dissident group overseas? Battles over Internet free expression are replacing struggles over freedom of the press of global news media and will continue to be of international concern.

6 Finally, concern is growing about the effects of all this greatly expanded communication flow on its global audiences. Most people spend no more than an hour a day reading newspapers or getting the news from television or radio, but the news volume cascades on. David Shenk wrote that in the middle of the last century, "We began to produce information much faster than we could process it. We have moved from a state of information scarcity to a state of information surplus – from drought to flood in the geological blink of an eye." In his recent book, *Data Smog: Surviving the Information Glut*, Shenk argues that information overload is bad for your health, promoting stress, memory overload, compulsive behavior, and attention-deficit disorder. Shenk argues that the well-known global village, created by mass communication, is at the same time growing increasingly fragmented and fractionalized as people, despairing of being able to master a grand overview, retreat into their own special interests. He argues that cyberspace, including the Internet, promotes a highly decentralized, deregulated society with little common discourse and minimal public infrastructure.[8]

Concerned persons are pondering the implications of all this. Society, in short, faces the danger of computer/communications technologies advancing faster than our ability to develop methods of controlling and using them for the general welfare of humankind. This has always been true of technologies, but today that gap is becoming ominously wide. Nonetheless, innovations in media technology will continue to shape international news.

Finally, Pelton of INTELSAT saw much more to come: "New and perhaps totally different architectures for space communications are likely to evolve in the 21st century and the long-term growth and development of space communication seem relatively well-assured. In short, the 21st century should see the beginning of the true long-term road to space communications, making it truly the beginning of the 'golden age' of space communications."[9]

Notes

1. "Most Online News Readers Use 5 Sites or Fewer," *New York Times*, March 15, 2010, B2.
2. Joseph Pelton, "Heading for Information Overload," *Inter-Media*, Autumn 1988, 19.
3. Pelton, "Heading for Information Overload."
4. Arthur C. Clarke, "Beyond Babel: The Century of the Communication Satellite," in *Process and Effects of Mass Communication*, W. Schram and D. Roberts, eds. (Urbana: University of Illinois Press, 1971), 952.
5. Pelton, "Heading for Information Overload."
6. "Old News and a New Contender," *The Economist*, June 18, 2005, 52.
7. Richard Posner, "Bad News," *The New York Times Book Review*, July 31, 2005, 1.
8. Michiko Kakutan, "Data, Data, Everywhere, and All the World Did Shrink," *The New York Times*, July 8, 1997, B6.
9. Pelton, "Heading for Information Overload," 21.

3

Global Media Under Stress

When an unexpected global calamity occurs, such as the recent earthquakes in Haiti, Chile, or China, news media immediately begin gathering all available details about the horrendous events. Earthquake and tsunami stories, like most major news stories, were essentially reported by journalists working for news organizations of Western nations. To their clients, news has – like electricity, water, and gas – become an essential service that is taken for granted. By merely turning on a radio or television set or picking up a newspaper at the door, or logging on to the Internet, people expect to find the latest news, whether it be from the Middle East, Europe, Africa, or wherever. (Such is not the case, however, among the rural poor of developing nations.)

Indeed, most people in the industrialized world cannot remember when important breaking news was not available immediately (like any other public utility) at the flick of a switch; the technicalities of news delivery are of little public concern and only dimly understood at best. The fact is, however, that global news communication is of fairly recent origin. The far-flung apparatus or "system" through which news flows around the world has evolved and expanded greatly since World War II, along with our modern information society. We learned, for example, about the important battles of World War II many hours or often several days after they began – and then only through radio or newspapers. About thirty years later, the daily clashes in Vietnam were delivered in full color on our home television screens at dinner time, sometimes on the same day they occurred.

Naturally, the public's perceptions of warfare have always been colored by the way journalists have reported them, but color television pictures of

The World News Prism: Digital, Social and Interactive, Ninth Edition.
William A. Hachten and James F. Scotton.
© 2016 John Wiley & Sons, Inc. Published 2016 by John Wiley & Sons, Inc.

modern wars, including US dead and wounded, had an unusually strong impact on public attitudes. And today, with the ongoing war in Syria and Iraq, the public follows many dramatic news events in real time. Hence, the impact is greatly enhanced.

In our time, and particularly since 1945, an intricate web of international communications has been spun about the planet, greatly expanding the capability for news and political interaction at a time when the need for information has become so much more urgent. This rapid growth of what Colin Cherry termed an "explosion" in mass communication around the world has had widespread significance: for international relations and world politics; for the flow of news and information; for the cultural impact abroad of motion pictures, television, and video from the West; and for the institutions of international communication, including news agencies, broadcast networks, international newspapers, magazines, and the now ubiquitous Internet and its digital progeny. Today, the world reacts politically and socially much more quickly, and perhaps emotionally, to events than ever before.

As we become, in various ways, a more interdependent world community with common problems and dangers, if not common values and goals, the world's ability to communicate effectively with all its parts has been greatly expanded. We now have an expanding global economy, and we are trying to develop institutions to deal with it. Reliable news and adequate communications are of prime importance in today's world.

This communication explosion has three broad dimensions: geographically, vast areas of Africa, South and East Asia, and Latin America have been drawn into the global communication network for the first time; the amount of traffic and the number of messages carried in the system have multiplied geometrically; and the technical complexity of both the new hardware and the skills and specialized knowledge needed to maintain and run the network has become increasingly sophisticated.

"For two thousand years and more the means of distant communications were various postal services, derived from the Roman cursus publicus, working at the speed of the horse (up to and including the Pony Express); and then the explosion hit us, not immediately upon the invention of the telegraph, but nearly a century later," Cherry wrote. "It is the sheer suddenness of the explosion which is of such profound social importance, principally following the Second World War."[1]

Advancing from crystal sets in 1920 to a television service in 1937 took, as Cherry pointed out, only seventeen years. The first transistor appeared

in 1948, and electronic memory chips, the silicon brains of microcomput-
ers, came soon after that. The first Sputnik went up in 1957, and only eight
years later Early Bird, the first generation of the global INTELSAT system of communication satellites, went into operation in 1965 and brought
television pictures from Europe. Just twenty-five years later, INTELSAT VI
was in the heavens and, compared with Early Bird, had fifty-five times
more power and a total communications capacity that had increased 170
times. Comparing the communications capacity of Early Bird INTELSAT I
to INTELSAT VI, a major carrier of international news, is like comparing the height of a toolshed with a skyscraper in New York City.[2]
Today, the Internet with its rambunctious progeny – interactive newspapers, online broadcast media, social media, and many bloggers – has added
more dimensions to international news, including gossip, advocacy, and
misinformation.

The International News Tradition

The expanded international news system is largely an outgrowth of Western news media, especially those of Britain, the United States, and, to a lesser
degree, France and Germany. A world news system exists today because the
peoples of Western democracies wanted world news, and the great independent newspapers, news magazines, news agencies, and, later, broadcast
organizations have cooperated and competed to satisfy those wants and
needs. Editors and correspondents, working for independent (that is to
say, non-governmental) and profit-making news organizations, have developed the traditions and patterns of providing the almost instantaneous
world news upon which people everywhere have come to rely. The credibility and legitimacy that such news generally enjoys rest on its usually
unofficial and independently gathered nature as well as its informational
or generally objective content. The enduring ethic of Western journalism
was summed up more than 100 years ago by an editor of *The Times* of
London:

> The first duty of the press is to obtain the earliest and most correct intelligence
> of the events of the time, and instantly, by disclosing them, to make them the
> common property of the nation. The duty of the journalist is to present to his
> readers not such things as statecraft would wish them to know but the truth
> as near as he can attain it.

That nineteenth-century statement represents a journalistic ideal; actual practice is often much different. Some transnational media have close, compromising ties to their governments, and all independent media are subject to varying kinds of controls and influences from the corporate interests that own them. Nonetheless, the news media of Western nations have more freedom and independence to report world news, and hence more credibility, than media of other nations. And because of greater financial resources and technology, Western media have a greater capability to report world news. Although the press in different nations will differ sharply about the facts and importance of particular news stories, the process is essentially one of international cooperation.

Cooperation is still an integral part of global news flow, but digital disruption is rapidly changing how foreign news is gathered and distributed. The names of the leading media are still familiar – *New York Times*, Associated Press (AP), British Broadcasting Corporation (BBC), *Wall Street Journal*, *Washington Post*, *Financial Times*, *Daily Telegraph* (of London), *The Economist*, *Time*, National Broadcasting Corporation (NBC), National Public Radio (NPR), and more recently Al Jazeera (in English and Arabic), which is very important for the Arab world. But today much of the world news collected by these media appears as well on the Internet or websites via Google, Yahoo, and other "search" sites and on thousands of online editions of newspapers, magazines, and radio and television broadcasters. Further, the well-known "old media" have gone digital in various ways. The *New York Times* and *Washington Post* have online editions that reach more people than their print editions. The BBC, long the leader in world news via short-wave and AM radio and now a leader in television news, has been a major presence on the global Internet.

These media are still reporting world news but, as emphasized elsewhere, their financial wherewithal to do it has been sharply restricted by falling circulations, declining audiences, and advertising losses to "free" online media like Google, Yahoo, and other "new media" on line. The dozen or more "old media," though weakened financially at home, still have the authority and stature to authenticate the serious news for the world and create a consensus for what is considered to be the major news from abroad.

Serious regional publications and other media, such as (to name a few) the *Guardian* of London, *Le Monde* of Paris, *Frankfurter Allgemeine Zeitung* and *Der Spiegel* of Germany, *The Times* of India, and numerous other media around the world still contribute to world news flow. So in 2010, global journalism faced this anomalous situation: the traditional providers of world news were financially weakened and less capable of covering the news, but at the same time, due to the abrupt digital explosion, vastly more information and news went out to even the most remote corners of the world.

Currently, however, comparatively little revenue ever finds its way back to the journalists and news organizations, who dug out the original facts and pulled the big story together. This has caused such important news organizations as ABC News and the Associated Press to restructure and downscale their news operations. For example, in early 2010, ABC cut 300 to 400 people, or roughly 25 percent of the news division of 1,500 staffers. ABC News called it a "fundamental transformation." The network, as well as NBC and CBS, have lost audiences, the result of competition from cable, the Internet, and changing consumer habits. CBS News, a chief competitor, said at the same time that it was laying off dozens of employees. ABC said it would replace some news bureaus with more flexible so-called digital journalists, who work on their own in foreign capitals.[3]

Some press and broadcasting organizations use their own correspondents to report foreign news, but the global workhorses and the linchpins of the world news system have long been the so-called world news services: the AP, BBC, AFP, and DPA, which are in effect "newspapers for newspapers." It is no coincidence that they all are in the Western nations of the United States, Britain, France, and Germany.

In 2005, the Associated Press, with 242 bureaus, a total staff of 3,700, and more than 6,000 subscribers, processed 20 million words and 1,000 photos daily and had an annual revenue of about $630 million. Yet, as a cooperative mainly owned by US newspapers, the AP is an important cog in the world news system but not as central as in previous times. After a decade of watching the newspapers and rival news services shrink, the 161-year-old AP said in 2007 that it was refitting itself to deal with the twenty-four-hour news cycle it had helped create. The AP said it would change the way it files, edits, and distributes news, opening four new regional editing hubs and expanding its multimedia packages for entertainment, business, and sports reports. And the company is moving toward an all digital platform it calls the "Digital Cooperative."

Some of the great newspapers of the world maintain their own correspondents abroad. The same is true of the extensive broadcasting systems BBC, CBS, NBC, ABC, CNN, and others, as well as the leading news magazines such as *Time*, *The Economist*, *L'Express*, and *Der Spiegel*. Other important regional dailies are *The Hindu* and *The Times* of India, and the *New Straits*

Times of Singapore. However, as print media continue to face the financial stress of a changing communication marketplace, these have fewer journalists to report and edit the news.

Several newspapers, such as *The New York Times*, *The Washington Post*, and the *Los Angeles Times*, as well as the *Guardian* of London, syndicate their news and sell it to other newspapers at home and abroad. As a result, their news stories and features supplement as well as compete with the world news agencies. It is well to remember that once a news event is reported – the death of a king or a major earthquake – this information becomes the common property of journalism and can be repeated anywhere; only the precise wording of a news story can be copyrighted, and this rarely becomes a factor in news flow.

People receive more and more of their news from electronic sources, smartphones, computers, and television. Two television news services, Reuters TV (formerly Visnews) and Associated Press Television News (APTN), as well as the great Western networks, have been playing an increasingly important role in the international news system. Live feeds from another continent are usually identifiable as the work of the network involved, but the source of the news on tape or film is not as evident. Most viewers are unaware that much of the foreign news viewed on television is supplied by two television news agencies, dominated by American and British interests.

Reuters TV, the biggest and best known, is the world's leading supplier of international news video and film for television, servicing more than 409 customers in eighty-three countries, and is distributed by both satellites and airmailed videocassettes. Reuters TV says it reaches 1.5 billion people daily. In 1992, Reuters bought out its co-owners, NBC and BBC, and changed its name from Visnews. Reuters TV staffs thirty-eight bureaus and works with contract crews in about seventy countries.

The pivot of these services is APTN, also located in London, which remains a center and clearinghouse for international news exchanges. APTN was founded in 1994 as Associated Press Television, and in 1998 it merged with Worldwide TV News (WTN) to form APTN. Both services have exchange agreements with the US networks ABC, CBS, NBC, and CNN, all of which maintain several bureaus overseas. The US networks sell some of their news products abroad and thus contribute to the interchange that makes the international news system work. Video news agencies like these do not produce programs that TV viewers can use. Rather, they provide footage of an event with only natural sound and very little editing. This is sent out via an encrypted video stream that is distributed on three satellites for global coverage.

Eurovision, the regional television exchange system in western Europe, gets about 40 to 50 percent of its material from Reuters Television and APTN. The majority of television systems around the world depend on these two services for all of their world news on television. In numerous small African nations, often a lone television service depends on a five-minute package of world news from Reuters TV for its entire foreign coverage.

These world-wide news agencies mean a Westerner's right to know is the world's right to know. Thus, any news story that gets into the European or US news media can, and often does, flow rapidly around the world and can appear in local media anywhere if it gets by the various gatekeepers that select and reject the news of the day. Stories about unrest in Ukraine, the war in Afghanistan or terrorist bombings in Pakistan often will be read or viewed or listened to in Africa, Asia, and Latin America.

There is some basis to complaints about this Western-dominated system. But the West does not enjoy a closed monopoly of world news; any news organization is free to report world news, but few as yet have the capability and credibility for so doing. Moreover, far-ranging and technically sophisticated as it is, the world's present news system is not as pervasive and efficient as it might be, considering the world's diversity and its need for information. Yet the new digital media have been providing more and more news and information to the global flow.

Global Television News

The successful establishment of the twenty-four-hour Cable News Network (CNN), with its global reach, has been a major innovation in international news as well as in the competitive US cable television news. Ted Turner, the Atlanta, Georgia, broadcaster, launched the around-the-clock news service to attract viewers to cable television and to compete in news with the three major US networks. Started in 1980, its growth and success have been impressive – and imitated. From a single network available to 1.7 million US households to its current twenty-three networks reaching some 260 million households worldwide, CNN is seen in more than 200 countries. So when a world crisis such as the 9/11 terror attacks occurs, CNN plays a major role in informing the world quickly.

During an international crisis, CNN plays a special global role. Whereas ABC, CBS, and NBC will issue news bulletins and then go back to scheduled programming and perhaps do a late-evening wrap-up, CNN stays on the air for long stretches of time, continually updating the story. The three major networks' version of the story will be seen in the United States; CNN's version will be seen all over the world. Overseas, travelers often can watch CNN in their hotel rooms, foreign television services pick up the whole service or some news programs from CNN, and individual television viewers can get it off their satellite dishes or subscribe to the service locally.

During prolonged crises, such as the first Gulf War, CNN can play a key role, with its extensive coverage of all facets of a story. Indeed, CNN's international position often makes it a player in diplomacy as well as a reporter of major events. With its reports available in all world capitals, political leaders and diplomats watch closely and are willingly interviewed on CNN in order to get their views widely known. (CNN recognizes its near-diplomatic status, and reporters are aware of the danger of being manipulated by their interviewees, whether they are President Obama or President Putin.)

Recently, CNN has not been without its problems and its critics. When there is not an international crisis or a celebrity scandal or trial, viewership of CNN drops off sharply, and revenues from advertising have declined as well. During the O.J. Simpson trial, audiences soared when CNN provided gavel-to-gavel coverage, often to the neglect of foreign news coverage. Lately, CNN has been lagging in its US cable ratings behind Fox, MSNBC, and CNBC.

Some argue that CNN is primarily a technological innovation in international news by reason of its ability to interconnect so many video sources, newsrooms, and foreign ministries to so many television sets in so many remote places in the world. In this regard, CNN has undoubtedly had a major impact on diplomacy as well as global news. Nonetheless, a television news channel of true global reach was an innovation whose time had come and, as proof of that, CNN now has serious competition at home and abroad.

In 1991, the BBC began its own World Service Television (WST), now called BBC World, and has been expanding it rapidly. Since 1997, BBC World has been challenging the dominance of CNN International. BBC World has a twenty-four-hour international current affairs TV channel with BBC news, documentaries, interviews, and so on. Unlike the radio service, it is commercially funded and is widely carried on satellite and cable.

With the 24/7 cable news television industry, called by some "the newest public utility," the old leader CNN has been bucking stiff competition from MSNBC and Fox News Channel. MSNBC is owned jointly by NBC and Microsoft, and has averaged a higher daily audience than CNN. Fox, which appeals to a more conservative audience than the other two cable news channels, has been making large gains. Just after the 9/11 tragedy, CNN pulled in record numbers of viewers, putting it far ahead of second-place Fox. However, within two years Fox moved ahead of CNN and has stayed there ever since. CNN did get stronger during the Arab uprisings in 2011 and 2012, showing again that it can be the leader in TV reporting of an ongoing international crisis. Rupert Murdoch, the owner of the huge Fox conglomerate, showed again in 2014 with his unsuccessful bid to take over Time Warner that he wants to dominate TV cable news throughout the world.

The success of CNN and BBC World illustrates the ways that media technology can shape the contours and impact of international news – and will continue to do so. International radio broadcasts, both short-wave and medium-wave, are also major purveyors of global news. But because of their roles in public diplomacy the BBC World Service and the Voice of America are discussed in Chapter 12.

With the greatly enhanced technological reach of international communication, the location of a sender or receiver is no longer as important as it once was. The key gatekeepers of the world news system are still concentrated in New York City, London, Paris, and similar metropolitan centers, but it is not necessary to be in those cities to follow the news of the world. A short-wave radio or a satellite dish, and now a computer with an Internet connection or a cellphone, can keep a person almost anywhere in touch with the day's principal events. Furthermore, distance has become increasingly less a factor in the cost of long-distance news communication, whether it takes place through a private telephone, computer or fax messages, television reception, or news reports bounced off satellites, or now even Twitter. Essentially the same technological process (and at the same cost) is required to send a news flash via satellite from London to Paris as from London to Tokyo. And the greater the traffic on the system, the lower the unit cost of the messages sent. International communication is tied to computer technology, and in that explosive field the costs of computers are dropping as rapidly as their efficiency is increasing. In addition, the capacity of communication satellites to carry information is expanding. Much of the content of the international news system concerns popular culture – video, movies, music in its many forms, youth lifestyles and attire – all of which appeal to a global youth culture found literally everywhere. Besides traditional news, the system carries news about the widely known and admired icons of pop culture, the singers, musicians, dancers, rappers, and movie stars. The commonalities of this youth culture were well shown in July 2005 by the Live 8 concerts in eight major industrial nations plus South Africa, in an effort to pressure leaders at the Group of 8, then meeting on aid, to mitigate poverty in Africa. Over a million young people attended, while another 5 million watched AOL's live video streams on their computers. The music, performers, and their message resonated around the world.

If technology is the good news, then performance in recent years is the bad news. In earlier years, the American "national media" – particularly *The New York Times, The Washington Post*, the *Los Angeles Times, The Wall Street Journal*, CBS, NBC, ABC, *Time*, and *Newsweek* – which set the news agenda for other media, did much of the gathering of news from abroad with the help of news agencies.

But that situation changed around 1989 when the Cold War ended. The television networks and the news magazines gave much less attention to serious foreign news. One indicator: In its heyday, CBS maintained twenty-four foreign bureaus; by 2002, it had nine reporters in only four capitals: London, Moscow, Tel Aviv, and Tokyo. Dan Rather admitted to Harvard students, "Don't kid yourself, the trend line in American journalism is away from, not toward, increased foreign coverage."[4]

Max Frankel, former editor of *The New York Times*, wrote, "A great shroud has been drawn across the mind of America to make it forget that there is a world beyond its borders. The three main television networks obsessively focus their cameras on domestic tales and dramas as if the end of the Cold War rendered the rest of the planet irrelevant. Their news staffs occasionally visit some massacre, famine, or shipwreck and their anchors may parachute into Haiti or Kuwait for a photo op, but these spasms of interest only emphasize the networks' apparent belief that on most evenings the five billion folks out there don't matter one whit."[5]

Foreign news is expensive to gather and often not of interest unless American lives – as soldiers or terrorism victims – are at stake. Instead, network television and the news magazines shifted their resources and considerable talents into high-profile stories of scandal, celebrity, and sensation.

However, a few major US daily papers still report the world. The best and most comprehensive foreign reporting, some of very high quality, comes from just four daily newspapers, *The New York Times, The Washington Post, The Wall Street Journal,* and the *Los Angeles Times.* This small group plus the Associated Press and Reuters are the prime sources for foreign news. It should be noted that a good deal of serious foreign news is available to radio listeners of National Public Radio's two daily programs, *All Things Considered* and *Morning Edition.* Major British and European newspaper still cover world news in large part because their readers demand it.

Notes

1. Colin Cherry, *World Communication: Threat or Promise?* (New York: Wiley Inter-science, 1971), 57–58.
2. Joseph Pelton, "Heading for Information Overload," *Inter-Media*, Autumn 1988, 19.
3. Brian Stelter and Bill Carter, "ABC News Plans to Trim 300 to 400 from Staff," *The New York Times*, February 24, 2010, B5.
4. Stephen Hess, *International News & Foreign Correspondents* (Washington, DC: Brookings Institution, 1996), 61.
5. Max Frankel, "The Shroud," *The New York Times Magazine*, November 27, 1994, 42.

4

Impact of Great Events

Great news events of our times have given us insights into the role that global news plays in assisting and accelerating political and social change. Intensive television coverage of such an event as the prolonged civil war in Syria does not determine the political outcome of such crises, but reporting (or non-reporting) has a clear impact on public opinion, which may well influence decisions made by government leaders of great nations.

Today fast-moving changes are being shaped by transnational communication. Not only have speed and volume increased along with greater geographical dispersal of international news flow, but the nature and effects of the content have changed and diversified as well. Instead of the mere words and numbers of yesteryear's news, today vivid color video coverage of news events is now delivered to the world's news publics, greatly increasing the impact of the message. As a result, a new kind of audience involvement in world events has emerged. The propaganda maxim that the report of the event can be as important as the event itself has greater impact than ever in the age of media events.

The following case studies illustrate how audiences of great international events increasingly share their concerns with each other. In this chapter, we will look at journalistic aspects of several news stories: violent political protests in Iran, the devastating earthquake in Haiti, the Israeli sea raid near Gaza; the tsunami in South Asia, the 9/11 attacks on the United States, the collapse of Soviet communism, the 1991 failed coup in Moscow, and interactions between terrorist attacks and global television. Each provides instructive examples of the interplay between news and media.

The World News Prism: Digital, Social and Interactive, Ninth Edition.
William A. Hachten and James F. Scotton.
© 2016 John Wiley & Sons, Inc. Published 2016 by John Wiley & Sons, Inc.

Election Protests in Iran

After presidential elections in Iran in June 2009, many thousands of Iranians took to the streets to protest the results. In the past, the regime could block out such unfavorable news by shutting phone lines and restricting a few foreigners. But in this new age of social communication with cellphone cameras, Twitter accounts, and other facets of the World Wide Web in play, governments cannot keep the outside world from learning what is happening. In the riot, a young Iranian woman was shot: she bled to death in a Tehran street, and became a world-wide martyr because a 40-second video of her death ricocheted around the world. The 2-megabyte video was emailed to a nearby friend, who forwarded it to the Voice of America, the *Guardian* in London, and to five other online friends in Europe, with a message that said "please let the world know." Another friend posted it on Facebook. Copies of the video spread quickly to YouTube and were televised within hours on CNN.

Despite Iran's efforts to keep a lid on the violent street events, the victim, Ms. Agha-Sotan, was transformed from a nameless victim to an icon of the Iranian protest movement. It was easier for Iranian authorities to limit images and information within Iran than to stop them from spreading rapidly to the outside world. Iran has severely restricted Internet access for Iranians, but a loose worldwide network of sympathizers has arisen to maintain connections between activists and spontaneous filmmakers. The pervasiveness of the Web has made censorship[1] a much more complicated task for Iran and the three dozen other countries – as varied as China, Cuba, Singapore, and Uzbekistan – that extensively control their nations' use of the Internet.

In Iran censorship has been more sophisticated than most and it uses the latest spying technology to locate opponents. But Twitter and phone video can operate in limited ways to a world of online spectators. Because of this determination, hundreds of amateur videos were uploaded to YouTube after the riots, providing television networks with raw and unverified videos from the protests. Global news gathering benefits from the fact that videos and tweets indicate to many that broadly based Internet devices and the spirit of young, tech-savvy people cannot be completely repressed by an authoritarian regime.

In addition to Twitter, YouTube has been an important tool to spread videos from Iran when traditional media have had trouble filming protests or the ensuing crackdowns. The BBC's Persian-language television channel said that during one of the protests, it was receiving about five videos a minute from amateurs, even though the channel was largely blocked within Iran. One video showed pro-government militia members firing weapons at a rally. "We've been struck by the amount of videos and eyewitness testimony," said Jon Williams, the BBC world news editor, adding: "The days when regimes can control the news are over." In Iran, however, as new media proliferate, traditional journalists have been having a more difficult time. Journalists were told they could not cover protests without permission, effectively confining them to their offices.

Earthquake Flattens Haiti

In mid-January of 2010, Haiti was devastated by an earthquake of 7.0 magnitude that shattered its impoverished and teeming capital of Port-au-Prince into rubble. The death toll was estimated at over 200,000. Global media became focused on the vast misery and helplessness of the small Caribbean nation. Television journalism was perhaps Haiti's greatest helper during the first days of dire need. Within 20 hours, two major US networks were broadcasting from the scene, followed by reporters and photographers of major print media. CNN said it was its biggest deployment, short of a war, of news media since the tsunami in 2004. Network television expanded its coverage, bringing vivid pictures into homes everywhere. At first, news networks and newspapers found themselves supplementing traditional reporting with Twitter and cellphone videos of witnesses in Haiti. The biggest challenge for the media was that the entire infrastructure of Port-au-Prince had collapsed. Reporters equipped themselves with satellite phones and clips that allowed them to draw power from car batteries for their laptops, cameras, and phones. Many of the press slept on the ground.

Yet Haiti's extreme distress remained mostly a network television story. Television quickly informed a mass audience globally of what had happened and, more importantly, helped to create a worldwide caring and sympathetic audience willing to help alleviate such unprecedented human misery – vividly shown right there on their TV screens.

Critic Alessandra Stanley wrote, "Disaster is both one of the hardest and easiest sights to watch on television: the medium feeds on paradox, presenting extraordinary images that horrify and also comfort. Since the earthquake struck Haiti, network and cable news shows have organized the chaos with raw, graphic footage, as well as with beautifully edited vignettes, some scored to music, that calibrate the balance of hope and despair."[2]

In such a calamity, television reporters are the heralds of the fundraising efforts. Television reporters repeatedly told people where and how to donate money for Haiti and allowed viewers to feel that they could do something to help. They also help the TV organizations by reminding viewers that journalists serve as a pillar of the rescue mission – on the scene to do more than just report the news. Another function of TV news is to remind government officials, UN groups, the Red Cross, Care, and other aid agencies just how desperate the situation in Haiti is and how much must be done to rebuild this shattered country.

Dueling Videos in Israeli Sea Raid

In June 2010, Israeli commandos attacked and boarded the so-called "freedom flotilla" of ships from Turkey carrying supplies to blockaded Gaza. In the melee nine activists were killed, in a confusing conflict in which both sides were well armed – with video cameras. Both sides promptly released a blizzard of video clips "proving" the other side was the aggressor. The flotilla movies proved popular on the Internet. A video from the Israeli defense forces notched 600,000 views on YouTube. Digital views from both sides were shown worldwide on television news programs. But these views did not establish the sequence of events or who attacked first.

James Hoge, editor of *Foreign Affairs*, said there has been a gradual increase in the use of video clips to bear witness and shape opinion. "On a matter like this, public opinion is awfully important in terms of determining which image is going to last. First, it was people in crowds with mobile phones. Now, as so often is the case, governments catch up and begin to use the tools for their own purposes."[3]

The activists had intended to stage a "media event" and were webcasting live from the open seas as the confrontation started. They were using the services of Livestream, a New York-based firm that hosts free webcasts. On board was a full multi-camera production uplinked to the Internet and to a satellite that allowed news channels to re-broadcast live pictures of the raid in progress. Video images from the vessel were viewed by a quarter of a million people on Livestream, and after the attack were watched by countless others on television. The episode again illustrated the propaganda maxim that what people believe happened can be more important than what actually happened.

Tsunami Batters South Asia, Killing Thousands

After an underground earthquake off the coast of Sumatra on the day after Christmas 2004, a giant wave radiated throughout the coastal areas of Indonesia, Thailand, Sri Lanka, India, numerous islands, and even to the coast of East Africa. The death toll climbed to over 220,000 dead or lost, and the homes and livelihoods of millions were devastated.

The disaster rippled beyond South Asia, making it a tragedy of global proportions. Among the casualties were thousands of vacationers of fifty nationalities from outside the area. The missing included 1,500 from Sweden, 700 to 800 from Norway, and over 100 each from New Zealand, Denmark, the Czech Republic, Italy, Germany, and Israel. The disaster's reach was an unsettling reminder that globalization can bring the world together in tragic ways.

The world's news media responded quickly, as thousands of images from around the region poured out to television networks. Video compression technology, fed by digital cameras and enabled by satellite and videophones, along with laptops with uplink capabilities, meant that the world was viewing the deadly aftermath just hours after it had ended.

Soon after that, real-time video footage of the tidal wave striking the shore, much of it taken by tourists on or near beaches in Thailand, began appearing on network broadcasts. In this disaster, there had been a reversal of the news-gathering process. Usually, reporters would get a story and then commission a photographer to go and get the pictures. In this case, the reporters were chasing the pictures and trying to create some context for what the viewers were seeing.

Some saw the tsunami story as a kind of tipping point in so-called "citizen journalism," where bloggers and social media play a part. Digital technologies – the Internet, email, blogs, digital cameras, camera phones – have enabled people on the scene of a news event to share with professional journalists the capability to reach a wide audience, and show the world what they saw and experienced.

"Tsunami videos" proved a boon for bloggers trying to attract viewers. Dozens of locations on the Internet hosted amateur videos of the Indian

Ocean disaster. Many video bloggers were deluged with requests to see more of the dramatic scenes. One blog created just after the disaster, Waveofdestruction.org, logged 682,366 unique visitors in four days. Another site, named "Cheese and Crackers," went from attracting about ten surfers a day to 640,000 visitors after showing the tsunami videos.

But the tidal wave and its follow-up stories of the relief and reconstruction efforts of the outside world were also a boon for the so-called "mainstream media." Tim Rutten, media critic of the *Los Angeles Times*, noted that the story vindicated the indispensability of the mainstream media. He said that in their response, "they have fulfilled the most basic of journalistic obligations – the duty of witness. They have placed the suffering and loss of millions before the conscience of the developed world, and the result has been a demonstration of human solidarity across national, religious and culture divides that seemed beyond reach just a month ago."[4]

Using front-page stories as a measure, in the first several days *The New York Times* published fifty-three stories on the tsunami, the *Los Angeles Times* thirty-eight, and *The Washington Post* thirty-one. In Britain, the BBC had audience increases of as much as 50 percent for its regular nightly news programming. CNN, with its extensive overseas staff, saw its daily audience increase by 38 percent and its prime-time viewers grew by 46 percent. CNN had eighty journalists on the scene within days of the disaster and the BBC had 100 people in the field. Rutten commented that "Real news is covered the same way that real wars are won: by putting enough boots on the ground."[5]

Most of the world responded generously with money and assistance for disaster relief. Finally, the tsunami story was a truly global drama that had victims and heroes but no villains – no human ones, anyway.

The 9/11 Terror Attacks on the United States

The news of a single day has rarely had such a profound effect on modern history. December 11, 1941 – the date of the surprise attack on Pearl Harbor that brought America into World War II – was such a day. September 11, 2001 – the terrorist attacks by hijacked airliners on the World Trade Center towers in New York City and the Pentagon in Washington, DC – was another historic day that set off a global upheaval with still unforeseen repercussions. After the collapse of the two skyscrapers, the scarring of the Pentagon, the crashing of four airliners, and about 3,000 lives lost, Americans and many others worldwide no longer felt personally secure and safe from the threats of a dangerous world beyond their borders. The United States and its allies promptly embarked on a war against terrorism.

News coverage of the many facets of 9/11 was comprehensive and magnificent. In New York and Washington, DC, journalists reported a local story of great national and international import. Global color television – nonstop and constantly updated – carried unfolding details to every corner of the world. Supplemented by radio, print media, the Internet, and cellphones, much of the world saw and heard nearly the same video images and news reports that Americans received. And the US audience was huge: 79.5 million viewers were watching news coverage on broadcast and cable television networks in prime time on September 11, according to Nielsen Media Research.[6]

On September 14, three days later, 39.5 million viewers tuned in to television news coverage in prime time. The Internet audience (which is international) was huge as well. The number of page turns (hits) on just www.cnn.com jumped to 162.4 million.

Moreover, that vast audience approved of the way both the US government and the media had responded. According to a poll by the Pew Research Center for the People and the Press, 89 percent of people felt the media had done a good or excellent job in covering the attacks.[7]

Professional journalists agreed.

So after more than a decade of looking inward and often ignoring the outside world, the news media, as well as thoughtful citizens, began showing a more serious interest in world affairs again; in particular, trying to understand radical Islam and the complex politics of the Middle East and Central Asia. The nature and motives of Osama bin Laden became a subject of intense public and media interest – at least for a while.

A Pew poll taken in October 2001 found that the terrorist attacks and the war in Afghanistan had created a new internationalist sentiment among the public. There was more support for a multilateral foreign policy than before 9/11, with roughly six of every ten people (59 percent) now saying that the interests of allies should be taken into account by US policymakers. By a two-to-one margin, the public thought that taking an active role in the world, rather than becoming less involved, would be a more effective way of avoiding problems such as terrorism in the future. And support for assertive US leadership also had grown.[8] These opinion shifts were dramatic, but did not last.

Since 9/11, the major national news media had been given a chance for redemption, reporting with great competence a global news story with many dimensions. Because of budget cuts and fewer overseas reporters and bureaus than earlier, the broadcast networks – ABC, NBC, Fox, and CBS – were the least prepared for this new "asymmetrical" war against terrorism, which has no standing armies to confront: its enemies are hidden, subversive, and of differing nationalities, but are found in "training camps" in remote areas of the developing world – in Afghanistan, and maybe in Iraq, Syria, Somalia, and Sudan. Or probably some terrorists have been living in the West for many years in deep cover and waiting for the chance to strike – a new challenge for reporting as well as for governmental counter-terrorism efforts.

The 9/11 coverage on network television was important, unprecedented, and revealing about television news itself. Network news showed it could still mount a powerful system of news coverage; no US network or cable system performed badly. Viewers depended on Tom Brokaw, Dan Rather, and Peter Jennings (all three no longer anchors) not only for news but for reassurance and solace. In the first weeks, television coverage was unabashedly patriotic, with American flags much in evidence, but the public apparently didn't mind. In those first days, television news ran up huge costs but carried few commercials. The major print media dispatched platoons of reporters and photographers to cover whatever could be found out in Afghanistan, Pakistan, or wherever. Similarly, many journalists from Europe followed suit.

Americans were also getting their news from other sources: BBC television reporters scored several major scoops in Afghanistan, because the British government was more forthcoming with news. Although the press received high marks for its initial war coverage, the news media still faced controversy when reporting news from the "homeland." Some thought that a few members of the press had forsaken their traditional skepticism and were too willing to be a pawn of government and accept only the official versions of events. But other critics argued that the press was unpatriotic at times – too sympathetic to war protesters, and tending to overplay stories about collateral damage to civilians and reports of atrocities by the US military.

All agreed this was a different kind of war – if, indeed, it was a "war." For the first time since the end of the Cold War, the press had a major international news story to focus on – one with staying power.

Electronic Execution of Soviet Communism

The collapse of communism in central and eastern Europe in 1989, along with the end of the Cold War, were two of the most significant political events since World War II (some said since 1848), and were all the more dramatic because they were so unexpected. Certainly Western mass communication – going over, under, and around the Iron Curtain – played a role in raising expectations and in breaking the communists' monopoly on information and popular culture.

Critic George Steiner commented on the impact of television soap operas:

> Once "Dallas" had come their way [it could be picked up several hundred kilometers east of Checkpoint Charlie], once tapes of Western soap operas and rock jamborees could be multiplied and sold beyond the "Dallas line," the cataclysm and saturnalia were inevitable. Television sparked the great wild surge toward a consumer economy, and television packaged (brilliantly) the actual rush. Why live by bread alone when there is peanut butter? Why endure as a Soviet satellite when the word "satellite" means cable television?[9]

The dramatic and sudden collapse of communism in eastern Europe came after a generation of communication interactions between the Western nations and the socialist nations of eastern Europe, the USSR, and the Third World – all set in the context of the Cold War. Recent economic successes of the West, along with the failures of socialist political economies, helped explain the media changes. Further, the sheer pervasiveness of Western communications accelerated modifications of and, in time, the abandonment of, communism and its press theory.

Western journalism rode the crest of the technotronic revolution that had reshaped global mass communication during the past generation and created the information societies of the West. (One Russian general said that the USSR lost the Cold War because it was hopelessly behind the West in computer technology.) Communication satellites, computerization, global television, high-speed data transfers, and especially new media products such as videocassette and audiocassette players, all spurred by profit-making opportunities, had led to a vast flood of Western television programs, movies, videocassettes, CDs (compact disks), and taped music recordings, moving inexorably from western to eastern Europe.

Grist for this vast mill consisted of not only Western pop culture (movies, TV shows, music videos, and rock and other popular music) but also newspapers, magazines, and books. Western versions of the news, along with Western methods of news reporting and presentation, became widely accepted and emulated. The AP, Reuters, CNN, the BBC and Radio Free Europe, Radio Liberty, and the *International Herald Tribune*, among other media, added diversity to the monolithic news structure of the communist regimes. Whatever their shortcomings, Western media had a crucial advantage over communist media: they were not government-controlled and hence they achieved a wide credibility. Consequently, centralized communist governments lost their monopoly over their own information.

Western news media acted as catalysts for political change in communist nations in several ways: People in eastern Europe did listen to Western broadcasts, which carried both world news and news about the satellite nations themselves.

Much of this news went by short-wave radio, some by AM and FM broadcasting and, for East Germany, via television from West Berlin and the Federal Republic. German-language television was received all over the GDR (German Democratic Republic) except in low-lying Dresden, which was locally dubbed the "Valley of the Ignorant" because of the poor TV reception there.

Some observers believe the beginnings of the breakup of the communist empire in Eastern Europe began with the successes of the Solidarity trade union in Poland. The Polish communist regime's monopoly on news was broken in two ways: first, by the rise of alternative newspapers that challenged the government and supported Solidarity goals; and, second, by a triangular communication flow between the alternative papers, foreign reporters, and international broadcasters. It worked this way: Foreign journalists reported news of Solidarity to their Western media; these stories were beamed back to Poland via international short-wave radio, particularly by the BBC, Deutsche Welle, and Radio Free Europe; then the stories were also picked up by the alternative papers in Poland.

This communication model was followed again and again. Michael T. Kaufman, who covered Poland for *The New York Times*, wrote:

It turned out that a few dissidents using non-violent means, and exploiting the freedom of the press and airwaves beyond their borders, could in this increasingly interconnected world bring down autocrat after autocrat. Foreign correspondents wrote for their own papers, but their reports were translated and beamed back to countries where such information as they were writing was banned. The spread of portable radios and videos made such information much more accessible. The official press was forced to offer more information, more truth, as it was forced to compete for credibility with the outsiders. ... Once informed, the people were mobilized. In most places, they marched and chanted and drew placards and with the world press watching such means proved sufficient to expose previous forbidden truths and to make revolutionary changes that had so recently seemed impossible.[10]

In the revolutionary events of 1989, the media played a variety of roles. One was to report that such things happen and that times are changing. Another was to show that the world was indeed watching and that the Berlin Wall could be turned into a sieve. A third purpose was to show potential demonstrators in other countries that the unthinkable was perfectly possible. So, uprisings in East Berlin, Budapest, Prague, and Bucharest all reinforced one another.

For William E. Henry of *Time*, the triumphs owed something to journalism but little to journalists:

> The function of news people was not sage or analyst but conduit, carrying the raw facts of an amazing reality to the startled citizenry in each revolutionary nation and to a waiting world beyond. ... The thrills of 1989 and early 1990 came as useful reminders that the most interesting part of the news business is, in fact, the news. For broadcast journalists, events proved anew that the chief element of their much discussed power is the simple capacity to reach many people quickly – and in cases of true turmoil, with a verisimilitude no other medium offers. TV's basic function was as the great legitimizer.[11]

The Failed Coup in Moscow

Communications was one of the major reasons why the right-wing *coup d'état* failed to topple the Soviet government in August 1991. The nine coup leaders arrested Mikhail Gorbachev, closed down all but a handful of Communist Party media, and held a television press conference proclaiming the new government. They assumed that the nation would passively accept the changeover. However, the coup masterminds failed to understand how much the Soviet Union had changed in six years of *glasnost*. With a more open communication system and a new taste for free expression, the resistance in Moscow rallied around Boris Yeltsin. They used fax, photocopying machines, and cellphones to let fellow citizens know it was not too late to resist the coup. Inexplicably, the plotters shut down neither international telephone lines nor the satellite relay station, and they did not jam short-wave radio. No actions were taken against the large foreign press in Moscow, which sent out a flood of words and pictures to a disapproving world. CNN was even received in some Soviet republics. It was as if the coup leaders became immobilized, like deer before car headlamps, by the television camera lights recording and transmitting the events within the parliament and the street barricades outside. Soviet journalists, emboldened by *glasnost*, refused to accept the coup restrictions. Blocked at the printing plants, dozens of independent publications ran off photocopies and passed them out on street corners. Moscow's subway was quickly papered with handbills. Interfax, the independent news agency, distributed underground reports along with its own stories.

The impact of Western radio was even more impressive. The BBC doubled its Russian-language program to eighteen hours, its largest increase ever. It also relayed the banned broadcasts of a Moscow station. Radio Liberty's twenty-four-hour broadcasts, in Russian and eleven other Soviet languages, reached an estimated audience of 50 million. Gorbachev later said he gratefully listened to the BBC, RL, and the Voice of America while under house arrest at his dacha in the Crimea.

As *Newsweek* commented, "The coup leaders apparently relied on popular indifference and fear of authority. But those are not the attributes of people in the know. And last week Russians proved that they have entered the information age."[12]

Ironically, the new communications openness that propelled Boris Yeltsin to political power after the failed coup also caused him severe political damage in the winter of 1994–95, when he sent the Russian army into Chechnya to put down a rebellion. In Moscow and throughout the nation, millions of Russians watched television pictures of the brutal suppression of the revolt and the killing of thousands of civilians. And many Russians did not like what they saw.

Terrorism and Television

The very nature of global television and telecommunications, that can bring people closer together while sharing the mutual grief of tragic events, such as the assassination of John F. Kennedy or the tsunami disaster in South

Asia, also can be manipulated to capture the world's attention. Unquestionably, certain acts of international terrorism, such as jet hijackings, political kidnappings, and civilian bombings as in Oklahoma City, are perpetrated primarily to capture time and space in the world's media. Terrorism has been called "propaganda of the deed" – violent criminal acts, usually directed at innocent civilians, performed by desperate people seeking a worldwide forum for their grievances. Experts disagree over terrorists' motives.

Terrorism, of course, is not new. But the flare-ups of the phenomenon since the 1960s – especially in the Middle East, Northern Ireland, Latin America, Turkey, Italy, West Germany, Spain, and now the United States and Britain – have been facilitated in part, some say, by global television coverage that beams images of terrorist violence into millions of television sets around the world. Many terrorist groups have mastered a basic lesson of this media age: Television news organizations can be manipulated into becoming the final link between the terrorists and their audiences and, as with all sensational crimes, the more outrageous and heinous the terrorist act, the greater attention it will receive in the world's news media. Walter Laqueur said, "The media are a terrorist's best friend. . . . Terrorists are the super-entertainers of our time."[13]

In this age of global television, the effects of 9/11 and the 7/7 attacks in London were deeply felt in many lands. Whether in Madrid, Jerusalem, Shanghai, or Jakarta, the news and video were filtered through the prisms of differing cultures, ethnicities, politics, and religion. But the most important reaction was in Washington, DC, where the Bush administration, supported by US public opinion, vowed to strike back hard at terrorism.

After 9/11, international terrorism became a major concern at the top of the foreign news agenda as well as the global political agenda. After being downplayed by news media for years, terrorism was major news again; the "acts of war" on September 11 immediately triggered a new kind of war with Islamic terrorists and any states supporting them. The risk of future attacks of such a devastating nature was raised from "possible" and "unlikely" to "probable" and "likely" in the minds of editors and security officials alike.

A positive result was that the American public woke up to the importance of foreign news; the nation was reminded that we live inseparably in one world – a world that can be threatening and dangerous. The news media were reminded of the perils of neglecting foreign news since the 1989 fall of communism. Historians may be critical of American presidential leadership for failing to respond sharply to terrorist acts against America during the 1990s. And much of the news media, particularly local media and broadcast and cable television, can be faulted for not informing the public (and government) adequately about the growing dangers coming out of the Middle East conflicts: the bombing of Marine barracks in Lebanon; the bombing of Air Force living quarters in Saudi Arabia; the blowing up of US embassies in Nairobi and Dar es Salaam; and the attack on the *U.S.S. Cole* in Yemen – all precursors to 9/11.

For the first time since 1812, when the British burned down the White House, Americans realized that their two-ocean defensive shield could be penetrated. (In 1941, Hawaii was still a territory.) People realized we were now vulnerable to bioterrorism and even nuclear attacks as well as suicide bombings. In addition, airliner hijackings returned to the news as a major threat to the security of commercial aviation. The possibility of being hijacked by suicidal terrorists who used the airliner as a deadly missile, killing all on board, had hardly been imagined.

No doubt the vivid television pictures multiplied the psychological impact of the terror – the depression, sense of loss, and insecurity – felt by so many people. This, apparently, is what the terrorists intended, but did global television assist the terrorists in achieving their aims? Perhaps, but there was no choice. Acts of terrorism are major news and, of course, have to be reported.

Be that as it may, terrorism and all its facets is news, and as such it poses worrisome questions for broadcast journalists: Does television coverage really encourage and aid the terrorists' cause? Is censorship of such dramatic events ever desirable? Raymond Tanter wrote, "Since terror is aimed at the media and not at the victim, success is defined in terms of media coverage. And there is no way in the West that you could not have media coverage, because you're dealing with a free society."[14]

Terrorism coverage is a journalistic problem of international scope, just as international terrorism itself is a transnational problem that individual nations cannot solve without international cooperation. Broadcast journalists argue about whether the violence would recede if television ignored or downplayed an act of terrorism. Most journalists doubt that self-censorship by news organizations is a good idea, or even possible, in such a highly competitive field. However, television organizations have established guidelines for reporting terrorism incidents in a more restrained and rational way.

As with much else in foreign news, a big story in one nation is not necessarily a big story somewhere else. And, further, actors in the same violent story can be called "terrorists" in one nation and "freedom fighters" in another. Yet, for Western news media, any terrorist attack will be an important news story.

Notes

1. Mark Landler and Brian Stelter, "Web Pried Lid off Censorship," *The New York Times*, June 1, 2009, A1.
2. Alessandra Stanley, "Haiti Broadcast Coverage: Compassion and Self Congratulation," *The New York Times*, January 16, 2010, 3.
3. Brian Stelter, "After Sea Raid, Videos Carry On Fight," *The New York Times*, June 2, 2010, A1.
4. Tim Rutten, "When Facts Trump Attitude," *Los Angeles Times*, www.latimes.com, January 8, 2005.
5. Rutten, "When Facts Trump Attitude."
6. "Add It Up," *American Journalism Review*, November 2001, 11.
7. "Add It Up," 11.
8. "America's New Internationalist Point of View," Pew Research Center for the People and the Press, online report, October 24, 2001.
9. George Steiner, "B.B.", *New Yorker*, September 10, 1990, 113.
10. Bernard Gwertzman and Michael Kaufmann, eds., *The Collapse of Communism* (New York: St. Martins Press, 1990), 352–353.
11. William Henry, "The Television Screen is Mightier Than the Sword," *Time*, May 10, 1990, 51.
12. "How Resistance Spread the Word," *Newsweek*, September 2, 1991, 39.
13. Neil Hickey, "Terrorism and Television," *TV Guide*, August 7, 1986, 2.
14. Hickey, "Terrorism and Television," 2.

5

English:
The Language of the World

If Jules Verne's adventurous Phineas Fogg traveled around the world in eighty days again today, he would find that as an Englishman abroad he would have little trouble keeping up with the news and entertainment. At almost every stopover, he would be able to buy a copy of the *Guardian* or possibly the *Financial Times*, and at his hotel's newsstand he would have a choice of the *Economist, Time,* or *New Yorker,* among other English-language publications. In his hotel room, he would be able to watch the day's televised news either from CNN via cable and Comsat from Atlanta or BBC World. On the local television station, he could see a world news package of stories put together by Reuters Television outside London. And if he had a small short-wave radio, he would be reassured by listening to the BBC World Service from London or the Voice of America. Also, on local television, he would likely find reruns of his favorite British programs, and if he sought out a local movie theater, he likely would have a choice of current Hollywood productions. Chances are that a local bookstore or airport newsstand would have a wide selection of English-language magazines and paperback books. Today he is likely to have a laptop computer, a cellphone, or an iPad which he would be able to keep up with the news and entertainment as well as stay current by email with personal and professional contacts. The increasing availability of such Western publications and electronic media fare (most of it in English, the lingua franca of international communication) is an example of the way the major institutions of news communication – world news services, satellite services, broadcast systems, great newspapers and magazines – have become increasingly internationalized or globalized in recent

The World News Prism: Digital, Social and Interactive, Ninth Edition.
William A. Hachten and James F. Scotton.
© 2016 John Wiley & Sons, Inc. Published 2016 by John Wiley & Sons, Inc.

years. Globalization offers business opportunities for media corporations to make money overseas. This is facilitated by innovations in media technology (facsimile printing and satellite distribution in particular) and a growing elite cosmopolitan audience. Whatever the cause, the fact is that more and more of the activities of the major news media now transcend parochial or national concerns and serve broader transnational purposes. This Brave New World is mainly expressed in the English language or its varied modifications.

English-speakers can travel anywhere in the world and often find that the "native" or local people already know English or some modified version of it such as "Manglish" (Malay and English) or "Konglish" (English in South Korea), or where people speak a mixture of local languages and English, as in Mumbai (formerly Bombay). Robert McCrum, in his important 2010 book, *Globish: How the English Language Became the World's Language*, says that alongside the Internet, the globalization of English and "of English literature, law, money and values is nothing less than the cultural revolution of my generation."[1] McCrum says that English is the language of aspiration and the lingua franca of international culture and commerce (including of course international journalism and popular culture). The most admired and imitated model of journalism evolved in England and the United States. A leader of any nation who wants to be widely understood in today's world must be able to speak English in a televised or radio interview. The same is true for public figures and celebrities. And the new media of digital distribution are mainly in English.

Media Conglomerates

Media conglomerates have been arising out of the capitalistic West that some critics feel may dominate, if not unduly influence, much of international communication and entertainment in the near future. Frequently mentioned among these "media baronies" are those of Rupert Murdoch of Australia, Britain, and America; Silvio Berlusconi of Italy; Time Warner, Disney Company (ABC), and Viacom (CBS) of the United States; the Bertelsmann group of Germany; and Sony of Japan – all multimedia and multinational.

In recent years, we are seeing that some of these media leviathans are not doing so well: they are being overshadowed or neutralized by digital media. However, in August 2010, two of the largest media companies, Time

Warner and Murdoch's News Corporation, reported strong earnings and large increases in advertising revenue. Both firms saw big gains in their television and cable units.[2]

As recently as 1989, the world was still defined by Anglo-American television networks like NBC, BBC, CBS, ABC, and CNN or by international magazines like *Time* and *The Economist*, and papers like the *New York Times* and *Washington Post*. The *Washington Post*, weakened financially by the digital upheaval, was sold in 2013 to Jeff Bezos, the billionaire founder of Amazon. His has provided some stability, at least in the short term, to what many consider the nation's second-best daily newspaper. The *Post* reported selling 485,000 copies on a typical weekday in 2014 but had fewer than 50,000 readers willing to pay for a digital subscription. In contrast, *The New York Times* has managed to gain more than a million digital subscribers by tying the print and digital subscriptions into a tight subscriber package.[3]

Today, the new media enable local cultures to define themselves in local terms through the local media. For the world's lingua franca, the stronger the local loyalty, the more urgent is the need for the supranational advantages of the world's English or Globish. And Globish, as Robert McCrum asserts, is "fulfilling its destiny as the worldwide dialect of the third millennium." In China, for example, an official slogan is "Conquer the English language to make China strong."[4]

But the globalization of mass communication is proceeding in response to the needs and economic opportunities of a shrinking world. The transnational media are doing more than seizing the chance for greater profits from new markets, albeit those factors are obviously important. Whether viewed as another example of Western "media imperialism" or as a significant contribution to global understanding and integration, the international media are becoming increasingly cosmopolitan, speaking English and or Globish, and catering to an internationally minded audience concerned about world affairs.

The daily, ink-on-newsprint newspaper is still a major prop of global journalism because such papers still gather most of the world's news and because they serve as a check on excessive political and economic authority. Moreover, printed newspapers are still doing well in other major nations, including Japan, China, and India. There are more than 8,000 dailies worldwide and many thousands more weekly journals. A few of the more serious "prestige" papers attract readers far beyond their national borders. Not many Westerners read foreign publications, so they are unaware of the extent to which people abroad depend on newspapers and magazines published in other countries. The intellectually demanding *Le Monde* of Paris, famous for its analyses of world affairs, is widely read in the Arab world and francophone Africa. The London-based *Financial Times* uses a plant in Frankfurt to print nearly 53,000 copies daily of an edition described as "Europe's business paper," and has a US edition printed in New York City for American readers. Gannett distributes in Europe copies of *USA Today* printed in Switzerland; the only difference is that the weather maps are of Europe and Asia. Britain's *Guardian, Independent,* and *Daily Telegraph* are found on many foreign newsstands, as are Germany's *Frankfurter Allgemeine Zeitung* and Switzerland's *Neue Zürcher Zeitung.*

But the newspaper that has evolved furthest toward becoming a truly global daily is the *International Herald Tribune* of Paris. The *IHT* was the sole survivor of several English-language papers, including the *Chicago Tribune,* the *Daily Mail* (of London), the *New York Herald,* and *The New York Times,* that earlier published Paris or European editions for English-speaking travelers. Started by James Gordon Bennett in 1887 as the Paris edition of the *New York Herald,* the *IHT* has outlived its parents and today is fully owned by the *New York Times* company. Today, the paper is the European edition of the *New York Times,* considered by many the world's greatest newspaper. This marvel of distribution appears daily on some 8,500 newsstands all over Europe, supplied by editions printed in Paris, London, the Hague, Marseilles, Rome, and Zurich; and more recently in Hong Kong and Singapore. African and Middle Eastern subscribers are served by mail; distribution in North America, Latin America, and the Caribbean comes from a Miami printing plant. The *IHT* thus has become the first newspaper in history to publish the same edition simultaneously on all continents.

Although it remains an American newspaper in outlook and perspective, the European edition of *The New York Times* has gradually acquired an important non-American readership. Nearly half its more than 100,000 readers are an elite group of European internationalists – businesspeople, diplomats, and journalists fluent in English. These non-American readers are part of an "international information elite" who, regardless of geographic location, share a similar rich fund of common experience, ideas, ways of thinking, and approaches to dealing with international problems.

Numerous other publications, particularly magazines, have reached and helped shape this international information elite. Hearst Magazines International has successfully published magazines abroad, with sixty-four foreign-language editions of eight magazines. Its leaders, *Cosmopolitan, Esquire,*

Good Housekeeping, and *Popular Mechanics*, were distributed in fourteen languages to sixty countries.[5]

Another success, *Reader's Digest*, established its first foreign edition in Britain in 1938. By 1995, there were forty-seven international editions printed in eighteen languages. Almost 13 million copies a month are sold abroad. In some countries, including nearly all Spanish-speaking countries, the *Reader's Digest* is the most popular magazine. So successful has been its adaptation to foreign soil that many readers are unaware that the *Digest* is not an indigenous publication.

Weekly newsmagazines such as *Time* and *Newsweek* have been hurt by the rapid 24/7 increase of the news cycle due to the digital media. *Time* still has three international editions – Europe, Asia, and South Pacific – with more stress now on commentary and features rather than hard news. *Time* and *Newsweek* both slashed circulation in an attempt to keep alive.[6] In October 2012 *Newsweek* disappeared after covering America and the world since 1933. Many other weekly magazines appear likely to soon suffer *Newsweek's* fate.

A major competitor of the news magazines abroad is *The Wall Street Journal*. With a satellite-assisted leap across the Pacific, the highly successful *Journal* launched, in 1976, an Asian edition in Hong Kong that covers a sixteen-country business beat from Manila to Karachi. Smaller than the domestic edition, *The Asian Wall Street Journal* tries for the same mix of authoritative business and political news, a risky experiment for a region with so little press freedom. And pressures were applied, mostly by Singapore's then ruler, the authoritarian Lee Kuan Yew. In November 1985, the editor of *The Asian Wall Street Journal* apologized to a Singapore court for any possibility of contempt of court raised by a *Journal* editorial commenting on Singapore politics. The incident prompted questions about the appropriate response when a foreign court challenges the editorial freedom of an American newspaper published abroad. By mid-1990, after three years of harassment and a lengthy legal dispute with Lee, the *Journal* announced that it was ending circulation in the island republic.

The Wall Street Journal also has a European edition, printed in the Netherlands and written and edited in Brussels, Belgium. The paper, which can be purchased on the day of publication throughout Britain and continental Europe, is edited for the international executive doing business in Europe. Major competitors are two highly regarded British business publications, *The Economist* and the *Financial Times*.

In Latin America, following the invasion of cable television, American newspapers and magazines have been gaining many new readers in the region. Magazine publishers have launched Spanish-language editions of *Glamour, Discover, People, National Geographic,* and *Rolling Stone.* The *Miami Herald* has become the international English newspaper of Latin America, with ten regional printing plants and an overseas circulation of about 35,000 to 40,000. Brazilian sales of *Reader's Digest* in Portuguese jumped from 35,000 to 600,000 in two years.

Changes in World News Services

The changes in the world news services as they have expanded abroad are further evidence of this growing globalization of transnational media. Although they claim to "cover the world," the agencies historically have tended to serve primarily their own national clients and those in their spheres of influence; that is, Reuters serviced British media and the British Commonwealth, Agence France-Press (AFP) worked mainly for the French press and overseas French territories, and United Press International (UPI) (in its prime), in addition to its US clients, long had strong connections in Latin America. But these world agencies have become more international in scope, selling their services to whoever will buy, wherever they may be.

In addition, the personnel of world agencies have become significantly internationalized. Formerly, the Associated Press, for example, boasted that its news from abroad was reported by American AP correspondents who had experience in running an AP bureau in the United States. The agency would not depend on foreign nationals to provide news from their own countries for AP use in the United States. That has changed. With the increased professionalism of journalists abroad, news agencies not only find it more useful to use qualified local journalists, but also may get better reporting from staffers who know their own country, its language, and its social and political traditions. In late 2005, the AP planned to introduce an Internet database system called eAP that will deliver news photos, and video and sound clips, with identifying codes that will enable the AP to track how many times articles are used by a client.

Another facet of internationalization is foreign syndication of news by major daily papers. The New York Times News Service sends more than 50,000 words daily to 550 clients, of which 130 are newspapers abroad. Its close competitor is the Los Angeles Times/Washington Post News Service, which transmits about 60,000 words daily to fifty nations or about 600 news-papers, half of which are outside the United States. This total includes papers in West Germany and elsewhere that receive the DPA (Deutsche Presse Agentur), with which the service is affiliated.

As noted previously, there is syndication as well of television news film and videotapes, especially those of America's NBC, CNN, CBS, and ABC, and Britain's BBC and ITN, most of it distributed by two Anglo-American firms – Reuters Television and Associated Press Television News – via videotape and satellite (and sometimes by airmail) to almost every tele-vision service in the world. There is probably more international cooper-ation than competition in the transnational video news business, in part because most nations have only one government-controlled television ser-vice. Unlike the print media, which usually carry a credit line on agency reports or syndicated material, syndicated television news is usually pre-sented anonymously. Whether watching news from Cairo or Shanghai, the viewer is rarely informed who supplied the foreign video.

Media Changes in Europe

The increasing economic integration of the European Community plus the demassification and deregulation of broadcast media are rapidly interna-tionalizing much of mass communication in western Europe. Although Europeans, like people everywhere, prefer to read, view, and listen to news and entertainment in their home or native language, the push toward transnational communication is still strong. This is due to the rapid expan-sion of cable and satellite options for viewers, as well as increased numbers of private or commercial television and radio channels and the increasing popularity of VCRs, DVDs, and the Internet.

As noted previously, major American and British print and broadcasting organizations are trying to increase their audiences in European nations. And other media conglomerates in France, Germany, Italy, and Japan are buying up media properties abroad. Deregulation and privatization of radio and television and the expansion of cable and pay television, assisted by satellite distribution, also have added potentially important new daily news outlets in English as well as many more entertainment options for Europeans. Europe's broadcasting systems, formerly run by governments or by public corporations (paid for by special taxes or fees), have heretofore generally offered high-quality programming but with limited choices. But western Europe is now following the deregulated American models, with greatly increased choices. As a result, there has been a rush for the huge profits to be made. Adherents of Europe's tradition of public service broadcasting feel that programming quality will be sacrificed by deregulation and commercialization. The money to be made from advertising, viewer fees, and revenues from movies and video programs is expected to run into the billions.

Western European nations, particularly France, are concerned about the influence and popularity of American movies and television shows with European audiences, and have established quotas on imports and subsidized their own productions. However, another, quieter, invasion has taken place: American companies have infiltrated nearly every corner of the European television business. Time Warner, Viacom, Disney/ABC, Cox Cable, NBC, and others are getting involved in European-based television programming, in broadcast stations, in cable and satellite networks, and in the coming convergence of telecommunications and entertainment. And they see a huge market: 350 million people in twelve major western European nations and 650 million overall west of Russia, many of them hungry for televised news and entertainment.

Expanding Media Baronies

Many of the innovative changes in European media, as elsewhere, are being made by the transnational media conglomerates, themselves a by-product of rapid changes in international communication. There is growing concern as well about the economic, and potentially political, influence wielded by these powerful forces in global communication. The prototype of the media barons is Rupert Murdoch with his News Corporation. With 150 media properties in Australia, the United States, and Britain, Murdoch has been carefully assembling a vertically integrated global media empire. In the United States, he owns the Fox television network, the *Wall Street Journal*, and the *New York Post*. In addition, he has a significant share of Twentieth Century Fox Broadcasting, which produces TV shows and owns thousands of hours of films and television programs. In Europe, he has pioneered in satellite broadcasting and owns 90 percent of the British Sky Broadcasting channel (a satellite television system), a new sports network, and a twenty-four-hour news channel that draws from his two London papers, *The Times* and *The Sunday Times*. He owns direct broadcast satellite services in Britain,

Italy, Hong Kong, Japan, and Mexico; he owns two-thirds of daily news-paper circulation in Australia; and he owns HarperCollins Publishers and other British papers, including the *Sun* and the *News of the World*. Con-stantly juggling his properties (and his considerable debts), his News Cor-poration, which had revenues of less than $1 billion in 1980, had expanded its revenues to $14 billion in 2000.[7] In 2011 Murdoch's London papers were beset by "Rupertgate" when Murdoch's employees were accused of phone-hacking, police bribery, and using improper influence in pursuit of stories. To help stem the legal onslaught Murdoch closed down his *News of the World*, a Sunday scandal sheet. Murdoch's reputation was badly blemished, but his business empire has prospered from investments in US entertain-ment media.

Murdoch's media acquisitions have apparently influenced several major US media mergers, all of which have had implications for the future of international communications. In August 1995, the Walt Disney Company announced its purchase of Capital Cities/ABC, in a deal valued at $19 bil-lion. The merger brought together ABC – then the most profitable televi-sion network, including its highly regarded news organization (with Peter Jennings then as anchor) – and its ESPN sports cable service with an enter-tainment giant: Disney's Hollywood film and television studios, cartoon characters, theme parks, and so on, and the merchandise they generate. (In one recent year, the Disney Company sold more than $15 billion-worth of Disney merchandise worldwide, a total more than seven times the global box-office receipts for Disney movies.) Disney is more interested in content, especially game parks, movies, and consumer goods, than in conduits (cable or satellites). For 2000, Disney's total revenue was $25.8 billion, putting it in second place among media giants.

The real giant among the mega-media companies was AOL Time Warner, whose 2000 total revenues hit $36 billion, well ahead of Disney. Viacom (CBS) stood in third place at $20 billion, followed by Vivendi/Universal at $18 billion, Bertelsmann at $16 billion, and Murdoch's News Corpo-ration at $14 billion. However, the bursting of the dot com bubble in late 2000 hit AOL Time Warner hard, wiping out almost $200 billion in shareholder value. Time Warner shed AOL and has since come back. However, the French-controlled Vivendi/Universal conglomerate went under.

Another major merger began with Westinghouse's takeover of CBS Inc., creating the nation's largest broadcast station group, with thirty-nine radio and sixteen television stations reaching 32 percent of the nation. About the same time, Viacom, a hot cable company, bought a legendary Hollywood studio, Paramount Communications, for $8.2 billion. Several years later, Viacom bought the CBS Corporation for $37.3 billion, creating the world's second-largest media company. In May 2000, the FCC (Federal Communications Commission) approved the Viacom/CBS merger, and for its money CBS brought to the merger $1.9 billion in radio properties, including 190 radio stations; $4.4 billion in television holdings, including the CBS network, CBS Entertainment, CBS sports, and seventeen television stations; and $546 million in cable properties. However, CBS and Viacom separated into two different entities in 2006.

These megamergers positioned the resulting giants – Time Warner, Disney/ABC, and Murdoch – to better penetrate and dominate the growing international markets for television, movies, news, sports, records, and other media programs. At the time of its merger with ABC, Disney president Michael Eisner spoke glowingly of India's huge middle class of 250 million as a great potential audience for Disney movies, cartoons, news, and sports programs. NBA and NFL games have been gaining large audiences overseas; hence the importance of the ESPN networks. Critics noted that news organizations (and journalists), such as *Time* magazine and CNN, or ABC News or CBS News, were just small players within these entertainment giants.

The competition among CNN, MSNBC, and Fox News Channel (FNC) to dominate a twenty-four-hour cable news channel in the United States has strong international potential as well. Broadcast networks have been looking to international markets as a way of gaining hundreds of millions of new viewers. NBC's international holdings currently are about 20 percent of the network's worth of $10 to $20 billion; in the next ten years, half of the network's value is expected to come from international holdings. As predicted, Asia is becoming the main area of global audience growth, because about 25 percent of the continent's vast population is expected to receive cable before long. By contrast, the US market, with cable in 65 million of its 97 million households, is nearing saturation. Numbers of cable viewers are expected to rise abroad in time for the startup of NBC Europe as well as related NBC services in Latin America. Since 9/11, the war on terrorism for a while gave an impetus to twenty-four-hour global news, and competition has become much more intense.

Other European Baronies

Among European media groups with far-reaching holdings is Bertelsmann A.G. of Germany. From a Bible-publishing house, Bertelsmann grew into a media giant with book and record clubs in Germany, Spain, Brazil, the United States, and eighteen other countries. Bertelsmann owns Bantam, Doubleday, and Dell publishing in the United States, and Plaza y Janes book publishers in Spain, in addition to thirty-seven magazines in five countries, record labels such as RCA/Ariola, and a number of radio and television properties. In 1998, Bertelsmann shocked US book publishers by buying Random House for an estimated $1.4 billion, consolidating its claim as the world's largest English-language publisher of trade books. Considered the crown jewel of American book publishers, Random House had $1.1 billion in sales in 1996. With the sale, half of the top twenty US publishing firms, with a 28 percent share of the total US market, were in foreign hands. With $15.5 billion total revenue in 2000, Bertelsmann ranked as the world's fifth-largest media conglomerate.

Possibly the most swashbuckling of the media barons has been Italy's Silvio Berlusconi, who built a multibillion-dollar media television and newspaper empire, Fininvest, of unusual power and influence. With 42 percent of Italy's advertising market and 16 percent of daily newspaper circulation, he has concentrated his power more into a single market than any of the aforementioned barons. He has owned Italy's three main private television channels, Rete 4, Canale 4, and Italia 1, as well as *Il Giornale*, a leading Milan paper, two leading news weeklies, thirteen regional dailies, and a large book publisher plus television holdings in France and Germany. Using his extensive media power, Berlusconi became prime minister of Italy in 1994. He has been in and out of political power since, but has continued to be a dominant political force in Italy. But currently Berlusconi is no longer a serious candidate for high office in Italy. Personal foibles and political antics have caught up with him, but he has so far just managed to avoid a prison term.

Diffusion of Mass Culture

A major impact of these global media giants comes from their diffusion of the popular culture of the West to all – literally all – corners of the world, with profound influences that can only be described as revolutionary. The world is beginning to share a common popular culture. Much of the diversity of the world's cultures and languages is being lost forever. This trend is part of a long-term historical process that predates modern media, but in recent years the pace has accelerated.

American films regularly acquire more than 50 percent of the French market; about 50 percent of the Italian, Dutch, and Danish markets; 60 percent of the German markets; and 80 percent of the British markets. Recently, among the world's 100 most attended films, eighty-eight were American. Seventy-five percent of all imported television programs come from America. Millions in Europe have watched *Oprah Winfrey*, subtitled or dubbed. American basketball, played in 192 countries, may become the world's most popular sport. The NBA finals have been broadcast in 109 countries in twenty languages. Here are random examples of US mass culture abroad: *Dallas* has been seen in ninety-eight countries; 40 percent of television programming in New Zealand is American; Mickey Mouse and Donald Duck, dubbed in Mandarin, have been seen weekly in China; *Sesame Street* has been seen in 184 countries; and the hottest game show on French television is *La Roule de la Fortune*. Popular culture also conveys lifestyles. Like their Russian counterparts, young Chinese prefer American jeans and T-shirts as well as rock music. Young people in Germany are using such slang terms as "rap music," "body building," "windsurfing," and "computer hacking" – and, what is more, they are doing these activities.

One of the most powerful influences on global youth culture has been Music Television, or MTV, which first appeared on US cable in 1981. Since then, it has grown into a global phenomenon reaching into about 250 million homes worldwide. Despite criticism and unease from some members of the older generation, the recording business, by hitching would-be music hits to television, has found a marketing tool that has brought it unprecedented profits. Much of MTV's success was based on adapting the musical programming to the musical tastes of the teenagers of the region receiving it. In 2010, MTV bowed to cultural change and scrapped the legend "Music Television" from its corporate logo. The change was a belated recognition of what had been obvious for years: MTV had evolved into a reality channel that occasionally runs programs that have to do with music.[8]

The West, it has been said, won not only the Cold War but also the battle for the world's leisure time. Popular culture has been one of America's most lucrative exports, but observers say that the worst, instead of the best, of American culture seems to be flooding the world. Critic Michiko Kakutani commented, "Some of America's culture exports are so awful that you suspect that we are using the rest of the world as a vast toxic waste dump and charging for the privilege."[9] Chinese pop singers produce songs so similar to those in the West that you have to listen carefully to find that the lyrics are in Chinese. But the West has been greatly influenced by popular culture produced by the rest of the world.

The Videocassette and DVD Revolution

The global dissemination of popular culture, especially movies and music videos, was first greatly facilitated by the rapid spread of videocassette recordings and videocassette recorders to play them on. (VCRs have been largely replaced by digital video disks (DVDs), but the impact and effects are similar.) The terms "explosion" and "revolution" have been used to describe this phenomenon. In less than a decade, VCR and videotape penetrated remote areas that the printing press and other information devices had not successfully reached after centuries. The spread has been to poor nations as well as the affluent West, but for different reasons. Depending on culture and political traditions, VCRs can have profound effects not only on viewers but also on broadcasting and other media. Widespread use of VCRs can challenge the usual system of government control of television by providing diversity of views and variety in entertainment. (The use of audiocassettes has done much the same thing to radio broadcasting.) VCRs circumvent the utilization of broadcast television for development and political control by bringing about a de facto decentralization of media. People in poor countries, including youth, now often have the freedom to view what they want to see – not what Big Brother, or even their parents, think is best for them. And apparently what they want are movies, pop music, and videos from the West. In Saudi Arabia, the only choice for viewers of over-the-air television has long been the puritanical, heavily censored and dull programming of government television. (For example, religious orthodoxy requires that a Saudi woman's face may not be shown on television.) As a result, VCRs and DVDs have proliferated by showing much of the forbidden fruit of Western movies, including X-rated videos, most of them smuggled into the country.

In India, many people, annoyed by the inadequacies of state-run broadcasting, have turned to private enterprise "alternative television" news on videocassettes. The producer of "Business Plus," a monthly tape on political and economic issues, said India has the only private-view news magazines in the world. The tapes, made in English and Hindi, rent for about 60 cents a day or sell for about $8. The audience, though small, is composed of middle-class, cosmopolitan Indians dissatisfied with the vacuity of official news and documentaries. The trend toward news-oriented videotapes began earlier with "Newstrack," a fast-paced monthly video of investigative reporting with a segmented format like that of "Sixty Minutes."

Throughout emerging nations, small shops renting or selling videotapes (and later DVDs) from the West have become commonplace. In the remote nation of Bhutan, on India's northern border, people had been watching videos on television sets for years before the nation had an over-the-air television service. To a Westerner, the VCR is an easy way to watch a movie or record a television program for later viewing, but to many millions in developing nations, VCRs and DVDs are a means of gaining alternative news sources or viewing sometimes prohibited Western entertainment shows – activities that authoritarian countries have largely failed to censor or control.

English as THE Media Language

Effective communication across national borders, regardless of other cultural and political differences, certainly requires that sender and receiver communicate in a mutually understandable language. More and more, that language is English, which is clearly the leading tongue of international communication today.

Among the "Big Ten" world languages, English usually ranks third, with about 300 million native speakers in twelve countries, after Mandarin Chinese, with about 885 million, and Spanish, with 332 million native speakers. English is ahead of Russian, with its 282 million speakers, Arabic, with 220 million, and German, with 118 million. Furthermore, English is the most widely used geographically. Several hundred million people have some knowledge of English, which has official or semi-official status in some sixty countries. What is more, this number includes most of the world's leaders. (As noted above, if a leader wants to get on global TV, he or she had better know English.) In all, there are about 4 billion English speakers, including those using Globish (a modified form of English) in the world, and the number is rapidly increasing, according to Robert McCrum.

Unquestionably, English has become the global language of science and technology. More than 80 percent of all information stored in 100 million computers around the world is in English, and 80 percent of all scientific papers are published first in English. English is the language of the information age: computers talk to each other in English. The Internet today reverberates with many languages, many of which can be translated into English by computer programs. English is the most-taught language in the world; it is not really replacing other languages but, rather, supplementing them.

In many developing nations, English is the language of education, providing an entrée to knowledge and information. But one unfortunate result is that many native English speakers, especially Americans, have much less incentive than, say, Israelis, Dutch, or Swedes to learn other peoples' languages. Currently, the US government has an acute shortage of Arabic-speakers. Few Americans not of Hispanic origin even learn to speak Spanish, although it is widely spoken there. The nation's Hispanics numbered 35.3 million in 2000, and to inform and entertain them were thirty daily newspapers, 265 weeklies, 352 magazines, and 594 radio stations – all in Spanish.

Globally, English has also become the leading media language for international communication. Most of the world's news is carried in English. Most news agencies carry some of their news in English. Six of the world's biggest broadcasters – the BBC, CBS, NBC, ABC, CNN, and CBC – reach a potential audience of about 300 million people through English-language broadcasting.

The imperialism of nineteenth-century Britain was a major reason that so many people from Singapore to India to Kenya to Nigeria to Bermuda converse today in English. Not unrelated is the phenomenon of numerous English-language daily newspapers flourishing today in countries where English is neither the official nor even the most widely used language. Beginning with the *Chronicle of Gibraltar* in 1801, English-language dailies, catering to expatriates, the foreign community, and local educated elites, have long survived, if not always flourished, in such diverse metropolises as Mexico City, Caracas, Paris, Jerusalem, Taipei, Rome, Athens, Cairo, Beirut, Manila, Bangkok, Singapore, and Tokyo, as well as throughout India and Pakistan and the former British territories of Africa, such as Nigeria, Ghana, Sierra Leone, South Africa, Uganda, Kenya, Tanzania, Zimbabwe, and Zambia. In parts of polyglot Africa, English has almost evolved into another African language because of the role it plays in education, commerce, and mass communication.

Most of the "content" of mass culture that moves across national borders is in English. Jeremy Tunstall has said that English is the language best suited for comic strips, headlines, riveting first sentences, photo captions, dubbing, subtitling, pop songs, billboards, disc-jockey banter, news flashes, and sung commercials. One appeal of English as an international language is that it is easy to speak badly.

This thrust of English as a world media language has become self-generating, and any educated person of whatever nationality who wishes to participate in this shrinking and interdependent world finds it useful to know English. In fact, because English is now spoken as a second language by more people around the globe than by British and Americans combined, it must now be considered as belonging to the world, as indeed it does. For when two persons of differing linguistic backgrounds are able to converse in person or through computers, the chances are they will be using English.

Notes

1. Robert McCrum, *Globish: How the English Language Became the World's Language* (New York: Norton, 2011).
2. Joseph Plambeck, "Profits Up at Time Warner and News Corporation Helped by Ad Rebound," *The New York Times*, August 5, 2010, B4.
3. Zoe Fox, "Top 10 U.S. Newspapers Ranked by Digital Circulation." *Mashable Charts*, August 11, 2014.
4. McCrum, *Globish*, 26.
5. Deirdre Carmody, "Magazines Find Green Pastures Abroad," *The New York Times*, March 20, 1995, C5.
6. Jeremy Peters, "The Economist Tends its Sophisticated Garden," *The New York Times*, August 9, 2010, B1.
7. Ken Auletta, "Leviathan," *New Yorker*, October 29, 2001, 50.
8. Scott Collins, "MTV Broadening its Brand," *Wisconsin State Journal*, February 11, 2010, C5.
9. Michiko Kakutani, "Taking Out the Trash," *The New York Times Magazine*, June 8, 1997, 31.

6

Brazil: Latin America's Communication Leader

As the only Portuguese-speaking country in Latin America and one of the ten top world economies, Brazil has risen above many challenges since its independence from Portugal almost 200 years ago. With a hectic political trajectory that has alternated populist charismatic elected presidents with military/civil dictators, the country entered the twenty-first century as a 200 million-population promising developing democracy. All in all, it has had more gains than losses despite its colossal social problems and inequalities. Brazil is a member of the BRICS (an acronym coined in 2001 for Brazil, Russia, India, China and South Africa as the next group of countries predicted to turn into dominant economies by mid-century), which represents almost 3 billion people in five countries. Brazil aspires to become a global power by obtaining a permanent seat at the UN Security Council, the body charged with maintaining international peace and security. Currently, two BRICS members (China and Russia) have permanent seats at the Security Council, along with the United States, the United Kingdom, and France. In Latin America, Brazil leads the region's economy and, particularly, the communication industry along with Mexico.

Internet Use

Brazil has been a fast adopter of media technology. Its Internet has grown unlike any other sector in the last decade, with an increase of almost 145 percent since 2005.[1] By 2014 some 53 percent of the almost 200 million

The World News Prism: Digital, Social and Interactive, Ninth Edition.
William A. Hachten and James F. Scotton.
© 2016 John Wiley & Sons, Inc. Published 2016 by John Wiley & Sons, Inc.

Brazilians were using the Internet, behind only China, the United States, India, and Japan in total number of users. Brazil's Internet access is higher than Mexico's (41 percent of its 124 million people), but smaller than Argentina's (about 60 percent of its population of 41.8 million) or Chile's (65.7 percent of 17.7 million people).[2] In fact, in some South American countries such as Argentina, Uruguay, and Chile, a larger percentage of the people own computers than in Brazil because of their higher level of literacy and smaller populations. In addition, some of these countries have special programs for digital development, which have no parallel in Brazil. In Uruguay, for example, the government gives laptops to all students enrolled in public schools. Uruguay, with a population of just over 3 million people, is considered the "Switzerland of South America" for its long democratic tradition, sophisticated banking system, high literacy, and strong middle class. It was the third South American country to legalize same-sex marriage in 2013, and it legalized the use and production of marijuana in the same year. Overall, Central America generally has much lower levels of Internet use than the countries of South America, with fewer people living in more developed urban areas.

In spite of advances in technology, within every Latin American country there are huge disparities in online access. In Brazil, the Internet penetration is only 10 percent in rural areas and only 6 percent among the people with the lowest income and lowest level of education, due partly to the high cost of computers and poor Internet connections.[3] While 54 percent of the 63.6 million households surveyed between 2012 and 2013 by Cetic (the Brazilian Center of Studies on Information and Communication Technologies) had a computer, mostly a desktop, only 40 percent of them had Internet connected by DSL (Digital Subscriber Line) or cable. As in other developing nations, the statistics are much better regarding mobile phones, which by 2013 were present in 90 percent of households in Brazil. Mobile Internet access is booming in the region with 3G technology, yet the more advanced 4G services reach only thirty-two Brazilian cities, and consumers complain the system is inefficient. Brazil has the largest mobile phone market in Latin America, and in 2013 it was moving to become the fifth-largest smartphone market in the world.[4]

In the same year, the country had 65 million Facebook users, second only to the United States, and became the second-biggest user of Twitter as well, with 41.2 million users. It was also the largest market for YouTube outside the United States, with 60 percent of its users under 34 years old. Moreover, Latin Americans have been among the most active users of Twitter, since the company launched a Spanish version in 2009. Argentina, Brazil, and Mexico are home to the world's top Twitter users after Indonesia and India, with the United States being the number one user of this social media platform. Latin Americans, known for enjoying endless informal conversations with friends and acquaintances at coffee shops and bars in their free time, found the perfect niche to continue chatting on social media. They spend over ten hours a month on social media – twice the global average. Furthermore, the youth (15–24) spend an average of 32.5 hours per month online – 6.3 more hours than the estimated global average of 26.2 hours.[5] Even LinkedIn found a home among Brazilians, who make up the second fastest-growing market for this popular, business-oriented social networking service, with over 11 million users by 2013 after only two years of operation. Yet Facebook tops every other social media platform, followed by Twitter.

In fact, Twitter is Latin American politicians' favorite platform. Top Twitter executives, thrilled by the company's success in Latin America, advised regional politicians to adopt the microblog in a more interactive way instead of using it as a broadcast platform. Politicians quickly embraced social media and developed a direct connection to citizens, bypassing the traditional media, which usually campaign against them. The strategy has been successful. An early adopter of Twitter was President Hugo Chavez of Venezuela, who combined modern platforms with long, old-school, Cuban-style speeches on radio and television. By the time he died in March 2013, he had 4.13 million Twitter followers – the highest number ever for a Latin American politician. In late 2014, Argentine president Cristina Fernandez de Kirchner had 3.13 million followers; Mexican president Enrique Peña Nieto had 2.91 million; Brazilian president Dilma Rouseff had 2.74 million; and Venezuelan president Nicolas Maduro had 2.11 million. Those are significant numbers for Latin America, although they pale when compared to President Barack Obama's 45.9 million followers on Twitter.

The data on Internet usage in Latin America indicate a major change in media habits. The dominant online activity for Latin American middle-class youth is social; young consumers are mostly digital-oriented with little to no attachment to legacy media. Also, they are protagonists of media convergence: for example, watching social TV (the union of television and social media) on Facebook and Twitter, where they share their experiences about favorite TV shows, is a growing trend. However, one must remember that social and economic inequalities in Latin America force the less educated population to stick to traditional television and radio, especially in Central America and in rural areas of South America. A quick walk in the streets of any major city in Brazil, though, confirms that even those who have little access to the digital world do know about it, talk about it, and dream about having their own digital experience.

Brazil's advance in technology parallels its economic growth in the first decade of the twenty-first century. This growth came as the country ended the twentieth century with a government reform that allowed foreign companies to invest in several areas. New government welfare policies and better jobs quickly improved living standards and created a better-educated workforce. A particular "inclusive growth" measure, a conditional cash transfer program known as Bolsa Familia (Family Allowance), is credited with helping to lift from poverty over a decade some 40 million people, who joined an emergent middle class in urban areas. Other Latin American countries have adopted different versions of the "family allowance" including Mexico (Oportunidades), Colombia (Familias en Acción), Peru (Juntos), Chile (Chile Solidario) and Guatemala (Mi Familia Progresa). In Brazil, the program has benefited 13.8 million households living in poverty or extreme poverty.[6]

A natural consumer boom followed, allowing millions of Brazilians to buy their first home, car or computer. More easily available credit, for example, made airplane tickets one of the top items purchased by the emergent middle class. By 2013, airports, roads, and malls in major cities were jam-packed by a population segment that was joining the mainstream consumer class for the first time. This new middle class, identified in Brazilian statistics as the "C class" in a system that divides Brazilian society into five economic groups from A to E based on income, began to buy computers. They deserted the traditional *lan-houses* (local area network places) or Internet centers wedged into *favelas* – shanty towns – and other poor communities that charged online users by the hour for computer use and Internet access. In addition, this middle class of Brazilians bypassed the print and online mainstream media, which hoped to attract the new consumers. In the blink of an eye, Brazilians joined global trends, becoming new addicts of social media. By October 2013, Brazilians using the Internet spent 36 percent of their online time on social media. Facebook had by then 46.3 million users, which placed Brazil second to the United States and ahead of India among Facebook users.[7] The 2012 Cetic survey noted that people preferred to spend their time online surfing social media websites (73 percent of respondents); watching films and videos (49 percent), downloading music (46 percent) and playing online games (33 percent). Cetic found that three-quarters of social media users were in the middle or upper class economically and had at least a high-school education. As in other Latin American countries, most Brazilians with access to the Internet lived in urban areas. The Cetic study examined almost 17,000 Brazilian households in 350 cities and found that Internet access was especially high in the wealthy urban centers in the south and southeast regions of Brazil (about 50 percent of the homes) compared to the less developed regions of the north and northeast, where only about a quarter of the people had Internet access.[8]

Overall, Latin America's effort to bridge the digital gap still lags behind, even though the number of Internet users is going up and access has become more affordable. National Internet access is very uneven in the region, and Latin America overall lags behind in Internet development. The World Economic Forum found that the region displays a poor innovation environment, and a weak educational system, especially in math and science, which restricts Latin American opportunities to develop a knowledge-based economy. In 2014 Internet World Statistics reported that 85 percent of people in North America had Internet access, compared to only 38 percent in Latin America. Even long-time leaders in traditional communications like Brazil and Mexico are well behind Canada and the United States in developing their Internet capabilities and far behind in social media such as Facebook, where the percentage of users in United States (43 percent) is more than twice as high as in Brazil's loquacious population (18 percent). As the world embraces big data production and transmission along with mass adoption of connected digital services by consumers, businesses, and governments, Latin America will need to multiply its efforts to fight the shortage of data scientists, and solve problems with poor-quality data and dilemmas with data privacy.

Internet-Enabled Protests and Civil Engagement

Given the context, which combined economic growth and access to technology, it was not a huge surprise that the mass demonstrations that took over the streets in major cities throughout Brazil in June 2013 were organized through Facebook and Twitter just as in the Arab Spring. Tired of spending hours stuck in traffic inside overcrowded commuter buses, citizens of all ages protested, initially in major urban areas, against an increase in bus fares. Soon, the protests gained further public support and a new agenda that attacked almost every national flaw, including the country's endemic political corruption and lack of accountability, government overspending on soccer stadiums for the 2014 World Cup, high taxes, violent crime, and lack of investment in infrastructure. Demonstrators complained that the government had built First World soccer stadiums, but offered Third World schools and hospitals.

Brazilian protesters embraced social media as a tool for civil engagement and recruitment during the protests as Facebook pages calling society to take action multiplied. As the rallies grew, several left- and right-oriented groups tagged along, including the Brazilian anarchists, an anti-globalization local version of the Black Blocs, formed by individuals who wear black clothing, dark glasses, hoods, scarves, and masks to avoid identification. Acting mostly in large urban centers such as Rio de Janeiro and São Paulo, where they are known for destroying property, several Brazilian Black Bloc groups have had a marked decentralized Facebook presence, alternately expanding and shrinking as they are driven by casual, sometimes one-time followers known as *slacktivists* rather than followers committed to long-term action. Mainstream journalists have defined the Black Blocs as a loose, mixed association between well-off college students and low-income residents of peripheral urban areas and, occasionally, members of the socialist political party Psol, and the government-supported Landless Workers Movement, a Marxist-inspired grassroots association that organizes farmland takeovers.

All these groups meet in cyberspace, currently a favorite arena for political participation in Latin American countries with high Internet access. For example, a study conducted in 2013 by the Igarape Institute, a Brazilian-based think tank, found forty-one Facebook pages claiming to represent the Black Blocs with a total of 1.45 million likes focused on recruiting and mobilizing protesters, gathering information on protests, reporting on the ground through videos, photos, and testimonies, and denouncing police brutality and infiltration as well as censorship.[9] Whether social media worldwide will make people more likely to participate in politics beyond liking, sharing, and copy-and-pasting content is still unknown, but research on Brazilian online activism has found positive results. That's the case with the Brazilian anti-corruption offline and online campaign Ficha Limpa (Clean Record), which in 2010 led to the introduction of a law that bars political candidates with a criminal record from running for office for eight years. Over 1.6 million Brazilians signed the document in favor of the Ficha Limpa and had the support of 3 million Internet users, possibly the highest number of online supporters for a cause in the country up to that point.[10] In another study about online political activism vs. slacktivism, Anita Breuer and Bilal

Farooq found evidence that the online engagement in Brazil, which forced the government to enact the Ficha Limpa law, had a high level of political interest, which contributed to engaging people offline.[11]

Since then, Internet-enabled social activism has grown. The protests of 2013 and 2014 caught Dilma Rousseff, Brazil's first female president, Congress, and governors off-guard. The Workers Party (PT), in power for over a decade, did not see the wave of popular dissatisfaction coming and did not know how to react. President Rousseff expressed empathy with the movement and, in keeping with the Brazilian tradition of political improvisation, tried to defuse it by proposing a number of political and social measures. A common media explanation was that entire communities that had improved their living standards had realized they were paying high taxes and were now finally asking for better services.

Out of tune with government institutions, the protesters felt equally disconnected from the mainstream media. The mainstream media initially reacted negatively to the street protests, calling the demonstrators vandals and placing news about the protests in the crime sections of newspapers and TV newscasts. While pictures and videos of police brutality flooded Facebook, Twitter, and YouTube, social media users attacked the protest coverage by the mainstream media so strongly that journalists of large, well-known news organizations had to hide their company logos to avoid been beaten up by people in the streets. In June 2013 demonstrators attacked the offices of the daily newspaper *Zero Hora* in southern Brazil. They called for the democratization of the media and argued that the paper's coverage distorted their social movement. Over 130 newspaper professionals of *Zero Hora* signed an open letter to the public asking for freedom to fairly report was happening.[12] By October that year, the National Association of Investigative Journalists (Abraji) reported that ninety-six journalists had been attacked by both protesters and police over a four-month period.[13]

Brazilian media critics have pointed out that the national media did not understand the nature of the emergent middle-class protests. In recent years, the Brazilian mainstream media have been accused of lacking diverse points of view and of avoiding discussion of important issues that affect most people.[14] Furthermore, objectivity has not been a staple of political coverage. A study of the online mainstream media coverage of the 2010 Brazilian presidential elections indicated the presence of biases toward candidates and political parties in the news.[15] Frustrated by the mainstream media coverage of the protests, online users turned to a citizen journalism experiment led by a group of young people called Midia Ninja ("Ninja" stands for

Independent Narratives, Journalism and Action). The new media group is a collective of collaborators, mostly unpaid volunteers, in 200 cities. Its goal is to promote "direct, participatory democracy" among people who are hungry for information through an alternative media model that has grown faster than its founders had imagined. Midia Ninja broadcast the protests and interviews with different people, including politicians, on tweetcasting and on its website, POSTV. Midia Ninja is also on other platforms such as Facebook, with over 300,000 followers, as well as on Tumblr, Instagram, Google Plus, and Flickr, with multiple live updates. Its editors say they "show what network television does not."

In an interview with well-known mainstream journalists of TV Cultura's program Roda Viva (Live Circle) of São Paulo, two Ninja creators argued that although traditional newspapers had migrated to the Internet, they had not updated their twentieth-century approach. Meanwhile, as Brazilian print newspapers have lost circulation and laid off hundreds of professionals throughout the country, a whole new generation of Brazilians who still want to become journalists have embraced the digital independent media. They look for freedom to report at a lower cost. The Ninjas believe that readers will also engage in a twenty-first-century approach by helping to finance new business models through crowdfunding, subscriptions, and micro-donations to particular news stories, which will replace the "like" on websites. In their view, Brazil's new alternative journalism formats will find what some mainstream media are missing: independence and credibility.[16]

Other independent and more professional online journalistic groups have emerged, such as Agencia Publica, a non-profit, non-partisan online investigative group led by a group of female journalists financially supported by crowdfunding and by international sources such as the Ford Foundation. Reporter Brasil is another non-profit online news agency created by journalists, social scientists, and educators dedicated to investigating human trafficking, modern slavery, and workers' rights, and to educating people about these topics as its founders explain in the organization's website. A third one, Viomundo ("I've seen the world") takes a more political viewpoint than the others. Viomundo claims over 700 subscribers who pay about $5 a month to keep the website publishing stories ignored by the mainstream media. In addition, it asks readers to finance in-depth investigations which are listed on its website with explanations of how much is needed to produce each story.[17]

The Internet-enabled uprising reached a climax in July 2014, during the World Cup, the most expensive soccer tournament in history and a huge public relations effort to improve Brazil's image abroad. Different sources claimed that the Brazilian government spent over $15 billion on the World Cup to fulfill the International Federation of Football Association's (FIFA's) demands amid numerous accusations of corruption against both the government and FIFA. Years earlier, former president Lula da Silva had promised that private money would cover the costs of major construction projects, but the government of president Dilma Rousseff ended up paying for the twelve brand-new or renovated stadiums. Some of them were built in cities that could not even support everyday football matches, such as Brasilia, the country's capital, and Manaus, a city in the heart of the Amazon forest. The consensus was that the money spent on the World Cup should have been earmarked to build hospitals and schools instead of stadiums built for just four games. Matters got even more complicated when the government evicted over 200,000 people from their homes in slum areas to make way for construction projects, generating further public disapproval.

In spite of the protests, the World Cup was a major source of festivity. Although six of the twelve cities that hosted the games were among the world's fifty most dangerous, according to the Mexican-based NGO Citizen's Council for Public Security and Penal Justice, foreign tourists did not feel intimidated by the negative media attention. Over 1 million people, mostly from North America, Europe, and other Latin American countries, visited Brazil during the World Cup – twice as many tourists as had visited South Africa during the 2010 World Cup. And while businesswise the event was successful, Brazilians were left with a bitter taste in the mouth, as their national team faced a staggering defeat (Germany beat Brazil 7–1) at the end of the tournament. Across the board, soccer fans grieved, even those who had protested in the streets. At the same time, twenty-one young leaders in charge of organizing the protests were temporarily jailed, while thousands of angry citizens quickly dispersed, frightened by the police brutality. Lawyers defending protesters and journalists beaten by the military during the demonstrations received international media attention, and human rights organizations complained about the Brazilian government's disregard for free speech.[18]

During the 2013 protests, 117 journalists suffered physical attacks and ten went to jail while covering the protests; one TV cameraman died after being hit by a protester. By late 2014, during the campaign for general elections, the protests timidly rekindled in the country's major cities, but their young leaders remained in the shadows, fearing arrest and police brutality. Ordinary citizens generally stayed away from street demonstrations, dreading the Black Blocs' violent actions. At the same time, the Midia Ninja website, which by September of 2014 celebrated 1 million live streams, expanded its agenda to include reporting on media diversity, abortion, drug use policy, problems with daily police violence, and Brazil's horrifying prison system.[19] The new independent online media that mix information with activism won't disappear; to the contrary, they are a sign of a fundamental change in journalism in Brazil, but one that is not yet present in other Latin American countries.

Legacy Media and Ownership

Brazil is a classic example in Latin America where new technologies and the Internet seem to assault the traditional media business instead of being absorbed and adapted with care and strategy by management. A successful print media market that excelled in the late twentieth century decelerated in the twenty-first century, while the online market has grown, albeit employing a much smaller number of professionals. Brazil has 727 daily newspapers, most of them small, with a total average paid circulation of 8.4 million in 2013. The press is concentrated in large cities and still controlled by a handful of wealthy families. In 2011–12, paid circulation grew by just 1.8 percent, but this increase was due to online access. Most daily newspapers in Brazil have paywalls and few of them plan to offer free access to readers. In an attempt to protect its content, for example, the top daily newspaper, *Folha de S. Paulo*, obtained a court order in 2013 forbidding the reproduction of its news and commentaries by a government agency to distribute to federal authorities.[20] *Folha*, like many other newspapers in Brazil, has developed metered paywalls allowing online readers access to a certain number of articles before having to pay. *Folha* claims its website had 21 million unique visitors per month by 2013, the same year that the Reuters Institute published its digital news report. Reuters found that 73 percent of almost 1,000 Brazilians interviewed had never paid for digital news content, but about two-thirds agreed that they would likely pay in the future.[21]

Meanwhile, other Latin American countries have adopted similar models. The Mexican Grupo Reforma, publisher of ten daily newspapers in five cities, charges online subscribers 20 percent less than a print subscriber, but it also offers plans that combine digital and print subscriptions because "print advertising still commands a dramatic premium over digital ads" according to media analyst Estefania Hernandez. He also noted that the major Colombian newspapers *El Tiempo* and *El Colombiano* upgraded their paywall projects in 2014, while the online kiosk system *Pasalagagina* successfully offered access to thirty Colombian magazines for a monthly subscription fee.[22] As yet few in number, the growth of digital newspapers may be the best way to guarantee the survival of media diversity and press freedom in certain countries in the region, as the case in Venezuela suggests. *El Impulso*, that country's oldest newspaper (established 110 years ago), temporarily closed in September 2014 for lack of printing paper, one of the many shortages in this media-polarized country. Paper shortages caused another thirty-seven Venezuelan newspapers to suspend or reduce their print editions, according to Reporters Without Borders.[23] Venezuela, led by socialist president Nicolas Maduro, the handpicked successor of deceased leader Hugo Chavez, has tried to control all news media. Opposition newspapers have been closed or sold to companies allied with the government in undisclosed deals. With the news dominated by propaganda and counterpropaganda, the population is suffering civil unrest, high inflation, food shortages, and economic stagnation.[24]

Printing paper was available in Brazil, but readership of daily print newspapers among adults fell dramatically from 49 percent in 2010 to 24 percent in 2013.[25] The daily paid individual circulation of Brazil's major newspapers (*Folha de S. Paulo*, *O Estado de S. Paulo*, and *O Globo*) is usually below 300,000, a very low number considering that São Paulo and Rio de Janeiro are megacities with populations of 11.9 million and 6.4 million respectively. The overall prospect for newspapers is not encouraging as the average circulation of paid print newspapers in Brazil fell by about 325,000 from 2012 to 2013.[26]

Frightened by the country's latest economic downturn and the growth of the Internet, the print media have as usual laid off journalists. In newsrooms across the country over 1,200 journalists lost their jobs in 2012. In São Paulo, Brazil's main media hub, 280 people were dismissed in the first half of 2013.[27] Some of them, well known in the field, have continued to practice journalism for free on their blogs.

By 2013, print editions of major daily newspapers were shrinking and newsrooms were operating with smaller staffs. Although newspapers were second to television as the preferred medium for advertising between 2010 and 2011, by 2013 advertisers flocked not to prominent online news websites as expected, but to Google and Facebook, where most readers look for news without a sense of loyalty to traditional brand media companies once represented by newspapers and magazines. Jayme Sirotsky, president emeritus of the RBS media group, one of the largest in the country, told *The Economist* in 2013 that the Brazilian media had tried to produce quality news content in a hostile economic environment. By mid-2014, his own company had laid off 130 journalists from its print newspapers while increasing the number of professionals working for digital content and diversifying by investing in software and other online businesses.[28] The once vibrant magazine industry faced recession as well. Editora Abril, Brazil's main magazine publisher, folded four of its fifty-three titles, consolidated its divisions, and eliminated 150 top editorial positions in 2013. In addition, Abril transferred ten publications to its Argentinian partner Caras. Publisher of the successful newsweekly *Veja*, with a 1.1 million circulation, and the Brazilian versions of *Playboy*, *Elle*, and *Cosmopolitan* (called *Nova* in Brazil), Editora Abril was moving to lay off or transfer to partnership publications hundreds of professionals.[29] Such measures indicated that the ten national conglomerates, largely located in the Rio de Janeiro–São Paulo area, that control the majority of the Brazilian media want to keep profitable and relevant in the Internet era at any cost. Seven of these companies are responsible for 80 percent of what is read, heard or seen in Brazil. Media companies located in the Rio de Janeiro–São Paulo area also generate 85 percent of TV and radio content distributed in the country.

Since 2002 foreign companies have been allowed to own up to 30 percent of local television, radio, print or any other media business, but Brazilian media companies are primarily family-owned with some foreign partnerships. Globo Network, for example, has joint ventures with 20th Century Fox, Sky, Universal, MGM, Playboy, and others. Globo's monopoly of the airwaves is attested by its control of 75 percent of spending on television advertising. The second-largest conglomerate in Brazil is Editora Abril, responsible for 73 percent of the best-selling magazines. The Marinho family owns Globo Network; the Silvio Santos family owns the SBT Network with its 108 affiliated stations; the Saad family owns the Bandeirantes Network, a group of television and radio stations, a free newspaper in association with the Swedish company Ab Kinnevik, and a system of classified ads. Other families, such as the Mesquitas (O Estado de S. Paulo Group); the Frias (Folha de S. Paulo Group), the Civitas (Abril), and the Sirotskys (RBS), control a great deal of the print media in Brazil. In recent decades, religious groups have begun operating television and radio stations. Igreja Universal do Reino de Deus (the Universal Church of the Kingdom of God) owns TV Record, the third largest network in Brazil, with eighteen TV stations and another twenty-eight affiliates. TV Record owner, the self-appointed Bishop

Edir Macedo, has been investigated for tax evasion and money-laundering in the recent past. Yet by 2013 he had become the owner of a bank. Another Brazilian characteristic is the recurring government distribution of broadcast licenses to politicians. Exactly 271 politicians are owners or directors of radio and television stations. The majority are mayors of small cities, but the list includes twenty senators and forty-eight members of the Brazilian House of Representatives.[30] Two former presidents, Fernando Collor de Mello (1990–92), impeached under allegations of corruption, and José Sarney (1985–89), both still politically active, are media owners in the impoverished northeast. In this region and others, the "colonel" system remains in practice. "Colonels" are not only landowners but also media owners who frequently clash with journalists. Journalist José Cristian Góes, for example, was sentenced to seven months and sixteen days in prison in 2013 in connection with a short piece of fiction mocking local political corruption that he posted on his blog, *Infonet*. Entitled "Me, the Colonel Inside Me," the story criticized people in positions of power and influence. It was told in the first person by an imaginary colonel, without any names, dates, or public positions being identified. Indeed, violence against journalists in small towns is common: in 2012, five Brazilian journalists and bloggers were murdered, probably in connection with their work. Two other journalists who specialized in police and public security issues had to flee the country. In 2013, thirteen Brazilian journalists suffered physical attacks in different cities.[31]

The concentration of media ownership in Brazil has its roots in the late development of the press in the country, where the first printing machines arrived with the Portuguese royal family in 1808 – 300 years after the colonization of Brazil by Portugal. Since its creation in the early nineteenth century, the press has been controlled by the country's elites and the structure remained untouched when the press converted into a mass media system. That is also the case with the mass media in other Latin American countries. Dissatisfaction with this rigid structure has grown. In the last decade or so, several Latin American countries led by left-wing or populist governments have discussed what has been called the democratization of the media – a subject on which there is a wide range of views depending on the source of criticism. Brazil, Argentina, Venezuela, Ecuador, Bolivia, Peru, Uruguay, and Mexico have adopted or are in the process of adopting new regulations for telecommunications and broadcasting. Some of these countries have passed laws changing media ownership rules in an attempt to break regional conglomerates, create state-sponsored community media, and stimulate diversity. Pressure for reform comes from political parties, NGOs, and organized sectors of society generally aligned with political factions, academia, journalists' unions, and other interest groups. Some of these projects do advance the notion of media pluralism, while others remain under a suspiciously authoritarian veil. Strikingly, Latin American countries that have approved media reform laws are the ones with limited press freedom, with the exception of Uruguay. Perhaps the definition of press freedom employed by governments in the region does not match the concepts employed by international organizations such as Freedom House and Reporters Without Borders. According to the 2013 Freedom House report, twenty out of thirty-five nations in the region are either not free (Mexico, Ecuador, Paraguay, Honduras, Venezuela, and Cuba) or partly free (including Brazil, Argentina, Chile, Colombia, the Dominican Republic, El Salvador, Nicaragua, Guatemala, Peru, Bolivia, Panama, and Haiti). Uruguay and Costa Rica are the only ones listed as having full press freedom. Furthermore, the 2014 index of press freedom developed by Reporters Without Borders indicates that journalists and the news media in Latin America are "political tools in highly polarized countries," where the private and public sectors engage in violent confrontation. Examples are Venezuela, Ecuador, Bolivia, Argentina, and, of course, Brazil.

Press freedom is far from being fully established in Latin America and the Caribbean. Media corporations defend their view of press freedom and complain about government interference in their businesses. In contrast, governments complain that the media lack divergent voices, especially when reporting on politicians. Sectors of civil society align with one or another, and different groups disagree. Following the trend, Brazilian sectors of civil society, supported by the Workers' Party currently in power and by former president Lula da Silva, have united around the National Forum for Democratization of Communication (FNDC) to lobby for an agenda that plans to break media monopolies and favors the creation of smaller communication groups to increase diversity and promote non-profit community media outlets. The FNDC also wants to combat vertical, horizontal, and cross-ownership of media outlets. Media groups and many politicians oppose these ideas, claiming they are a direct attack on their view of press freedom and that the door will be wide open to government censorship and control. Brazil's President Dilma Rousseff, who seemed to support the FNDC proposals earlier, has not spoken in their favor since taking power in 2010 and did not mention the issue during her 2014 campaign for reelection. Nonetheless, Brazil has approved some laws meant to improve access to information and democratization. After eight years of negotiation involving the government, Congress, journalists, and NGOs, the Access to Information Law became effective in 2012. It is helping to fight the administration's culture of secrecy and improving the work of journalists. Language that critics say is too vague allows government to deny access to information in cases of national security, risk to the population's health, and threat to economic stability, among other things. Ultra-secret information can be classified for twenty-five years, while secret information can be classified for fifteen years.[32]

In April 2014, Brazil enacted the Marco Civil da Internet Law, also known as the Internet Constitution, which includes rules for freedom of expression, net neutrality, privacy, and protection of personal data on the Internet. First introduced in Congress in 2009, the bill was finally signed by the president following allegations that the US National Security Agency spied on Brazilians' phone calls and Internet use. Concerned with the lack of data security and proper data storage, Brazilian authorities initiated consultations with the UN and the ITU (International Telecommunication Union) on policies to prevent monitoring of political, commercial, and industrial information. There is a lot of work to be done on the legal arena in the near future. The Brazilian Telecommunication Code, created in 1962, needs to be updated for the Internet era and adapted to new technological developments. Since the 1970s, the Code has survived more than twenty proposals to change it. Furthermore, Brazil's new 1988 Constitution limited the number of broadcasting licenses and rejected the idea of media monopolies, but there is no practical regulation to enforce these laws. In the meantime, Brazilian media experts interviewed on the topic continue to defend the concept of media democratization, but they believe that the current situation won't improve because several politicians who own TV and radio stations are linked to the government and benefit from state advertising.

Journalists' Profiles

In spite of the recent technological changes and the lower salaries paid to journalists, journalism is an attractive profession in Brazil. Most Brazilians journalists start their careers very young, often moved by a passion for their craft and a belief they will help to construct a better world. Not long ago, the typical Brazilian journalist employed in the industry was about

40 years old with at least fifteen years of professional experience: self-employed professionals, who tend to be older and more experienced but have a harder time trying to find an industry job.[33] A more recent study of 538 journalists in São Paulo, Brazil's main media hub, indicates a new profile has emerged. The new generation is predominantly female and between 23 and 35 years old. They are tech-savvy, have a master's degree (65 percent), change jobs frequently, and do not plan their professional future.[34]

The new media reality has changed the job market and confirmed a new hiring trend. Several news organizations have hired journalists as temporary workers or "permanent freelancers" without formal job contracts or benefits as a way to cut costs. The new trend brings insecurity to older professionals and frightens hundreds of new professionals who graduate every year from over 400 journalism schools in the country and flood the market in large urban areas on the coast, where most Brazilians prefer to live. The once powerful journalism unions can do little to help change these job contracts because the law requiring journalists to have a university diploma in journalism was revoked in 2009 and, consequently, fewer professionals join the unions. Compulsory university training for journalists was instituted in 1969 by the military dictatorship (1964–85) to expel political activists without a journalism degree from newsrooms. However, journalism unions found that the diploma rule (not considered a license by Brazilians) helped to keep out cheap labor and professionalize journalism. In the meantime, the number of journalism schools grew rapidly, and soon the National Federation of Journalists (Fenaj) turned into a political force to defend journalists' rights. Lately, both journalism school administrators and Fenaj have tried to reinstate the ban on practicing journalism without a diploma and a bill is circulating in Congress with journalists' support and news organizations' opposition.

Telenovelas

No analysis of the Latin America media can ignore the role of *telenovelas* (soap operas), a fictional, serial narrative genre with great economic power and cultural influence across all countries. Television is the most popular medium in Brazil, with a penetration of over 90 percent. Top TV networks offer mostly national programming focused on entertainment, and the number one locally produced entertainment has been the *telenovelas*. On a weekday night in November 2013, the soap opera *Amor a Vida* (*Love for Life*) broadcast at prime time by Globo TV Network showed the gay character Felix breaking chairs and throwing vases at mirrors after admitting he has committed a list of despicable crimes against his wealthy family, the Kourys. Following the punches and screams, Felix lies down on the floor in fetal position, feeling sorry for himself, and cries. It was a masterly scene that elevated TV Globo's audience to 40.2 points from the usual 35/37, while its competitors in the same time slot remained at 5.4 points (SBT Network) and 3.9 points (Record Network). Globo's drama division executives could not be happier. French TV executives visiting the Brazilian TV network saw the scene and decided on the spot to buy *Love for Life*, one of the many products that the largest media group in Brazil has exported to a long list of countries for decades.

Created in 1965, one year after the military coup, and with the initial support of the Time Life group, Globo is Brazil's largest media conglomerate, and one of the most successful multimedia companies in the world. It has 122 owned and affiliated TV stations accessible to 87 percent of Brazilian households. Headquartered in Rio de Janeiro, the conglomerate also owns cable and satellite companies, a radio network, several newspapers, magazines, and websites, a film company, a book publishing company, and a recoding label. Its *telenovelas* are popular in Europe, Asia, and Africa as well as in Latin American countries. They are also the bread and butter of Brazilian television. Typically, a *telenovela* runs for nine months, in episodes of 45 minutes plus commercials. Globo broadcasts three *telenovelas* between 6 p.m. and 10 p.m. Monday through Saturday. Millions of Brazilians watch them daily and talk about them with their peers both in person and online. TV executives monitor online chats and listen to focus groups before resolving the destiny of major program characters.

Besides their approach that mixes fiction and reality, tragedy and comedy, *telenovelas* have a key component that entices the audience: the inclusion of preselected social issues in the plots, such as racism, homosexuality, homophobia, domestic violence, drug abuse, and government/business corruption. These social issues capture the audience's attention, generate public awareness, and swell the audience. In a very particular way, *telenovelas* somewhat set the agenda of which social issues the public will discuss during their season. Another key component of *telenovelas* is the widespread use of product placement, also known as embedded marketing. Different merchandise and advertising, from clothes to furniture to cars to credit cards, are incorporated into the plots, displayed in the backdrop or modeled by the actors. On a separate website known as Globo Marcas (Globo

Brands), the network lists its partnerships with retail companies that sell the merchandise showcased in the *telenovelas* as well as in other TV productions. Since 2000, Globo Marcas has licensed more than 3,500 products and 170 brands. To complete the cycle, retail stores advertise on television, in print, and online the products featured on *telenovelas*.[35]

Some Hope For Brazil and Latin America

Brazil embodies one of the most emblematic predicaments of our time. Like most Latin American countries, it has jumped into the future without resolving major issues of its past. One of the world's top ten economies and with the fifth-highest number of Internet users, Brazil has been a fast adopter of media technology. Brazilians with Internet access spend more hours online than the global average, consider themselves Facebook and Twitter addicts, and comprise the second largest market for YouTube outside the United States. Oddly, Latin American presidents tweet frequently to offset negative media criticism, although never abandoning the nostalgic tradition of emotional, loud speeches broadcast on radio and television.

As elsewhere, online media are in the process of displacing legacy media, even though television remains the number one medium in the region. The networks' *telenovelas* still attract millions of viewers on prime time. And while newspapers and magazines surf the online wave through paywalls and lay off hundreds of journalists, alternative forms of journalism have emerged. Some are non-profit and non-partisan, others more partisan, but all are in search of a new model that will allow them to survive economically. More specifically in Brazil, an enthusiastic youth, part of a growing middle class, spearhead the media convergence and have organized street protests through social media, hoping for faster growth and social development.

The future, though, seems fuzzy just because in Latin America the path to a better life is never a straight line. At the moment, Brazil and its neighbors face a serious digital gap that only adds to a long list of social problems that include a weak education system, economic inequalities, endemic political corruption, lack of government accountability, and limited media freedom. Across the region, governments and media corporations disagree about almost everything. Media corporations complain that governments interfere in their business, while governments complain that the media lack pluralism and diversity. Both sides distrust each other, but at times they promote distressing alliances in exchange for political and economic gains. In recent years, several left-wing governments have passed legislation to limit media ownership, create state-sponsored community media, and approve regulations to manage and upgrade old telecommunications and broadcasting systems. Some of these measures have divided public opinion in Latin America. Yet a silver lining has emerged in Brazil, where Congress has approved two positive laws: the long-waited Access to Information Law, which fights the government's culture of secrecy; and the so-called Internet Constitution, which defines the rules for freedom of expression, net neutrality, privacy, and protection of personal data, including other rights and obligations for the use of the Internet. In Brazil, and perhaps throughout Latin America, there is hope.

Cuban Media after the Castro Era

Media in Cuba are tightly controlled by the government but cracks can appear. In Havana, neighborhood entrepreneurs have set up TV satellite dishes and Cubans hook up to them for a fee. Government crackdowns come periodically, but the neighborhood cable systems are operating again soon after the police leave. These Cubans are primarily interested in sports and soap operas (Brazilian ones are the favorites) plus dubbed American films, where many Cubans say they learn their English. Their complaint about Cuban TV has little to do with politics; they just find the government channels boring.

Media in Cuba are bound to change after the dramatic December 17, 2014 announcement by Presidents Barack Obama and Raul Castro that after fifty years the US embargo will end and normal diplomatic relations will resume. Just what will change and how fast is unknown. Cuba's authoritarian government insists that control of communication is essential to maintaining "La Revolución."

Cuba uses a combination of tight government control, economic pressure, harassment, and even imprisonment to control its media. All newspapers, magazines, radio, and television are run by the government. Radio Marti and TV Marti, both sponsored by the United States, attempt to breach this control but with limited success in overcoming Cuban government jamming. (Radio Mambi, a 50,000-watt Miami station with a decidedly anti-Castro tone, can reportedly be heard across Cuba, especially late at night.)

(contd.)

Cuba has its own Intranet system, limited to the island. There is very limited access to the Internet through a small number of Internet cafés and tourist hotels. Anyone entering an Internet café must show an ID card and the $5 an hour charge for an Internet connection is an effective barrier since the average Cuban earns $20 a month. There are a few independent journalists in Cuba, but their only outlets are publications outside Cuba. Some of them have photocopied their articles and distributed them to friends inside Cuba. Some bloggers try to stay free of government control by working through private fax or email networks to spread their views. Perhaps the most influential is Yoani Sanchez, who even publishes an Internet magazine (*Contodos*) which criticizes some Cuban government policies, although in carefully worded comments. Bloggers can be harassed and even physically attacked by government sympathizers and jailed for over-critical comments. Their posts can be garbled or changed to discredit them and serious transgressions can lead to prison.

The Cuban government's main TV channels are Cubavision and Cubavision Internacional, providing news, films, soap operas, and a variety of other programs including *Momentos historicos de la Revolución*. There is also a sports channel with an emphasis on soccer and baseball but also showing tennis matches and even bobsledding. In addition there are two education channels. Telesur, headquartered in Venezuela but reporting news from all of Latin America, is popular in Cuba. It is owned by a group of Latin American countries, but Venezuela (51 percent ownership) and Cuba (19 percent) effectively control it.

Cuba's important newspaper is *Granma*, an eight-page tabloid that is probably seen by most Cubans. It carries the name of the boat that brought Fidel Castro, Che Guevara, and their eighty confederates from Mexico to invade Cuba in 1956 and to overthrow the Batista regime in 1959. A paper targeted toward younger readers is *Juventud Rebelde*, while *Trabajadores* (*The Workers*) is a strongly Marxist publication by the government-controlled union.

About 90 percent of the films shown in Cuba are American, either dubbed or subtitled in Spanish. Many Cubans prefer the subtitled films as they think it helps them to learn English. Cuba publishes an increasing number of books in English as the tourism industry grows rapidly. There are, however, shortages of educational materials, and Americans have been bringing pens, pencils, notepads, and even stuffed animals to distribute to schools while visiting Cuba. Officially these are illegal gifts. This may explain why Cuban Customs confiscated three packages of school crayons when the author visited in December 2014.

J.F.S.

Notes

1. Mariana Sallowicz, "Acesso à internet no Brasil cresce, mas 53% da população ainda não usa a rede," *Folha de S. Paulo*, May 16, 2013.
2. Internet World Statistics.
3. Brazilian Internet Steering Committee Survey on the Use of Information and Communication Technologies in Brazil (2012), 178.
4. Cetic: http://www.cetic.br/publicacoes/2012/tic-domicilios-2012.pdf.
5. Jason Kohn, "The Internet is Booming in Latin America, Especially Among Younger Users," *Cisco Blogs*, October 7, 2013.
6. Elaine Fultz and John Francis, *Cash Transfer Programmes, Poverty Reduction and Empowerment of Women: A Comparative Analysis* (Geneva: International Labor Organization, 2013).
7. World Bank, "In Brazil, an Emergent Middle Class Takes Off," November 13, 2012; http://www.worldbank.org/.
8. Brazilian Internet Steering Committee, *Survey*, 487.
9. Igarape Institute, "Black Bloc Rising: Social Networks in Brazil," October 2013; http://pt.igarape.org.br/.
10. Débora Bressan Mulbeier, " Politicians in Brazil Must Have Clean Criminal Records," Ficha Limpa, June 22, 2010; http://dialogo-americas.com/en_GB/articles/rmisa/features/regional_news/2010/06/23/feature-03.
11. Anita Breuer and Bilal Farooq, "Online Political Participation: Slacktivism or Efficiency Increased Activism? Evidence from the Brazilian Ficha Limpa Campaign," Social Science Research Network, May 1, 2012; www.ssrc.org/.
12. "Jornalistas de Zero Hora pedem o fim de ameaças," June 24 and 25, 2013; www.coletiva.net.
13. Tambor da Aldeia, October 28, 2013, Press Freedom in Brazil, bulletin 44.
14. Marcio de Souza Castillo, "A midia alternativa em tempos digitais," edition 771, May 11, 2013; http://www.observatoriodaimprensa.com.br/news/view/_ed771_a_midia_alternativa_em_tempos_digitais.

15. Heloiza G. Herscovitz, "Online Coverage of the 2010 Brazilian Presidential Elections: Framing Power and Professional Ideology," *Communication Studies* (Portugal), 12 (2012), 1–23.
16. Interview with journalist Bruno Torturra and producer Pablo Capilé, founders of Mídia Ninja, August 5, 2013.
17. De Souza Castillo, "A mídia alternativa em tempos digitais."
18. Amnesty International Report, July 24, 2014.
19. Anonimous Rio (Facebook).
20. "Folha de S. Paulo confirma crise no jornal impress," *Brasil 247*; http://www.brasil247.com/pt/247/midiatech/101610/Folha-de-SPaulo-confirma-crise-no-jornal-impresso.htm.
21. Estefania Hernandez, "Diversity in Latin American Markets Drives Paid Content Strategies," April 20, 2013; http://www.kbridge.org/en/diversity-in-latin-american-markets-drives-paid-content-strategies/.
22. Barbara Sachitielo, "Circulação de revistas recua 3% em 2013," *Meio & Mensagem*, March 20, 2014.
23. "Around 40 Venezuelan Newspapers Hit by Newsprint Shortage," Reporters Without Borders, September 12, 2014.
24. "Venezuela's Oldest Newspaper Forced to Stop Printing," *Guardian*, September 10, 2014.
25. National Association of Newspapers (ANJ), Brazil.
26. National Association of Newspapers (ANJ), Brazil.
27. "A revoada dos Passaralhos," *O Globo*, Agencia Publica, October 6, 2013.
28. "Folding Papers: As the Middle Class Embraces Online Media, Newspapers Are Struggling," *The Economist*, July 13, 2013.
29. Sachitielo, "Circulaçao de revistas."
30. "6 Basics About Brazil's Media Market," *Donos da Midia*, database; Almeida, Bruno, June 30, 2011.
31. Adriana Braz, "Number of Politicians Controlling the Brazilian Media" (infographic), *Informação Comprometida*, 60, October 2013; *Report on Brazil*, Reporters Without Borders, 2013.
32. "Brazil: New Access to Information Law Becomes Effective Today," *Article 19*, May 16, 2012; http://www.article19.org/resources.php/resource/3208/en/brazil:-new-access-to-information-law-becomes-effective-today.
33. Heloiza G. Herscovitz, "The Brazilian Journalist in the 21st Century," in *The Global Journalist in the 21st Century*, David Weaver and Lars Willnat, eds. (New York: Routledge, 2012), 365–381.
34. Carlos Eduardo Lins da Silva, "Mundo do Trabalho Muda." May 13, 2014; http://www.observatoriodaimprensa.com.br/news/view/_ed798_mundo_do_trabalho_muda.
35. *Globomarcas*: http://www.globomarcas.com.br.

7

Russian Media: Struggling Against New Controls

Russian media were perceived as at least partly independent until the middle of 2014, when President Vladimir Putin initiated a crackdown on all critical outlets. In May, after citing the Internet as "a special CIA project," he signed a new law requiring many online sites to register with the government. In September Russia's parliament endorsed a law to tighten control over Russian media, including the leading business daily and the Russian edition of *Forbes*, by limiting foreign ownership to 20 percent. The vote was 434 to 1.[1]

The media in the country have had many different voices even if the state attempts to dominate them, especially television, where most Russians get their news. Numerous political forces have their media outlets and various populations generate information, produce and receive analysis, and, perhaps most important to the mass audience, get the entertainment they want. The media are also the place where the various forces of Russian society interact or confront each other and supply the instrument for extending their influence. To some extent the state controls the traditional media, but the new media have been taking over the audience and evading state controls.

More Than History

To paraphrase the famous Russian poet Yevgeny Yevtushenko, who said that a poet in Russia is more than a poet, the media in Russia have historically always been bigger than simply "the media." The Western, especially

The World News Prism: Digital, Social and Interactive, Ninth Edition.
William A. Hachten and James F. Scotton.
© 2016 John Wiley & Sons, Inc. Published 2016 by John Wiley & Sons, Inc.

American, journalistic tradition emphasizes facts and commerce. The US press, for instance, was created for two purposes: to provide commercial information (the first American newspapers printed trade tariffs for maritime shipping) and to be sold – so news had to be in demand, and this demand had to generate money. The first Russian private newspapers and journals were created for cultural and educational purposes. In the eighteenth and nineteenth centuries, outstanding cultural figures, such as Russian poet and playwright Nikolai Novikov; Aleksander Sumarokov, considered "the father of Russian theatre"; writer Denis Fonvizin; famous fable writer Ivan Krylov; and even Russia's most famous poet Aleksander Pushkin, started journals. Fyodor Dostoevsky, one of Russia's most famous novelists, co-edited a journal with his brother. Lenin's newspaper *Iskra* played a key role in preparing the Bolshevik Revolution of 1917, in line with his perception of the press as "the collective propagandist and agitator." Also noteworthy is the phenomenon of "thick journals" that emerged at the dawn of journalism in Russia and survived throughout the three socio-political systems that Russia has gone through in the last hundred years. These journals, combining fiction with political essays, served as a platform for socio-political discussions and a kind of a proto-parliament, formulating social ideas and shaping the public environment.

When I studied journalism at a Soviet university in the 1970s, we were not taught to strictly delineate between genres, to provide dispassionate reporting, or, when reporting a conflict, to seek opinions on various sides of the story. Though there were several layers of "scientific" and literary editing, proofing, and copyediting, we were well aware that the facts could still be either not reported at all, or interfered with for political and ideological reasons. Yet in my academic group we were all obsessed with politics, with doing good, making ourselves valuable, making the country and the world better places. The press in those days enjoyed a huge readership and had a real-life impact. If something was published, there was a reaction. In the summer before the sophomore year, I interned with a local newspaper *Slava Sevastopolya* in the Crimea, now Ukraine. People brought us letters with their complaints, sacks of them, on a daily basis, expecting in this way to make their situation public and to solve their problems. Years later, after Soviet leader Mikhail Gorbachev eased controls on the media, Russian journalists were able to practice this freer journalism. When I co-taught a 1993–94 seminar with Professor James Scotton at Marquette University, however, the class concluded that journalists in the post-Soviet era were finally free to live up to their early hopes but also doubted that in an impoverished Russia this freedom could continue for long.

Granted, the national newspaper *Pravda* was required reading for 20 million members of the Communist Party. Yet other newspapers and magazines had multi-million circulations as well, due to the high level of education in the country and the lack of other information sources. However, even though most readers trusted every word published or broadcast in the government-controlled media, there were plenty of people who did not. Many journalists used hints and innuendos to try to get their message through, and the educated audience was skilled at reading between the lines, finding bits and pieces of information hidden deep inside the texts, and deciphering the meaning.

In the perestroika (reform) and glasnost (openness) period initiated by Mikhail Gorbachev in the 1980s, journalists became the heroes of the time. Contrary to the common belief, Gorbachev's glasnost was not yet freedom of the press. He only opened the door a crack. It was the mass media that rushed in and opened it completely. The press became freer by the day thanks to journalists: first they criticized Stalin, then Lenin, then the state structure, the Communist Party of the Soviet Union, and even the KGB, the secret police. After that all the skeletons came out of the closet. Crowds gathered at the newsstand in front of the *Moscow News* office on Pushkin Square eager to read each new edition. People cut out and saved the best articles – the logic being that even if their liberties were taken away, they would at least have reading matter. Historical documents uncovering true stories of the past were seen as topical and timely. Television gathered dozens of millions of viewers for the new live political shows.

Of all public professional groups in the early 1990s, journalists enjoyed the greatest trust, more than the military, national politicians, or social activists. Freeing itself from ideology and repressive control, journalism pursued the truth and, as in Russian journalism in earlier times, their own means of self-expression. Mass media may not always have been the most professional, but periodicals competed with one another in the depth and import of their content, elegance of language, grandiosity of phrasing, and strength of headlines. The emotions and opinions of Russian journalism in those days were much like contemporary blogging.

Journalism in the 1990s was in a way a continuation of traditions inherited from Russian literature. This journalism was more open and critical than in Western countries, though it continued to function in harsh economic conditions that were more like those in Latin America and Asia, where government control of the media was much stricter. The Russian free press of the 1990s was passionate and denunciatory. One study said the Russian media of the period had "unprecedented freedom from censorship."[2]

The Good, the Bad, the Ugly . . . and the Legislative

The good

In the crossfire of criticisms from all sides, liberals and communists, inside and outside the country, east and west, one simple fact is often not recognized: Russian media in the two decades since the disintegration of the Soviet Union in 1991 are greatly changed. For one thing, Russian media have moved away from being part of the literary culture toward a more commercial orientation. There are some 78,000 registered media outlets in Russia, with 60,000 actually operating. In the early 2000s, fifteen new magazines would launch every day. Leading journalists, TV and radio hosts became some of the country's best-known public figures. The sheer numbers and better quality of TV sets (in the Soviet days some early Russian color TVs exploded), computers, and mobile phones have created a completely different media situation. Yet it was not technological progress but political change that was the major factor driving changes in the mass media. After the downfall of communism, the new 1993 Constitution of the Russian Federation stipulated that "The freedom of the mass media shall be guaranteed. Censorship shall be prohibited."[3] The 1991 law "On Mass Media," the first in a post-communist state, remains the main piece of legislation governing the production and dissemination of information in Russia, and outlaws any restrictions on the media, "with the exception of those prescribed by the legislation of the Russian Federation on mass media."[4] Using a Chinese saying, it is a garden where all flowers bloom – though the conditions for them are far from equal and are getting harsher.

Back in the Soviet days, criticisms of the authorities were not possible and only "certain problems" and "certain individuals" could safely be exposed. Some economic information found its way to readers, but political information was totally censored. In the Soviet days, information about the world behind the Iron Curtain was portioned and doctored, but now Russians can compare their own country with other countries while freely traveling abroad, navigating the Internet, or even watching government-sponsored TV. The foreign press was not accessible to Soviet citizens before the dramatic political changes in the 1990s. The *New York Times* or *Washington Post* could be bought only in luxury hotels that "simple citizens" were not allowed to enter. Libraries kept these newspapers in special storage *spetskhran* for restricted use only. Well into the 1980s, there were only two TV channels, and even they transmitted only until 10 or 11 p.m., with a long interruption (*setka*) during the day. Foreign radio transmissions were jammed.

Nowadays, several national and dozens of local TV channels and numerous satellite "dishes" transmit an endless number of Western channels, Euronews is broadcast on the national Kultura TV channel and is also part of the basic cable package. The world's major newspapers are sold in many cities. Russia's leading national business daily, *Vedomosti*, is published together with the *Financial Times* and *Wall Street Journal*. Digital media are opening new frontiers.

In the Soviet days, hurricanes and wildfires made their way into the news only if they happened in other countries. Soviet reality would allow none of them. Planes crashed and trains went off track only elsewhere, not in Russia. Currently, newsworthy events happening in Russia and in the wider world are fully covered by local media. Even in extreme cases, such as during the 2008 war in the Republic of Georgia, Russian media gave a more comprehensive report than Western sources. In Soviet times the most strictly controlled outlets were Western newspapers and magazines with caricatures of government and Communist Party chiefs. Humor and sarcasm now abound in the non-government media and there are no sacred cows or untouchable topics any more, at least in the print media and, especially, in the blogosphere. Shenderovich's "Soft Cheese" on the Echo radio station of Moscow and the new TV project "Television on One's Knee" may upset some authorities but they are hilariously funny. Comedian Dmitry Medvedev, dancing to the "American Boy" music at the graduation party of St. Petersburg University's legal department was a big hit on Russian TV and in the blogosphere, while President Putin's alleged adventures are a source of endless jokes in print and electronic media.

Some Western methods found their way into Russian media through expanded contacts, increased exposure, and also through various schools and training sessions organized by Western organizations, especially in the 1990s. Investigative journalism has become widespread. Young people go into the profession, and the best Russian universities offer advanced multi-media training to journalism students. Russian journalists have been awarded many international prizes for reporting.

The not so good

The distribution of media around Russia is very uneven. Those living in rural districts have much less access to quality broadcasting and newspapers. In most of Russia's vast territory only the national TV channels (TV 1, Rossia 1, NTV, and Kultura) and radio Echo of Moscow and Mayak are available. The picture of what is happening in the world is generally conveyed by the national TV channels.

Media freedom generally expanded during the 1990s rule of Boris Yeltsin, Russia's first freely elected president. Since Putin succeeded Yeltsin in 1999, direct and indirect control over the Russian media has steadily expanded. In trying to control the mass media so that they could no longer expose and denounce government errors and lies, Putin moved as early as 2000 to limit their freedom, especially national television. Pressure on radio, newspapers, and magazines soon followed. Government control over the media continues to grow. Not a single region in the country has a completely free mass media, and those territories with relative freedom allow no criticism of the local leadership.

Economic problems contribute to media instability and also push the press into the hands of local authorities and businesses. For example, in the Altai region, according to Yuri Purgin, president of a publishing house that owns twelve newspapers and magazines, a radio station, and four websites, "80 percent of the regional press in one way or another belongs to the state."[5] Leonid Nikitinsky, in his 2013 book *Tomorrow's Issue*, argued that in all of Russia's regions there are contracts between local media and the regional authorities for "informational services." This brings income to the media but at the same time blocks material critical of the authorities and can virtually turn the media into the mouthpiece of the state. According to Nikitinsky, younger journalists do not differentiate between public relations and journalism.

The income of newspapers and journals in Russia is lower than in Western countries. The distribution chains disintegrated in the 1990s, subscriptions plummeted, and advertising – a relatively novel source of media income in Russia – has not made up for the circulation losses. The state plans to spend 172 billion rubles (about 5 billion US dollars) to support mass media over the next three years, but this may not improve the economic situation for most media.

Because of economic problems, the number of serious – and expensive – articles has been steadily declining. According to Nikitinsky, "before, the news smelled of sweat and blood," but now there is a lot of sensationalism, sports, and society news. Journalists, avoiding conflict, turn into columnists, and news reporting has moved toward news entertainment. Journalism and journalists have lost much of the trust and authority they enjoyed in the early 1990s. Putin's changed policies since his 2012 return to the presidency are reflected in the media as well, with a growing tendency toward anti-Western, and particularly anti-US, posturing. Although the new policies have been criticized by the opposition media, the Russian people overall are being told that the United States wants to dominate, that the West has an inherent prejudice toward Russia, and even that current international conflicts are the result of deliberate schemes instigated by Western politicians.

Journalism education also does not seem to hold a solution for current media problems.[6] Deputy Minister of Mass Communications Alexey Volin told journalism students and professors at Moscow State University in 2013 that journalists should serve their editors and be prepared to do what they are told without aspiring to a higher mission.[7]

The ugly

Direct government attempts to discredit the media have also been on the rise. In the Duma, Russia's parliament, Deputy Andrey Isayev, an ally of President Putin, said, "The media is the most corrupt sphere in the life of the country. Journalists, as of today, are unfortunately the most backward class of our society."[8]

There have been many cases of persecution of journalists, beatings, and arrests. Photographer Denis Sinyakov was jailed for two months after he was arrested along with the Greenpeace activists who boarded a Russian oil rig in the Arctic Ocean in 2013. Igor Domnikov, correspondent of the *Novaya Gazeta*, was beaten in 2000 after publishing articles criticizing Lipetskaya Province authorities; he died two months later. In 2008 reporter Mikhail Beketov, who had exposed wrongdoings in the Moscow satellite city of Khimki, was brutally beaten and crippled, as was Oleg Kashin, a journalist and blogger who had published articles on road construction, youth movements, extremists, and opposition demonstrations. After a series of critical articles, Sergey Sokolov, investigative reporter with the newspaper *Novaya Gazeta*, was kidnapped and threatened with death. Russia is fourth in the world in the number of murdered journalists, according to the Committee to Protect Journalists. Correspondent Anna Politkovskaya and six other *Novaya Gazeta* reporters were murdered while performing their professional duties. Many cases remain unsolved, including the murder of ORT TV's news anchor, Vladislav Listyev.

Journalists and editors risk their jobs by displeasing local authorities, particularly around election time. And there are, of course, many other ways the authorities can block journalists. Natalia Morar, the Moldavian correspondent of the liberal magazine *The New Times*, was denied entry into Russia after she wrote some critical articles. Manana Aslamazyan, who headed an organization that trained regional television journalists, was forced to leave the country. Newspapers and magazines have also been swamped with court cases for publishing supposedly libelous articles. Aksana Panova, a successful journalist who created the Ural region's leading news service Ura.ru, was prosecuted on four charges of alleged tax evasion and financial manipulation. Panova initiated an innovative campaign to force municipal authorities to repair the roads. She painted the face of the responsible bureaucrat around each pothole.

The authorities have their own public relations staffs writing thousands of posts praising current leaders and criticizing the opposition, liberal leaders, and America.[9] Fake issues of opposition publications have even turned up, filled with material expected to alienate their allies. Opposition and independent websites, such as Grani.ru and the website of the radio station Echo of Moscow, have been targeted by numerous computer attacks.[10]

The legislative

Efforts to control the mass media have included repressive legislation and direct government takeovers. In 2012, 79 staffers at Lenta.ru issued a statement of angry protest, reading, "Over the past couple of years, the space of free journalism in Russia has dramatically decreased. Some publications are directly controlled by the Kremlin, others through curators, and others by editors who fear losing their jobs. Some media outlets have been closed and others will be closed in the coming months. The problem is not that we have nowhere to run. The problem is that you have nothing more to read." Ilya Krasilshchik, an employee of one of Lenta.ru's sister companies, wrote: "Advice for beginning journalists: pick a new profession."[11] The fear of libel prosecutions under new laws also limits criticism of government officials. Irek Murtazin, editor in chief of the newspaper *Kazanskie Vesti*, received a prison term for an allegedly libelous article in the social media source *Live Journal*. Putin again made libel a criminal offense soon after he returned to the presidency in 2012.

The most frequently blocked websites have been those of electronic libraries, blog platforms, and personal blogs, as well as sports portals and even poker games.[12] In November 2013 Internet provider Rostele.com blocked some of the resources of Russia's leading social network VKontakte by order of a Moscow court.

Confronted with criticisms, state officials promised to amend the law and called on Internet companies to consider self-regulatory measures. At the meeting of the Council on Human Rights in September 2013, Putin said that he recognized that "intellectual rights should be provided for and one must not overdo [it] in order not to kill the Internet." Still, the trend toward more regulation of the media is increasing. The Federal Security Bureau wants to require Internet providers to record all communication and allow the FSB direct access to this material. This is in clear violation of the Russian Constitution, which guarantees the right to privacy in postal correspondence, telephone discussions, and other communications.

In 2013 the Russian Ministry of Communication proposed to centralize all telephone and electronic communication. Leading Russian Internet companies and providers have publicly opposed the proposal.

All Those Media: Broadcast, Print, and Digital TV Under Siege

Although 2013 registered the first decline in TV viewers, the vast majority of Russians still get their news from the television. Of those polled by the Levada Center, 88 percent said that they preferred TV, a drop from 94 percent in 2009. In a country where the four national channels (TV1, Russia 1, NTV, and Kultura) are available to the overwhelming majority of the population, it is not surprising that the authorities use television as the main instrument to influence the people's minds and win their hearts.[13] Within ten years of Putin succeeding Yeltsin, the government had control over the national television channels. Unlike the situation in the United States, in most of Russia outside Moscow, St. Petersburg, and some other big cities, only the national TV channels are freely and easily accessible. There are various TV satellite and cable packages available for a fee. Some 56 percent of the TV audience receives cable transmission, while 35 percent get satellite transmission, and 9 percent receive TV via the Internet.[14] The government is trying to spread cable, perhaps trying to distract the population from the Internet toward media that are easier for the state to control.

Broadcast television gets the bulk of advertising money in Russia. Cable and satellite advertising, though growing, only receives around 2 percent (3 billion rubles against 139 billion rubles) and its revenue is only growing slowly. Advertisers use special TV channels only when they believe that they can reach a precisely targeted audience.[15] This vast disparity in commercial financing between the national channels and other TV stations results in huge differences in production quality. For this and other reasons, the five national channels lead in the size of their TV audience. The government's Channel 1 remains the most popular, with 14 percent of the TV audience, closely followed by the state-affiliated Russia 1 channel and privately owned NTV (both around 13 percent). The Kultura channel attracts a smaller but generally better-educated audience. NTV, the first private television station and the flagship of independent journalism, was essentially taken over by the government in a murky sale to a new owner. After the changes, all the channel's star reporters and news anchors left. Meanwhile, the "new" NTV in 2012 and 2013 showed two documentary films under the overall title "The Anatomy of Protest." The films generally portrayed protests as being led by unpatriotic groups with funding from Western and anti-Russian sources. The NTV's directorate for legal programs, which produced the films, is staffed mostly by former security services recruits. The films were sharply criticized by the journalism community. The four dominant national channels are followed by a group composed of TNT, STS, Channel 5, and RenTV, each with about 5 percent of the television audience. Other channels with small audiences include TV Center, TV-3, Domashniy, Perets (Pepper), military-patriotic-oriented Zvezda, Russia 2, U, Pyatnitsa (Friday), Russia-24, Ru.TV, Euronews, and Muz-TV.[16]

The channel dedicated to news, Russia 24, created several years ago, leads the list of most often quoted TV channels. Also on this list are the liberally orientated channel Dozhd (Rain), government-affiliated Russia Today which transmits both locally and abroad in many languages, the three primary national channels, Channel 1, NTV, and Russia 1, followed by EuroNews, Kultura, and TV Center. There have been recent efforts to overcome government controls and reach Russian TV audiences. A new low-budget TV project, Televideniye na kolenke ("Television On One's Knee," which in Russian implies self-made television) was started in 2013. The project's slogan is "Better make television on one's knee, than have television on its knees." The first three programs, released on YouTube, were enthusiastically received in the blogosphere, but the project has yet to prove its financial viability. Sergey Parfenov, a former megastar of the NTV channel before the change in ownership, had a 2012 political program on the liberal Dozhd TV channel financed by crowdfunding over the Internet.

LifeNews TV, launched in 2013 with substantial financing and the slogan "To be the first on urgent news," has said its goal is to become the number one information source in the country. Eighty percent of its news is not scheduled since it tries to be first to cover breaking news events. Viewers using smartphones provide information to supplement the station's own reporting. By the end of 2013 up to 30 million Russians had access to Life-News and it hoped to reach 50 percent of the country's population by the end of 2014 via various cable networks.

The state uses television to formulate its agenda, raise the popularity of the country's leaders, and influence the population. On government-controlled channels such as Channel 1 there is heavy coverage of the trips and meetings of the president and the premier. Government control over the national channels is concentrated primarily on news and political programs, but combined with the dictates of the ratings system, also defines the style and quality of other television broadcasts. Since the beginning of President Putin's third term in 2012 the tone of the political news programs has become more anti-Western. Top opposition politicians and commentators or experts who are identified with the opposition are generally not shown on government-controlled national TV. Still, the TV audience in Russia does not fully trust what it sees. Although a recent poll found a slight majority of 51 percent that still considered TV the "most trusted" information source, that was a sharp decline from the 79 percent who did in 2009.

Content on the main Russian TV channels is similar to that in the United States, although the Kultura channel, with its predominance of educational and cultural programs, is more like the BBC. One difference between US and Russian TV content, however, is the much larger percentage of both political news and entertainment news on the main US channels. On Russian television there are both significantly more soap operas and, at the same time, more cultural programming, in particular programs dealing with history theater, literature, and classical music.[17]

There are many foreign programs on Russian TV. Films are split almost equally between Russian and international productions along with new and old blockbusters, action films, and world classics. Many of the programs are franchised local variations of Western shows. *Let Them Talk* remains the most popular show on Russian TV, with up to 30 percent of viewers watching it, and its host Andrei Malakhov is cited in polls as the most trusted TV anchor. Though high in the ratings, the program has been criticized for its sensationalism. On one show a man and a woman had their DNA tested to see if he was the father of her child. The results were reported live on the program. The second most trusted TV figure is Vladimir Pozner, formerly number one and a giant of Russian journalism. Pozner was explicit in his liberal pro-Western views although he has become more cautious in a period of growing authoritarianism. He made what he claims was a "slip of the tongue" during his show when commenting on a new law prohibiting American adoption of Russian children. He called the State Duma the "State Dura" which in Russian means state fool: the Duma hurried to initiate a bill prohibiting citizens of other countries from working on Russian TV. Pozner, although he had lived in Russia for many years, was born in France, has a French mother and American father, and holds US, French, and Russian citizenship. His Russian citizenship was revoked by the government despite his apology.

Standing apart in Russian TV programming is *Wait for Me*, which looks for people who have either disappeared or lost each other. In Russia there are still millions who were displaced, imprisoned, or who lost relatives and friends during World War II and the Stalin era. Over the year, the program has become a grand opera of people lost and people found. Helping families and friends reunite after years of separation, filming their stories and broadcasting their reunions stirs human emotions and attracts a huge television audience. Russian-made series constitute the favorites of TV's most ardent watchers: housewives and pensioners. The program list is split into two categories: (1) banal themes, awkward plots, lots of tears, and clichéd dialogue that make the hardiest proponents of democratic freedoms want to ban them; and (2) high-quality productions, with fine actors, unique scripts, and amazing filming, such as the 2005 *Bandit Petersburg* film or the 2007 film *Liquidation*. There have also been several screenings of Russian classics on Russia 1.

There are also many TV channels that through digital transmission are becoming increasingly available throughout the entire country. The Public Television Channel, started in 2013 with government funding, was meant to sway "opposition" viewers, attract intellectuals, and offer educational, socially oriented broadcasting, with an additional regional focus: "Utopian television, created by Utopia," as it was characterized by its own director.[18] Public Television has so not far lived up to expectations and has run into financial problems. As part of the Kremlin's effort to build conservative support and counter liberal opponents, in 2005 the Spas TV (Savior TV) satellite channel was launched, featuring religious programs. Official figures claim an audience of 10 million, but Spas TV has been criticized for uninteresting content and broadcasting old shows. Only 7 percent of Russians are regular churchgoers.

Radio: "The Rest Is Just Appearance"?

Short-wave and medium-wave radio in the Soviet Union were reserved for the military. Every apartment was equipped with a radio receiver (the monthly fee was included in the rent) to be used for announcements in case of war. Many educated Russians turned to the Voice of America, the BBC, Radio Free Europe, and Radio Liberty for information. Although the number of radio listeners has decreased dramatically in recent years (41 percent of the population in 2009, 16 percent in 2013), radio continues to be an essential part of the media landscape, especially in remote areas. In some areas of Kamchatka on the eastern edge of Siberia the only accessible media outlet is a single local radio station. The most popular radio stations combine small talk with local or Western pop music and discussions of all sorts. All stations, unlike in the Soviet days, transmit mostly around the clock. The same "light music" heard in the United States ("elevator music") is broadcast on many Russian stations.

The Echo of Moscow is a major source of independent news in Russia. The radio station is owned the state gas monopoly Gazprom. The station has become the most popular in Moscow and was number 13 nationwide in 2012, according to the Russian Public Opinion Research Center.[19] In 1991 the station reported citizen resistance to the attempted coup by communist hardliners; Moscow television was showing the ballet *Swan Lake* over and over again while ignoring the dramatic events on its doorstep. Echo of Moscow correspondents were in Kiev in December 2013 to report on clashes there over whether Ukraine would join the European Union or keep its ties with Russia.

Although TV has been the main target of state control, radio has also experienced government pressure in recent years. Regions and cities have blocked unfavorable radio stations or specific broadcasts. When radio station Serebryanni Dozhd (Silver Rain) was broadcasting a live interview with Aleksey Dymovski, a police officer who posted an Internet video criticizing abuse rampant in the Ministry of Internal Affairs, the transmission was blocked to cities in Moscow Province.

In 2012 the US-funded Radio Free Europe switched to online service only and dozens of journalists in its Moscow bureau lost their jobs. Since the Soviet times Russians have listened to Radio Free Europe to hear independent opinions and unbiased news.[20]

Print Media Keep on Kicking

Compared with television, print media have retained a certain measure of freedom, probably because their smaller audience reduces their significance to the authorities. The number of people reading newspapers has gone down to 20 percent of the population, from 37 percent in 2009. Magazines and journals are read by only 4 percent, compared to 8 percent in 2009.

As opposed to Western countries, where printed newspapers are increasingly giving way to digital media, the Russian print media have just started feeling competition from the Internet. The problem, however, lies in distribution. Distribution chains were destroyed with the disintegration of the Soviet Union, and the state-owned postal service is so unreliable that even in Moscow newspapers are often not delivered. Local authorities often try to "cleanse" their cities of kiosks, stands, and pavilions, so the number of places selling newspapers in some cities has fallen dramatically, though their number was already significantly lower per capita than in most European countries. Also, the orientation of newspapers still alienates what could be a mass readership since they pay little attention to people's everyday problems and the issues that interest them most. In Russia there is also no tradition of adapting the use of language to a less educated audience.

The tabloids *Moscovsky Komsomolets* and *Kovsomolskaya Pravda*, as well as the newspaper *Argumenty i Facty*, have a nationwide circulation, and big cities throughout the country have centrally published "serious" dailies. Although the national tabloids have bigger circulations than regional newspapers, some local papers known for their independence are very influential. In some localities there are also free municipal newspapers.

Though, compared to the television, the printed press is less controlled by the state, the government uses it for its purposes as well. *Rossiyskaya Gazeta* is the source of much official information such as new laws. With 200,000 to 400,000 subscribers and many copies going to libraries and government institutions, overall readership is estimated at 1.35 million daily. Unlike the Soviet Union days, however, there is nothing like *Pravda*, the official

Communist Party newspaper that circulated millions of copies daily then, but now sells only about 100,000 copies a day.

Although the number of objective, high-quality Russian newspapers has declined, you can still get the picture of what is happening in the country and follow domestic and international developments by reading the printed press. The leading Russian socio-political newspaper *Kommersant*, the business newspaper *Vedomosti*, and *Novaya Gazeta* and many local newspapers continue to give an unbiased picture of what is happening. *Novaya Gazeta*, an outspoken opponent of Putin, has published articles by Putin's chief opponent, business oligarch Mikhail Khodorkovsky, who has been in prison on fraud charges since 2003.[21] Although newspapers all over Russia have cut print-runs, many are reaching new online audiences.

Magazines continue to have influence. The Russian version of *Forbes* has investigated some murky business deals in the country and had a circulation of 2.9 million in 2013. One of its editors, Paul Klesbenikov, a top investigative reporter, was murdered in 2004. Other influential magazines include *Russian Pioneer* (236,000), *Snob* (99,000), *Itogi* (65,000), *Expert* (62,000), *GQ* (61,000), *The New York Times* (53,000), *Afisha* (50,000), and *Russian Reporter* (44,000). *Snob*, a literary magazine started in 2010 by New Jersey Nets basketball team owner Mikhail Prokhorov, was the fastest-growing in 2013.[22]

But pressure on print media is increasing. Local newspapers have directives dropped on them from above about the publication of particular material, sometimes with special lists of "recommended" keywords for articles. There have been reported instances of direct censorship.

Where All the Young People Have Gone: The Internet

The Internet and its social networks is the domain where remarkable changes are taking place. Russian has become the second most frequently used language over the Internet. Over half the population of Russia, around 70 million overall, use the Internet, and half of these from a personal or household computer. Over half of Internet users and one-third of those using social networks do so on a daily basis.[23] Each Internet user spends about one hour daily online. Though Internet saturation is still lower than in western Europe, Russia is catching up fast.

The Internet has introduced an additional layer to society, separating its users from those without access. Moreover, the Internet itself also remains divisive, with each category of users having the specific sites they visit and their own social networks. So far people active in social networks are no more likely than the general Russian population to support political protests, according to research by Russia's New Economic School.[24] Also noteworthy is that social networks are not much used by Russia's rising nationalist groups.

According to a 2013 poll,[25] the number of Russians using the Internet (21 percent) and social networks (14 percent) as a primary news source is growing rapidly. Moreover, twice as many respondents perceived the Internet and social networks as the most trustworthy source of news (14 and 11 percent respectively). In Moscow,[26] social networks have overtaken radio as the most popular source of news. In Russia local social networks dominate, with one, Yandex, more widely used than Google.

Though TV still gets over half of all advertising, the Internet's share (15 percent) is rapidly growing and in 2013 surpassed that of print media. Leading online publications include the digital versions of the country's main dailies *Kommersant*, *Vedomosti*, *RBC Daily*, and *Moscow News*, as well the solely digital Gazeta.ru. Internet versions of the political journal *Expert*, business and entertainment journal Slon.ru, and *Forbes Russia* are popular. The online business resources also include the portal Prime with real-time market quotations, financial indexes, and commercial analysis, the business news portal BFM.ru, business and career publication *Delovoy Kvartal*, and *Ezhednevnik* (*Daily*). The political digital resources are represented by Newsru.com and Lenta.ru, carrying the latest news, and InoSMI and InoPressa with translations of most important materials in other languages, primarily English. In some regions online resources have been capturing audience from the traditional media. The international company Socialbakers is working to attract international advertisers and to detect inflated subscription figures of the so-called bots.[27]

Some social networks focus on anti-corruption revelations and the political opposition's activities. The famous site Rospil traces corruption and wrongdoing by state officials during state purchases. Financed entirely by public donations, Rospil publishes articles, investigative materials, and documents, and also collects complaints about corruption. Studies by the Center for New Media and Society show that Rospil's revelations do indeed have a significant influence on the share prices of exposed companies, showing that investors do use blogs as an information source.[28]

Groups in social networks were a major resource for Alexey Navalny during his campaign for Moscow's mayoral elections in 2013, where he ended up second with 27 percent of the vote. Navalny also used Russia's key search engine Yandex to collect money by developing the Kredit Doveriya (The Credit of Trust). An individual who contributed the legal limit of 1 million rubles could be compensated by contributors to an "Internet purse." A social network monitoring system was also set up to monitor this election with SMS messages with results sent directly from voting stations. Within an hour the voting figures were on the site of *Novaya Gazeta* newspaper and on the Dozhd television station. Rosuznik is another famous non-commercial site which publishes information on people detained during political protests. It organizes and finances experts, coordinates the work of lawyers, and assists activists in detention. Existing solely on public donations, Rosuznik focuses on political prisoners. The Dissernet site investigates and publicizes cases of dissertation plagiarism, which is especially common among state officials.

The government has invested a lot of time and energy in the Internet, but for a long time lagged behind. Electronic Russia was launched in the early 2000s to extend the Internet to the entire country and digitalize government communications and services. Professionals, and in particular young people, have been far ahead of the government in developing social networks and their audiences. Since the start of Putin's third presidential term in 2012, the government's Internet initiatives have largely been replaced by increasing attempts to control the Internet. The press reported that the Kremlin strongly recommended that state officials not maintain their own blogs or interact in social networks. Although later the president's press secretary Dmitry Peskov denied this, it did seem to indicate a growing preference for control over maintaining open communication channels and opportunities for getting feedback and engaging with society. The latest international Internet ranking rates Russia's Internet as "partially free."

Conclusion

Old-time Russian journalism which tended to feature cultural material may be dead in an age of mass audiences, especially on the Internet and television. The regime, though far from that of Soviet totalitarianism, is growing increasingly more authoritarian and is trying to fit the media within its system of vertical power and to use them for its own propaganda purposes. Despite the state's repressive measures, however, media in the country are burgeoning. As a profession, journalism, despite lingering post-Soviet handicaps, has long traditions of endurance and excellence and thrives on the rising public activism and sense of social responsibility within Russian society. Young journalists continue to search new frontiers, raising important themes and using innovative formats to overcome barriers. In a period that Russians would call *bezvremeniye*, which literally means "between times" and for which there is no English equivalent, it is hard to make predictions. However, some key conclusions on the more practical side would be:

- A society cannot function normally without independent and objective mass media. Independent mass media, uncontrolled by the government and perceived as a true fourth estate, are critical for the development of Russia.
- The press need not necessarily follow in the traditions of the West, but it must be professional, reliably presenting the facts and granting opposing sides an opportunity to express their opinions.
- Media principles should be developed by journalists themselves based on professional self-regulation and expert opinions.
- A professional journalism community must also develop house rules that place "political technologies," falsehoods, manipulation, and "black PR" outside the realm of acceptable practice.
- It would be beneficial for the state to eliminate the value-added tax for on the press and to subsidize paper, printing, and distribution for the printed press, as well as rent and other costs for radio stations. Such measures would improve the media's economic situation and help build their editorial independence.
- All those who use the Internet and other new means of communication must resist government efforts to take it over through close regulation.
- In line with the Russian tradition of journalism, it is essential to oppose the de-intellectualization of the press.

Vaclav Havel, the author and former president of the Czech Republic, told a group of journalists that to keep their freedom "It is important not to get afraid. Be able to confront the opposing force if you are sure that the truth is on your side. Be prepared for sacrifice. Not to lose pride, which has nothing to do with arrogance and haughtiness. And to breed within yourself what I call personal responsibility of everyone for the entire world." These words seem to be particularly relevant now.

Notes

1. Neil MacFarqhuar, "Russia Quietly Tightens Reins on Web with 'Bloggers Law,'" *The New York Times*, May 6, 2014; Andrew Roth, *Russia Moves to Extend Control of Media*, *The New York Times*, September 23, 2014.
2. Laura Beldin, "The Russian Media in the 1990s," *Journal of Communist Studies and Transition Politics*, 18(1), 1 (2002).
3. Article 29.5 ; http://archive.kremlin.ru/eng/articles/ConstEng2.shtml.
4. http://www.democracy.ru/english/library/laws/eng_1991-1/index.html.
5. Round table, "The Dystrophy of the 'Organs of Truth.' "
6. See, for example, S. G. Korkonosenko, *The Basics of Journalism: A Textbook for Universities* (Moscow: Aspect Press, 2001), 85, 169, 176, 262, 266, 275.
7. http://www.youtube.com/watch?v=vunrXEhqAuU.
8. Newsru.com site http://www.newsru.com/.
9. Alexandra Garmazhapova, "Gde zhivut troli" [Where Trolls Live], *Novaya Gazeta*, September 9, 2013.
10. It is not only the opposition and independent websites, however, that become the target of cyber-attacks. For instance, state-owned RIA Novosti reported such assaults on its accounts throughout 2012 and 2013, the latest of them on August 7, 2013, when hackers published fake information about Gorbachev's death first on German-language resource RIA Novosti Deutsch and then on the Twitter accounts of RIA Novosti's International Multimedia.
11. David Remnick, "Putin Moves Against the Press," *The New Yorker*, March 12, 2014.
12. Andrei Soldatov, "What's Russia blocking on the Web?," *Index*, June 13, 2013; Matthew Bodner, "Russians' Internet Increasingly Subject to Control," *The Moscow Times*, September 19, 2014.
13. For a detailed account of the situation with Russian television, see "Pro et Contra, Televideniye v poiskakh ideologii" [Television in Search of Ideology], *Carnegie Moscow Center*, 4, 2006.
14. Mike Butcher, "Russian Online Video Market Booming, Becomes Biggest in Europe," IKS-Consulting, March 25, 2014.
15. Sofya Inkizhinova, "Taksist Ashot vyhodit na svyaz" [Taxi Driver Ashot Comes Online], *Expert*, 44, November 4–10, 2013, 29.
16. TNS Russia.
17. Data are based on research by the Carnegie Moscow Center's interns Attila Juhasz and Sean Kesluk, August–November 2013.
18. Petr Skorobogaty, "Utopian Television, Created by Utopia," *Expert*, November 25–December 1, 2013.
19. http://www.wciom.com/.
20. Radio Free Europe/Radio Liberty Archives. Retrieved February 21, 2015.

21. Free Media Online http://freemediaonline.org. The first of these lectures, "The Modern Social Liberalism in Russia," was published in *Novaya Gazeta*, 122, on October 31, 2011; the second, "The Modern Social Liberalism and Economics," came out on April 16, 2012; and the third, "Between Empire and National State," on June 15, 2012.

22. Rebecca Mead, "Black Hole: Snob Magazine," *The New Yorker*, November 28, 2010; http://snob.ru/ (retrieved February 22, 2015).

23. "The Source of Information for Muscovites, the Ninth Text Press Issue," Levada Center, July 17, 2013.

24. Sam Greene, "Twitter and Russian Protest: Mems, Networks and Mobilization," Center for New Media and Society, Moscow, May 22, 2012.

25. "Where Russians Get the News From," Levada Center, July 8, 2013.

26. "The Source of Information for Muscovites, the Ninth Text Press Issue," Levada Center, July 17, 2013.

27. Yevgeny Krasnikov, "VKontakte is Awaiting Foreign Advertisers," *RBK daily*, October 7, 2013.

28. Reben Enikolopov, Maria Petrova, and Konstantin Sonin, "Do Political Blogs Matter? Corruption in State-Controlled Companies, Blog Postings, and DDoS Attacks," Center for New Media and Society, September 2012; federation.ens.fr/ydepot/semin/texte1213/MAR2013DOP.pdf.

8

India: Liberalization Spurs Phenomenal Media Growth

Since the liberalization of India's economy in the 1990s, its media have attained a new vibrancy. In the world's largest democracy, newspapers are thriving and cable television channels are vying with each other in English and numerous other languages, all seeking audiences and advertising in a large but fragmented market. In 2011 the entertainment and media industry that includes television, print, radio, and other media was worth $17 billion; by 2016, this figure is expected to more than double to reach $38 billion. In the last two decades, India has undergone its own information revolution and has emerged as a major Asian technology hub with its computer scientists and engineers in great demand worldwide. Yet India's per capita income of $3,900 per year is among the lowest in the world. Only about 200 million Indians – just one-sixth of its 1.2 billion population – have Internet access.

Social media are in their infancy in India but are poised to register an upsurge in the near future. There are an estimated 82 million Facebook users, about 55 million YouTube users, and about 20 million LinkedIn users. According to the *Social Media in India 2012* report of the Internet and Mobile Association of India, the estimated number of social media users in 2013 in urban India was 66 million and the active mobile Internet user base in India was about 40 million in 2012. The number of social media users is expected to increase to more than 200 million by 2017. Freedom of information on the Web is limited by India's Central Monitoring System that gives the government access to emails, text messages, and social media such as Twitter, Facebook, and LinkedIn as well as voice data on software such as Skype.

The World News Prism: Digital, Social and Interactive, Ninth Edition.
William A. Hachten and James F. Scotton.
© 2016 John Wiley & Sons, Inc. Published 2016 by John Wiley & Sons, Inc.

History

Advanced civilizations flourished in the Indus Valley and by the Ganges River earlier than 2500 BCE. Over the millennia, various invaders entered India and gave rise to a multicultural and multilingual society. After 200 years under British rule, India emerged as an independent nation in 1947 and established itself as a sovereign, socialist, secular, democratic republic. India has twenty-eight states and seven union territories and in area is the seventh-largest country in the world. A majority of India's population is Hindu (over 80 percent) followed by Muslims (13.4 percent), Christians (2.3 percent), and Sikhs (1.9 percent). About twenty-two major languages and over 600 dialects are spoken in India. About 73 percent of the population is literate. Hindi and English are official national languages. More than 53 percent of the labor force is in agriculture, with the rest in industry or services. The service sector alone contributes more than 65 percent of India's gross domestic product (GDP) while industry produces about 18 percent and agriculture about 17 percent. About one-third of India's people live in urban areas while the rest live in smaller rural communities.

India's newspaper history goes back to 1780 with the founding of *The Bengal Gazette* by James Augustus Hicky. An Indian press soon followed and played a prominent role in the struggle for independence despite an 1878 colonial law forbidding these papers from criticizing the British.[1] In the early twentieth century newspapers to promote the struggle for independence were founded by political leaders including Mahatma Gandhi (*Young India* and *Harijan*) and Jawaharlal Nehru (*National Herald*). Since independence and even before, India's print media have always been relatively free, but were suppressed for nineteen months between 1975 and 1977 when then prime minister Indira Gandhi declared a state of emergency. Even during this period, newspapers such as the *Indian Express* ventured to criticize the government. India's newspaper industry has remained strong, with notable newspapers such as *The Times of India* (founded in 1861), the *Statesman* (1875), *The Hindu* (1878), and *Malayala Manorama* (1890) continuing to thrive.

Why Newspapers Are Thriving

Contrary to the painful experiences of newspapers in the West that are struggling to find a viable business model to survive while transitioning to an online environment, newspapers in India appear to be thriving. *The Times of India* alone has a daily circulation of 3.3 million copies, followed by the Hindi-language *Dainik Jagran* (2.67 million) and the Malayalam-language *Malayala Manorama* (2.1 million). *The Indian Express*, started in 1932, now has thirty-five editions and dailies in seven languages with a total reach that exceeds 19 million people. Grouped by languages, Hindi-language daily papers lead with a total daily circulation of over 15 million copies, followed by English (more than 9 million) and Marathi (5.4 million). There are daily newspapers in Malayalam, Tamil, Telugu, Bengali and Kannada, each with a circulation ranging from over 2 million to over 4 million copies. The total circulation of daily newspapers averages 48 million copies each day.

There are several reasons for the print media's continued success. One is increasing literacy rates that in 2011 reached 73 percent (80 percent for men, 65 percent for women), up from 65 percent in 2001. Also, higher income levels mean more people, especially low-income rural residents, can afford a newspaper. Newspapers are inexpensive, 10 cents or less a copy, and subscribers can even retrieve some of the cost by recycling the papers. One study found that a single copy of *Dinathanthi* (*The Daily Wire*), a Tamil newspaper, was being read by groups of people in villages. The paper used simple language that was easy to read aloud. This working-class newspaper is read out loud and discussed by people who share a copy, often in a teashop, enabling even illiterate people to receive the information. The study reports: "The *Dinathanthi* newspaper arrives, most days, in the village by bus at around 8:30 in the morning, when most people have already been up for two or three hours and are on their way to work, either in the fields or in town. As soon as it arrives, the twenty-two page broadsheet is immediately taken apart and distributed so that every man interested and able can read a page. Over the course of a day, it is common for a single copy of *Dinathanthi* to pass through up to one hundred pairs of hands at this teashop, and it then moves through neighboring villages. It is only a few days later that the paper will be brought back to the teashop and recycled for use as a wrapping for fried snacks or as a container for small parcels of grain or lentils."[2]

Innovative business methods are also boosting income for India's newspapers. For example, brothers Samir and Vineet Jain charge celebrities for the stories about them in *The Times of India* rather than provide free publicity. The Jains own the Bennett Coleman Company Limited (BCCL) that also controls other newspapers plus magazines, satellite news, and entertainment channels and a radio network. In his 2012 article in the *New Yorker* magazine, Ken Auletta reports that BCCL accepts ads in exchange for equity in a company. Ownership stakes in more than 350 companies accounts for about 15 percent of BCCL's revenues. Other strategies the company employs include selling an entire front page for an advertisement or even changing the masthead to promote the name of a company that pays the price. Many publishers also inflate circulation figures by printing excess papers and sending these directly to the "raddhi" or paper recycling market.[3] Paying for favorable comment appears to be widespread. During elections, paid news is particularly lucrative for many newspapers, with politicians offering money to have good things published about themselves and criticisms by rivals blocked.[4]

Language Press Reaches Rural Areas

The expansion of the rural market was a catalyst to the growth of newspapers. As literacy rates improved and incomes rose rural residents became potential consumers of a wide array of products, including newspapers. Improvements in print technology as well as more advertising led some newspapers to establish district editions. Old letterpress machines gave way to offset printing, and satellites and computers allowed faster transmission of information. Many regional Indian-language newspapers are published in Hindi, Bengali, Malayalam, Punjabi, Marathi, Kannada, Telugu, Tamil, Urdu, Gujarati, and other regional languages. India's regional languages evolved centuries back and have their own scripts. These Indian-language papers must reflect their regions and be intimately in touch with their readers, but as one study noted they must also connect with national interests that provide a large part of their revenue.[5]

Political involvement is an important factor related to newspaper-reading habits. In the state of Kerala, the literacy rate is 93 percent and newspaper circulation is far greater than in other parts of India. That could be attributed to the people's desire to get more information and to participate in local politics. Another example of how politics can drive newspaper circulation is *Eenadu*, a leading Telugu newspaper in Andhra Pradesh. Ramoji Rao, the owner-editor of *Eenadu*, helped create the Telugu Desam Party and was active in the 1980s in state elections. During this period, *Eenadu*'s circulation rose by 37 percent.

In multilingual India a large percentage of citizens speak more than one language. In urban centers it is quite common for each household to subscribe to two or three newspapers in English and other languages. In 1996, there were 4,453 daily newspapers, and 2,004 of these were in Hindi compared with about 320 English newspapers. According to the Registrar of Newspapers in India, the total number of publications in March 2012 was 86,754. Hindi publications numbered 34,651, followed by 11,938 in English. *The Hindu* newspaper's Chennai edition was the largest daily, with a circulation of 1,606,711, followed by *Anand Bazar Patrika*, a Bengali newspaper from Kolkata with a circulation of 1,282,942. *The Times of India* was the largest circulated multi-edition daily (4,575,895) followed by the Hindi language newspaper *Dainik Bhaskar* (3,089,013).

Internet Access

Although we are in the digital age and India has become an important technology hub, the number of people with access to the Internet continues to be low. Of the more than 1.2 billion population, 198 million, or about a sixth, utilize the Internet, some via mobile devices. High cost of connectivity, instability in power supply, lack of language compatibility, and scarcity of local language content are some of the reasons for the slower diffusion of the Internet in both urban and rural areas. This is another factor that allows the traditional media to continue to flourish. Major media organizations do have a digital presence and provide breaking news, tweet the latest information, have Facebook, blogs, mobile apps and other features. However, digital advertising support is weak and digital technology has not had a noticeable impact on the traditional media industry. According to a prominent Indian journalist, "There can be little doubt that within this digital age paradox, both the print and broadcast media in India continue to benefit from the country's relative backwardness in Internet use and broadband access – and from the digital divides that stand out."[6] The International Telecommunications Union lists India among the least connected countries. A national survey found that newspaper editors and managers believed that the newspapers faced competition from television rather than the Internet. The survey also found that Internet users were not primarily seeking news but entertainment.[7] The tipping point might very well be access via mobile phones, that have spread at a phenomenal rate. There are 903 million mobile phone subscribers in India, and 358 million are rural subscribers, more than the total of 345 million in the United States. However, many of these are not smartphones although the number of smartphones is on the rise. According to the Telecom Authority of India, 99.25 percent of the nearly 600,000 villages are connected by village public telephones.

Magazines

India has a variety of magazines in various languages that cover a wide range of reader interests. *India Today*, India's leading English news magazine, is also published in Hindi and three other South Indian languages. Most of the newspaper companies also own magazines. The Times of India Group's magazines include *Femina*, a women's magazine launched in 1959, *Zig-Wheels*, an automobile magazine, and the movie publication *Filmfare*. The Hindu Group of publications owns *Frontline* and *Sportstar* magazines. Since 2008, India's Ministry of Information and Broadcasting has allowed foreign magazines to publish lower-priced Indian editions. This policy change attracted such magazines as *Harper's Bazaar*, *Business Week*, and *Playboy*, while those already available in the country, such as *Newsweek*, *Fortune*, and *Harvard Business Review*, could charge lower prices. Reaching India's growing wealthier classes with advertising for expensive products is a major reason for the influx of foreign magazines. *Maxim*, a London-based magazine, reported that it got a year's worth of advertising commitments for the Indian version even before it was launched in 2006.[8] One problem for India's magazine industry is recent increases in newsprint costs that have forced many magazines to reduce the number of pages and raise prices. Also, regional magazines have been losing circulation.

Television

Television in India was seen as an educational service of the government at its beginning in 1959 as a UNESCO project. Initially, television growth was very slow due to the need for heavy capital investment and the perception that it was a toy for the rich. The government-owned Doordarshan TV service launched, in 1975, a satellite project that beamed programs on health, hygiene, nutrition, agriculture, and adult literacy to 2,400 villages. Television for general audiences grew slowly until 1982, when color broadcasting started and more sports and entertainment programs appeared. In the mid-1980s there was a sharp increase in the number of television transmitters across the nation, rising from 40 in 1982 to 510 by 1990. Most television sets were still in urban areas and English-language programming was limited to a few national news bulletins and imported programs such as the American comedy *I Love Lucy* and the British comedy *Are You Being Served?* During its early years Doordarshan was considered a propaganda tool for the government, and much of the programming appeared to be relevant to neither rural nor urban residents. However, programs that did capture national audiences were serials based on the *Ramayana* and the *Mahabharata*, two of India's great Hindu epics. Some popular early soap operas during the 1980s were *Hum Log, Ye Jo Hai Zindagi*, and *Buniyaad*. These programs plus other serials based on mythology such as *Vishnu Puran* and *Ma Shakti* were hugely popular and racked up advertising dollars for the government-run television service.

Cable television began to have a significant presence in India in the 1990s as India's economy began to liberalize. But it was the Gulf War that brought dish antennas to watch war-related news on CNN. Many Indians worked in the Gulf area, and relatives back home were anxious to get information. STAR TV entered the country in 1991 with four twenty-four-hour channels and soon became part of Australian Rupert Murdoch's media empire. While some felt that the international satellite channels would cause a cultural invasion, others welcomed more choice in programming. But, as one report put it, "With the increase in transmission hours and in the number of STAR TV channels, the domination of American mainstream network fare became evident."[9] STAR Movies, a twenty-four-hour pay channel featuring American movies was launched in 1994. By then other satellite movie channels and services including CNN, Zee TV, Sun TV, and Jain TV, had become available in India. Other movie channels, either free or subscription-based, began to provide more choices to audiences, but India, like many other countries in Asia, soon became a dumping ground for American programs such as *The Bold and the Beautiful* and *The Simpsons* as well as programs from Europe and Australia.[10]

Murdoch's STAR TV had a big advantage in its access to popular programs produced for its Fox Network in the United States such as *Baywatch* and *Ally McBeal*. STAR channels also increased local news and Hindi-language programming. STAR's biggest success came in 2000 with the game show *Kaun Banega Crorepati?* (*Who Wants to Be a Millionaire?*), hosted by India's Bollywood superstar Amitabh Bachchan, that was watched by 100 million people.[11] In 2008, Murdoch added six regional

Indian-language television channels and launched a Dow Jones report for the Indian stock markets. STAR India has more than thirty-five television channels, including several high-definition channels in English and various Indian languages providing news, movies, sports, and other entertainment. In 2013, STAR India joined with Indian telecommunication conglomerate Reliance Industries and IMG Worldwide to reach soccer fans in India, where cricket is the major sport. Murdoch plans to further expand in India since selling his television stake in China at the beginning of 2014 due to continuing challenges of censorship and restrictions on foreign investment.[12] One successful Indian challenger to STAR TV has been Zee TV, launched in 1992, with programming mainly in Hindi and other regional languages. Zee TV is available via cable channels in various countries around the world.

In 2013 there were 153 million TV-owning households in India, 140 million with cable and satellite, and 59 million with a digital platform, and more than 700 television channels available on either network or cable. About 300 channels have permission to broadcast news and current affairs. There is an array of sports, movies, music, and other channels in English, Hindi, and a range of regional languages. Digitization of the cable TV sector was carried out in a phases, with all of India covered by the end of 2014.[13] Prominent journalist N. Ram says that the growing number of twenty-four-hour news channels in English and other languages is not yet a threat for newspapers as they form only about 10 percent of the TV market. The estimated 560 million Indian television viewers mainly tune in to entertainment programming.[14]

Game Shows

Game shows, particularly those related to music, have exploded in India. Top ten reality shows in 2012 include: *Ring Ka King*, a wrestling game show with a cricket player as the celebrity host; *Dance India Dance*; *Jo Jeeta Wohi Super Star*, a music-based reality show; and *Sa Re Ga Ma Pa Challenge*. This Zee TV show has evolved over the years, and different versions are aired in the Middle East and Pakistan. *Laugh India Laugh* is Star TV's stand-up comedy show. Indian versions of American game shows include *Fear Factor India*, *Deal Ya No Deal*, and *Survivor India*. In 2013 *Kaun Banega Crorepati* (*Who Wants To Be a Millionaire?*) became *Kaun Banega Maha Crorepati* (*Who Wants To Be a Multi-Millionaire?*) with the rupee prize money upped from the equivalent of $160,000 to just over $1 million. The large market for television shows provides ample opportunities for, as well as a constant demand for, new content. A current trend is to make television programs based on literary works.

Elitist Bias

The rise of the consumer society since liberalization in the 1990s has led to a shift in focus from developmental programs to programs for the growing urban middle class. The growth of the middle class as a distinct and important news consumer group is linked to the growth in television advertising in India's liberalized economy. But after decades of government programming that had little relevance to the urban viewers, television is now being accused of an elitist bias. According to researcher Nissim Mannathukkaren, who is now at Dalhousie University in Canada, "It is fairly obvious that the English-language media are generally catering to the interests of the urban, educated and relatively well-off sections of the population rather than the interests and problems of the nation as a whole."[15] The media coverage of the 2008 terror attacks in Mumbai was considered elitist, with the focus on two five-star hotels and little attention given to other locations such as the main train station and a government hospital. According to one researcher, English-language television's extensive coverage of Gandhian Anna Hazare's anti-corruption movement in 2011 came at the neglect of other significant news coverage.[16] A 2010 study found that the market-driven television news industry in India does indeed focus on the urban elites. It pointed out that the English, Hindi, and Bengali news operations try to appeal to this audience by hiring journalists who belong to the same urban elite category. The study also found that the idea of "objectivity" in the newsroom varied, and the news industry is viewed more as a business where journalists work for an employer than as an opportunity for independent news reporting.[17]

While there is criticism about news coverage by Indian media, they may unfortunately be emulating their international media counterparts. The Delhi gang rape that occurred in December 2012 resulted in a huge number of stories in media around the world. Poulami Roychowdhury found that in the United States the incident triggered 1,515 articles within two months. In general, she found that the stories in international media tended to be framed as a conflict between the modern and underdeveloped sides of India. The rape victim who was murdered was a medical student and portrayed as Westernized, while her male assailants were depicted as migrant workers and slum dwellers. She points out that in reality, the victim's family belonged to a similar social and economic class to that of the assailants.[18]

In an attempt to ease one "elitist bias" a government committee recommended that more homes, especially in rural areas, be included when determining viewership. Also recommenced was a revenue model that is not dependent on advertising support.[19] TV broadcasters will no doubt resist this suggestion and already are not happy with a rule that allows only twelve minutes of commercials per hour.

Radio

Radio originated in the early part of the 1920s as a private enterprise. A number of amateur radio clubs banded together and formed the Indian Broadcasting Company but had financial problems. The government took over the company and introduced license fees for radio owners. Initially known as the Indian State Broadcasting Service, it became the All India Radio in 1936, and in 1957 Akashvani (Voice from the Sky). In post-Independence India, radio was considered as the medium to carry developmental messages and reach rural audiences with educational programs in various regional languages as well as in English on topics such as farming practices, family planning, and adult literacy. Unlike newspapers and magazines, radio did not require literacy. Also, radios were cheaper than television sets and radio stations did not need as much capital as television stations to get started. All India Radio has 237 stations, reaching more than 99 percent of India's population. With the liberalization of the 1990s, private radio made a comeback. Today, numerous radio stations broadcast Bollywood music and other Indian music and programming via online channels that can be accessed from anywhere in the world. News media, including the *Times of India, Hindustan Times*, and the BBC, own radio stations and are pushing the government to allow news transmission. The government allows reruns of news but not original newscasts. A law suit before the Supreme Court of India is asking that private FM radio and community radio be allowed to broadcast news just as television is allowed to do. The Telecommunication Regulatory Authority of India lists 242 private FM radio stations currently operating in eighty-six cities in India.

Reaching Rural Areas

Although many see Indian television as catering to the urban middle class to the exclusion of the rural and the poorer classes, India's public service television broadcaster Doordarshan continues on its mission to provide developmental communication programming in addition to news and entertainment. Doordarshan's series on health communication, titled "Kalyani," launched in 2002 was recognized by the World Health Organization as one of the fifteen top global innovations because it included community outreach through audience groups called Kalyani Health Clubs. Doordarshan has recently launched *Swasth Bharat* (*Healthy India*), a thirty-minute prime-time magazine program through thirty regional stations of Doordarshan and twenty-nine stations of All India Radio covering twenty-seven states This is the first large-scale outreach program to reach various levels of the population via mass media.

Citizen Journalism

Citizen journalism provides another avenue to reach rural areas and report on issues that otherwise don't get media coverage. For example, Video Volunteers (http://www.videovolunteers.org/) trains citizens to create videos about local community issues. This organization was started in 2002 and has 117 correspondents across the country to provide videos for IndiaUnheard. The 900 or so videos shot so far have focused on a wide range of problems such as health facilities, water shortages, and lack of adequate infrastructure. Another service, CGnet Swara, can be used by anyone in the Central Gondwana region to report on local issues via their phones (http://cgnetswara.org/). Parul Agrawal, multimedia producer for the BBC Hindi Service, reported that based on a farmer's phone call to CGnet Swara, a forestry officer was charged with bribery and returned the bribe money. Citizens have been able to generate content through various blogs, including those hosted by media organizations. For example, CNN-IBN and IBN 7 channels have used videos, articles, and photographs from citizens to cover disasters such as the tsunami and the Mumbai terrorist attacks. At the height of the Mumbai terror attacks in 2008, tweets numbering more than one per second with the word "Mumbai" in them were being posted. Citizens were the main sources immediately following the crisis as little official information was available.[20] There are citizen journalism portals in various Indian languages, such as Merikhabar.com in Hindi. The website Assam-times.org reports news gathered by about 200 registered citizen journalists in India's northeastern region. The information on its website is also used by mainstream media. IBN Citizen Journalist website (http://ibnlive.in.com/) has posted information on a mobile photography contest, "Change One Person, Change the World," to encourage citizens to contribute ideas to change their community. IBN has also posted simple guidelines for citizens to follow, such as that the story should be original and factual, and provides a list of unacceptable items. Merinews.com claims to be India's largest platform for citizen journalism (http://www.merinews.com/).

Freedom of Information

According to the 2013 report of Freedom House, India's media were considered "partly free" with a press freedom ranking of 38 compared with 18 for the United States and 21 for Britain, both considered "free." Article 19(1)(a) of the Indian Constitution guarantees freedom of speech and expression. However, press freedom may be restricted based on factors such as national security and any threat to the sovereignty and integrity of India. Unlike newspapers, relatively free except during the nineteen-month emergency period in the 1970s as mentioned, both television and radio were entirely government-controlled until the 1990s. In reality the social context plays an important role in whether or not people can exercise their right to information. The Press Freedom Index of Reporters Without Borders ranked India 140 out of 179 countries based on criteria such as legislation, violence against journalists, and Internet censorship. Its report stated that since the bombings in Mumbai in 2008, the government of India has increased surveillance of Internet content. In 2012, when communal riots erupted in eastern India due to rumors on social media about retaliation among different ethnic groups, the government ordered Internet providers to block access to more than 300 social media sites. Google alone reported that during the 2012 disturbances it received five government requests to remove content, including sixty-four YouTube videos, and 1,759 comments associated with some YouTube videos. Google complied with some of the requests, according the report. New government rules require cyber cafés to maintain a record of users and allow photos of the users via webcam. A cyber café must keep records of each user's website access history for a minimum of one year. Perhaps because of this, the number of cyber cafés fell from 7,930 in March 2013 to 5,395 at the end of June 2013.

Bollywood

India's film industry, the largest in the world, turned 100 in 2013. It produced a total of 1,602 films in 2012 and 1,255 in 2011. Bollywood, India's Hollywood, is the Mumbai base of the Hindi film industry. Bollywood films are wildly popular both in India and in many other countries around the world. A typical Hindi movie is made for entertaining the masses. It has heroes, songs, dances, villains, great locales, and is filled with dramatic moments. Although Hindi movies are better known and more popular, in 2012 Indian movies were produced in thirty-five different languages, with the largest number produced in Tamil (262), Telugu (256), and Hindi (221). India produces more films than any other country, but some films may not actually be shown in a theater but instead go directly to television or DVD. All films produced for public showing have to be certified by the Central Board of Film Certification. While a number of these films are successful at the box office, some are small-budget, offbeat films that belong to the category of art cinema and focus on realistic social and political themes. One of India's best internationally known filmmakers was Satyajit Ray, whose offbeat films in his native Bengali language, such as the Apu trilogy (*Pather Panchali, Aparajito,* and *Apu Sansar*) won many international awards. Considered one of the top filmmakers in the world, he won an honorary Academy Award for lifetime achievement in 1992. More recently, there are films that fall into a "realistic but entertaining" category. For example, *The Lunchbox* is a romantic, lighthearted film about an older man who becomes connected to a younger woman when he gets the wrong lunch box at work. The film won the Critics Week Viewers' Choice Award at Cannes in 2013.

Bollywood movies are popular not only in other Asian countries but also in other parts of the world, including the United States, the Middle East, Australia, Canada, Africa, and Europe. Two Bollywood films that reached a worldwide audience in recent years were *Lagaan* and *Guru*. Harvard-educated and New York-based award-winning film director Meera Nair makes films that appeal to those in the East as well as the West. Her films include *Salaam Bombay, Mississippi Masala,* and *Monsoon Wedding*. After the 2008 film *Slumdog Millionaire,* a movie about a boy who grows up in the Mumbai slums and appears on the Indian version of *Who Wants to*

Be a Millionaire?, won eight Academy Awards in 2009, the popularity of Bollywood movies and Bollywood dancing shot up in the Western world. The film was directed by Englishman Danny Boyle and co-directed by Loveleen Tandan in India. A. R. Rahman won two Academy Awards for best original score and best original song for "Jai Ho." Both the song and the Bollywood dance accompanying the song were international hits. In a 2013 article in the *Journal of Media and Cultural Studies*, film critic Patricia O'Neill said Bollywood today exerts "at least as much ideological and cultural influence as Hollywood."[21]

The underlying themes of "boy meets girl" and "poor boy achieves success" have universal appeal, but many Bollywood films have broken away from the boy-meets-girl story formula. For example, the blockbuster film *3 Idiots* is a coming-of-age journey of three engineering students, and *Kahaani* is an award-winning thriller about a woman searching for her missing husband after a poison-gas attack on Kolkata rail station.

Indian films have contributed to television content in a major way. Not only are films shown on television channels, but there are programs based on film songs such as *Chitrahaar* (*A String of Pictures*). Many movie stars have also found another outlet in television hosting their own shows. Popular Hindi movie songs are also increasingly being used as titles of soaps on television to attract and connect with viewers. For example, the Indian version of a Pakistani serial *Dhoop Kinare* has the title *Kuch Toh Log Kahenge*, which is a popular song from the movie *Amar Prem*, and the soap *Kya Hua Tera Vaada* is named after the song in the 1977 movie *Hum Kisi Se Kum Nahin*. Other examples of such shows are *Pyar Ka Dard Hai Meetha Meetha Pyara Pyara* based on the film *Dard*, and *Golmaal Hai Bhai Sab Golmaal Hai* based on *Golmaal* (1979).

Film industries in other languages in India also have names fashioned after Hollywood. For example, the Telugu-language film industry is known as Tollywood. At the 2,000-acre Ramoji Film City in Hyderabad, a comprehensive and modern film production facility said to be the largest in the world, films in different languages are made. This film city is an important tourist attraction and even has replicas of India's best-known gardens such as the Brindavan Gardens in Mysore and the Mughal Gardens of Delhi.

News Services

India's four major news agencies are the Press Trust of India (PTI), United News of India (UNI), Hindustan Samachar, and Samachar Bharati. Press

Trust of India (http://www.ptinews.com/aboutpti/aboutus.aspx) was started in 1949 and has a network of more than 900 journalists and stringers all over India and in major world capitals. According to its website, PTI has more than 90 percent of the news agency market share in India. United News of India (http://www.uniindia.com/eng/) began in 1961 and has nearly 600 correspondents and stringers all over the country and in many major cities around the world. UNI has more than 1,000 subscribers in India and globally. Both PTI and UNI also have news exchange agreements with other international news agencies. UNI provides wire services in English, Hindi, and Urdu, and it was the first to launch financial services. Hindustan Samachar, started in 1948, focuses on social and national development issues. In 1975 it merged with other news agencies to become Samachar. Economic problems closed it in 1986, but in 2000 it was resurrected and now supplies news in fourteen languages. Samachar Bharati, established in 1965, prides itself as a supplier of news in Hindi and English, and of photos generally left out by the mainstream media. Samachar Bharati has about 100 correspondents in cities all over India and in major cities around the world. The independent Indo-Asian News Service provides stories from India and South Asia in English and Hindi.

Cross-Ownership of Media

The phenomenal growth of print and broadcast media coupled with new media technologies has resulted in a few media companies and businesses owning many print and broadcast media. Such horizontal integration has helped conglomerates gain a wider media reach and fattened their coffers. There has also been a trend toward vertical integration, with broadcast media companies owning distribution segments and distribution companies venturing into television broadcasting. Such cross-ownership patterns are creating fears that media pluralism will be limited and monopolies will grow. For example, SUN TV and Essel Group own publications, TV channels, FM radio stations, and direct-to-home (DTH) and multi-system-operators (MSO) distribution platforms. STAR India owns TV channels, FM radio stations, and distribution systems but does not own any print media. The Times Group and India Today own print media, television channels, and FM radio stations. One of India's largest business conglomerates, Anil Dhirubhai Ambani Group, owns television channels, FM radio stations, distribution systems, print media, and telecommunications.

A 2013 government report supported some regulation because of the need for pluralism and the media's important role in forming public opinion. The report states, "Regulating ownership of media outlets is thus essential in the public interest, as a guarantee of plurality and diversity of opinion." The report also states, "The Media Ownership Rules should be so designed as to strike a balance between ensuring a degree of plurality of media sources and content, and a level playing field for companies operating in the media sector on the one hand and providing freedom to companies to expand, innovate and invest on the other hand."[22]

Comic-Book Culture

Comic books have served to educate as well as entertain children in India. The widely popular Amar Chitra Katha comics are based on the great Hindu epics *Ramayana* and *Mahabharatha*, These comics promote Indian culture, mythology, history, and folklore and are very popular both in India and among the diaspora of Indians worldwide. There are about 400 different Amar Chitra Katha comics with more than 90 million copies sold so far in more than twenty languages (http://www.ack-media.com/). Heroes featured in the comics include Mahatma Gandhi, Nobel Laureate Mother Teresa, and Indian American astronaut Kalpana Chawla, who died while returning from space on the Columbia in 2003. Anant Pai started Amar Chitra Katha in 1967 with the goal of educating Indian children about their own culture. Samir Patil gave up his job in New York City to return to India and purchase Amar Chitra Katha and make it part of his Bombay-based ACK Media group. In a *Harvard Business Review* blog in July 2012, Patil said he had to rebuild the company and then launch TV shows, animated films, a social networking site for children, an online shop for parents, and mobile games. The company also distributes magazines, books, and DVDs to thousands of vendors across the country. ACK comics are available in digital format and may be downloaded to phones, tablets, and other electronic devices. In March 2012, ACK Media was sold to the Future Group, India's largest retailer.

There are also other comic books that capture the diversity of India in stories based on folk culture. Liquid Comics was founded in 2008 by a group of entrepreneurs including Gotham Chopra, an award-winning journalist and documentary filmmaker who is the son of spiritual guru and author Deepak Chopra. The company aims to entertain audiences worldwide with original stories distributed via various digital platforms. Vimanika, another recent comics company, has the serious goal of establishing that the past history is not a myth but a reality based on scientific facts. For this reason, founders Arora and Kanika Choudhary work with a scholar specializing in the epic *Mahabharata* and a scientist with experience at NASA. The tremendous growth in the comic culture may be attributed to the post-liberalization multinational production networks and the expanding consumer market. India also has a rich history of regional comic books. The Comic Book Project plans to digitize and archive Indian-language comic books published since the 1950s.

Journalism Education

The extraordinary growth in mass media in India has also led to a mushrooming of journalism programs around the country. The first journalism programs were offered in the 1940s, but until the 1990s journalists were mainly trained on the job. The UNESCO-supported Indian Institute of Mass Communication was established in New Delhi in 1965, the year that regular television programming began in India's capital. In 1973, under the leadership of K. E. Eapen, a pioneer in journalism education in India, the first communication department in the country was set up at Bangalore University in South India. Eapen, who had graduate degrees from US universities, modeled the Bangalore program after American examples. However, it was not until the 1990s, with the liberalization of the economy and the explosion in television stations as well as cable channels, that there was a major increase in journalism programs. By 2013 there were about 300 departments in various universities offering postgraduate diplomas and degrees in journalism and mass communication, and hundreds of other institutions offering diplomas and certificates in the communication field. About 20,000 students graduate annually from these programs with knowledge and skills in electronic media, journalism, advertising, public relations, and other communication areas.

Conclusion

India has a vibrant media market that has registered explosive growth, especially since the government opened it to more Indian and foreign competition in the 1990s. Until then, the broadcast media were government-owned and provided limited choices of channels and programming. Presently there are hundreds of cable channels and FM radio stations with programming in numerous languages. Rising literacy levels and a growing middle class have meant larger media markets, both urban and rural. Thousands of newspapers in English and Indian languages continue to register a healthy growth with little sign of being taken over by their online counterparts. While both broadcast media and newspapers have an online presence, these are used by a comparatively small percentage of news consumers due to the limited diffusion of the Internet. On the other hand, mobile news holds much promise due to fact that more than 75 percent of Indians own mobile phones. Social media diffusion is low but has the potential to grow rapidly. Comic books have acquired new life with their modern, online reincarnations.

Although the Internet is monitored by the government, citizen journalism appears to be a way to showcase local community issues from the people's perspective. Entrepreneurs are seizing the moment by starting new e-media businesses. As an information hub in Asia, India has been catapulted into the digital age on the one hand, but on the other it remains firmly grounded in traditional newspapers. Dichotomies are very much a part of the multicultural Indian society, with its diversity in language, religion, income, and education levels. Its media are equally diverse and cater to a fragmented market. Among the issues that confront the media in India are ethical coverage of news, evolving regulation of broadcast media, and cross-ownership of news media. Although the media are accused of elitist bias, as a developing country, India continues to use public media, including information and communication technologies, for communicating development messages about such important issues as health, literacy, and education to India's still largely rural population.

Notes

1. K. Vishwanath and Kavita Karan, "India," in *Handbook of the Media in Asia*, Shelton A. Gunaratne, ed. (New Delhi: Sage Publications, 2000), 84–117, 88.
2. Francis Cody, "Daily Wires and Daily Blossoms: Cultivating Regimes of Circulation in Tamil India's Newspaper Revolution," *Journal of Linguistic Anthropology*, 19(2), 2009, 286–289.
3. N. Ram, "Sharing the Best and the Worst: The India News Media in a Global Context," *The Hindu*, October 6/7, 2012.

4. Anuradha Raman, "News You Can Abuse," *Outlook*, December 21, 2009,

5. Robin Jeffrey, "Advertising and Indian-Language Newspapers: How Capitalism Supports (Certain) Cultures and (Some) States, 1947–96," *Pacific Affairs*, 70(1), 1997, 57–84.

6. Ram, "Sharing the Best and the Worst."

7. Gita Bamezai et al., "Impact of Internet on Changing Patterns of Newspaper Access and News-Reading Habits in India," *Media Asia* 38(2), 2011, 110–121.

8. Binny Sabharwal, "India, Glossy Magazines on the Same Page," *The Wall Street Journal*, January 16, 2007.

9. Keval J. Kumar, "History of Television in India: A Political Economy Perspective," in *International Satellite Broadcasting in South Asia,* Srinivas R. Melkote, Peter Shields, and Binod C. Agrawal, eds. (Lanham, MD: University Press of America, 1998), 19–46, 30.

10. Kumar, "History of Television in India," 31.

11. Arvind Singhal and Everett Rogers, *India's Communication Revolution: From Bullock Carts to Cyber Marts* (New Delhi: Sage Publications, 2001), 113.

12. Christopher Williams, "Rupert Murdoch Gives Up on China with Sale of Star China TV," *The Telegraph*, January 2, 2014.

13. Telecom Regulatory Authority of India, "The Indian Telecom Services Performance Indicators, April–June, 2013," New Delhi, December 2, 2013, 87.

14. Ram, "Sharing the Best and the Worst."

15. Nissim Mannathukkaren, "Media Terror! Understanding Television and the Media in India in the Context of '26/11,'" *South Asian History and Culture*, 1(3), July 2010, 416–434.

16. S. Khorana, "English-Language Television News and the Great Indian Middle Class: Made for Each Other?," *Studies in South Asian Film & Media*, (4)1, 2012, 23–37.

17. Somnath Batabyal, "Constructing an Audience: News Television Practices in India," *Contemporary South Asia*, 18(4), 2010, 387–399.

18. Poulami Roychowdhury, "'The Delhi Gang Rape': The Making of International Causes," *Feminist Studies*, 39(1), 2013, 282–292.

19. Prashant Jha, "Is it Time for a New Broadcasting Regulator?," *The Hindu*, April 18, 2013; Amarendra Kumar Dash, "Media Impact on Corporate Governance in India: A Research Agenda," *Corporate Governance*, (12)1, (2012), 89–100.

20. Brian Stettler and Noam Cohen, "Citizen Journalists Provide Glimpses Into Attacks That Transcend the News Cycle," *The New York Times*, November 30, 2008, 16.

21. Patricia O'Neill, "Imagining Global India: Bollywood's Transnational Appeal," *Journal of Media and Cultural Studies*, 27(2), 2013, 254–266.

22. Telecom Regulatory Authority of India, "Consultation Paper on Issues Relating to Media Ownership," Consultation Paper No. 01/2013, New Delhi, February 15, 2013, 7.

9

China: A New Media Face But Tighter Control

China has been tightening its already strong control over media within the country and over information that tries to enter China or leave it. In the last months of 2014 Chinese authorities moved to further limit foreign TV dramas, block foreign journalists from reporting "sensitive" stories, and even tightened control over Internet business services. This comes at a time when China claims it is reaching out to the world to show a "harmonious society" with peaceful intentions. *China Daily*, the English-language version of the government's flagship newspaper, *People's Daily*, had an expensive makeover to attract a wider audience and is available from vending machines just a few blocks from the White House in Washington, DC.

Xinhua (New China), the national news agency, launched CNC World, a twenty-four-hour English-language television channel. China Central Television (CCTV) is expanding overseas with broadcasts in English, Spanish, French, Russian, Arabic, and Japanese. "Our principle is to be real, to be objective, to be accurate and transparent," said Zhang Changming, CCTV deputy president. "CCTV will present the world with the real China."[1] At the same time China is presenting its culture through more than 300 Confucius centers in eighty countries. The centers, primarily to showcase Chinese culture, are often attached to universities in the United States and elsewhere.[2]

In 2014, however, the Foreign Correspondents Club of China reported increased pressure on its members to avoid articles on restive western China and Tibet and topics such as the wealth of relatives of the nation's leaders. Online Western TV dramas, banned or greatly limited on regular television sets, will face new online controls. Google, which moved its servers from

The World News Prism: Digital, Social and Interactive, Ninth Edition.
William A. Hachten and James F. Scotton.
© 2016 John Wiley & Sons, Inc. Published 2016 by John Wiley & Sons, Inc.

mainland China to Hong Kong in 2010 to avoid censorship, has had almost all its websites blocked since mid-2014. "Internet security is being raised to a much higher degree," said Xiao Qiang, a Chinese Internet censorship specialist at the University of California. "It overrides the other priorities, including commerce or scientific research."[3]

The new media of China were carefully crafted and developed at enormous cost to show a new face to the world. But at the same time it is difficult to ignore the old face that keeps appearing whenever Chinese authorities are rattled by events within or outside the country. When protesters in Egypt flocked into Cairo's largest public square in January 2011, the word "Egypt" disappeared from Sina.com, one of the most popular Chinese websites. Echoes of China's 1989 student uprising in Beijing's huge Tiananmen Square were no doubt felt in the nation's corridors of power. Two months later, when Chinese dissidents tried to mobilize "strolling protests" of citizens along Nanjing Lu, Shanghai's main shopping street, foreign journalists who tried to find out what was going on were detained and harassed. This is the "Censorship Pendulum" that almost predictably swings between repression and moderation[4]

Almost all the media in China – Xinhua, CCTV, some 2,100 newspapers, 9,000 periodicals, nearly 400 television stations, 200 radio stations, and every book publisher – are owned by the government in China. The exceptions are some Internet search engines which are privately owned but kept under close government surveillance. All media, including blogs and email, as well as all foreign media entering China, are subject to censorship. Foreign journalists risk intimidation, harassment, and even expulsion if their reports are seen as unfavorable to the regime. Reporters Without Borders consistently ranks China near the bottom in its world survey of press freedom.

Chinese journalists who displease the government face harsher penalties than foreign reporters and editors. A journalist working for a Chinese radio service received a life sentence for translating a call for protests by Uighurs in northwest China where there was ethnic rioting in 2009. One of China's best-known dissidents, Liu Xiaobo, was given a long prison term in December 2009 on the vague charge of "incitement to subvert state power." Ai Weiwei, an internationally famous artist and also a citizen journalist, was barred from leaving the country and his Shanghai studio was demolished by authorities in January 2011. Hu Shuli, an internationally famous magazine editor, was forced in 2009 to leave *Caijing*, which had irritated business and political leaders for years with exposés of corruption and incompetence.

Google gave up its mainland China operation in 2010, rejecting Chinese censorship rules. Media mogul Rupert Murdoch, who sold his last assets in China in 2010 after years of negotiating with Beijing, noted that the Chinese government was "quite paranoid about what gets through."[5] When President Barack Obama's 2009 inaugural address mentioned communism and fascism in the same sentence, CCTV cut him off. Such recent history does not suggest that China's international media ventures will escape censorship. Yan Lieshan, a columnist for China's *Southern Weekend*, which has battled censors for years to report corruption and incompetence, warned that any sign that international reports by Xinhua or other Chinese media are censored will doom what he calls "the great external propaganda campaign."[6]

In the twenty-first century China continues to be a nation that wants the benefits of an open, capitalist economy for its 1.3 billion people, while still tightly controlling its media. For the past thirty years, the Chinese leadership – nominally still communist but in fact strongly committed to a capitalist economy that it calls "market socialism" – has been unsure about how to carry this off. Can China run a free market economy without a free market in ideas? Many suggest it is impossible to do so. Others insist that it is just a matter of time before the Chinese people add democracy to the list of modern lifestyles imported from the West. The Chinese government officially accepts press freedom, but the constitution includes a list of situations in which government can restrict this freedom. The Chinese call this "a pragmatic approach" to freedom of the press that includes strong opposition to the notion of press "freedom to spread lies and rumors."[7] This "pragmatic approach" to press freedom has meant that China's leaders have alternately encouraged its media to be independent – at least economically independent – but then cracked down when that independence seemed to threaten those in control. The head of Central China Television, Hu Zhanfan, did draw criticism when he said the nation's journalists are not professionals but serve as "mouthpieces for the government."[8] But government officials consistently warn that "dangerous" Western values, no doubt including an independent media sector, must be avoided.[9]

Chinese journalists are caught in a media paradox. China's government has transformed almost all the nation's subsidized media from being a huge financial drain into a profit-making global industry. This means advertising, which implies popular content that attracts lots of readers, listeners, and viewers. But Chinese communist officials do not want any content, popular or not, domestic or foreign, that could threaten their grip on power. Foreign media conglomerates can, for example, bring sports or entertainment programs into China via satellite and even run fashion magazines. But China forced media mogul Rupert Murdoch's STAR TV to drop all BBC news reports when they criticized China's human rights record.

Western media conglomerates try hard to satisfy Chinese authorities. This is a major reason the Chinese think it is safe to allow some foreign television channels in the country, or at least some parts of the country. When AOL-Time Warner got permission to start a Mandarin-language channel in a limited area of southern China, it agreed to carry CCTV's English-language channel on its cable systems in New York, Los Angeles, and Houston. For China, AOL chose to pick up a Singapore TV channel. Its motto was: "No sex, no violence, no news."[10]

Television

The allure of Hong Kong forced China to let Western television in, mainly into booming Guangdong province, just next to the former British colony. Hong Kong's Western values, including democracy and independent media, are apparent on Hong Kong television. Large numbers of people in southeast China were watching Western-style Hong Kong television programs, since their antennas and illegal satellite dishes could easily pick them up. By 2005, China had authorized six foreign companies to beam twenty-four-hour channels to southeast China. Government officials hoped these television channels would lure Chinese viewers from Hong Kong television, while the channel owners would protect their licenses by carefully avoiding any anti-government programs.

Television reaches 95 percent of the people in China, with Central China Television's programs from Beijing dominating. In recent years, programs from provincial and large city stations have provided serious competition. Entertainment dominates, with news taking up about 12 percent of air time. That news is carefully controlled by the Chinese government. All stations, for example, must carry Xiwen Lianbo, CCTV's 7 p.m. thirty-minute newscast. This provides a daily Chinese view of world events. CCTV is burdened by the huge bureaucracy that surrounds it. In 2009 a fire at CCTV's almost completed new headquarters building lit up Beijing's night skies, but the Ministry of Information ordered no coverage until it had readied a report. Internet bloggers, who spread the news quickly, joked that CCTV employees looking out their office windows could see the biggest story of the year but could not report it. Like audiences everywhere, Chinese television viewers will abandon channels that block important news. When New York's World Trade Center was destroyed by suicide bombers in 2001, CCTV kept the tragedy off China's television channels for nearly an hour, awaiting the Ministry of Information's guidance, and thus lost its audience to Hong Kong's Phoenix channel.

Increasingly, Chinese citizens are getting access to foreign television programs. One survey found Chinese adolescents were watching, on average, two American movies or television programs a week. Foreign films and television programs screened by the censors are available on many channels, dubbed in Chinese or with Chinese subtitles. But most Chinese get their foreign movies from street vendors and small shops selling pirated copies. US industry experts estimate that 85 percent of DVDs, videotapes, and CDs sold in China are pirated copies with dubbed Chinese that the censor never gets to review. This influx of foreign ideas has drastically reduced the power of China's rulers to isolate and dominate society. Television has, in fact, forced changes in China's economic and political policies. As one media executive said, "Even if the Chinese tried to keep foreign cultural icons out, piracy would make them available."[11]

Dating, talent, and contest shows

Despite all the media controls, even some television shows produced in China can upset government officials. In 2010 authorities ordered the end to live dating shows after a female contestant on *If You Are the One* said the main quality of a husband for Chinese women was how rich he was. In summer 2005, a wildly popular singing contest attracted record audiences. *Super Girl*, a Chinese version of *American Idol*, had more than 400 million viewers watch its finale. Most viewers, no doubt, just saw this as television entertainment, but some people said the show made a political statement because the winner was popularly elected by 3.5 million cellphone voters. The contest originated with a provincial television station, far from the watchful eyes of the Ministry of Information, and was sponsored by a local dairy – thus the name of the show: *The Mongolian Cow Sour Yoghurt Super Girl Contest*. CCTV was startled when the program drew an audience larger than CCTV gets for its Chinese New Year extravaganzas. It said the show had "debased Chinese culture." The show also cut into CCTV's advertising revenue.

China's "Oprah Winfrey"

A very popular television program is *A Date with Luyu*. All sorts of celebrities and ordinary people share the sofa with Chen Luyu, "China's Oprah Winfrey," on the Phoenix satellite channel. Chen Luyu says she avoids politics because "my viewers do not want to listen to things like that."[12] But the program is a window on what concerns Chinese citizens. Inevitably, the talk includes comments on such topics as crime, corruption, and even AIDS, formerly taboo subjects. *A Date With Luyu* averages 240 million viewers per show. Former US Secretary of State Hillary Clinton had a date with Chen Luyu in 2010.

Newspapers

Despite their desire for tight media control, China's rulers want to create at least the appearance of transparency and more openness to the public and the media. In 2005, the State Information Office told Communist Party officials to start holding news conferences. This was a big change. In China, journalists can be severely criticized for seeking even routine information from Party officials. And almost anything can be declared a state secret in China. When scores of children died from poisoning at a school near Nanjing in 2002, Chinese officials ordered the death toll be kept secret. Only in 2005 did China announce that the death toll, at least in natural disasters, would no longer be considered a "state secret."[13]

Even though the print media are directly owned by the government, controlling Chinese journalists has not always been easy. There are probably 100,000 people in China who claim they are "journalists." One Chinese journalism professor found more than 300 schools in China claiming to have a journalism program although, as in many countries, most of the graduates will not end up as journalists. The top requirement for Chinese journalists, according to the Communist Party's *Handbook for Journalists*, is "faithfully propagating and carrying out the Party's principles and policies." But a major survey found many journalism students in China still thought they could fill the classic "watchdog" role and report government corruption.[14] And this role is actually recognized in the Chinese media system. Back in 1986, Communist Party Secretary Hu Yaobang told editors that they should include stories on problems in China, but 80 percent of their articles should focus on China's achievements.[15] The Communist Party lists the press as one of the eight major means for overseeing party and government officials. Despite such official pronouncements, however, being a "watchdog" journalist in China can be very risky.

"The best journalist in China"

Zhao Yan identified himself as "the best" journalist in China.[16] That may explain why he was whisked off to prison from a Shanghai Pizza Hut and charged with leaking state secrets. Zhao worked for a decade for *China Reform*, a newspaper with a reputation for exposing official corruption, then took a job with the Beijing bureau of the *New York Times*. Zhao's arrest may have been caused by a single sentence in a *Times* story that suggested two top Party officials were having a dispute over promoting a general. Suggestions of any disagreements within the Chinese leadership always bring a strong reaction from officials. Editors are routinely warned before Communist Party meetings that they are not to speculate on who might end up in leadership positions. China's leaders believe they can handle the social and economic strains that are testing them, as long as there is no sign of disunity.

Journalists working for foreign publications are sometimes charged with being spies. Ching Cheong, a reporter for Singapore's *Straits Times*, was charged with spying for Taiwan in August 2005. He apparently obtained documents showing discord among the Chinese leadership over the 1989 student uprisings in Beijing's Tiananmen Square. Another journalist, Shi Tao, was sentenced to ten years in prison for emailing a dissident in the United States that his paper, the *Hunan Business News*, could not report on any demonstrations on the anniversary of the Tiananmen Square protests. The government is also cracking down on Chinese journalists who want to find information on their own. They found that their newspapers were much more willing to print exposés if their stories exposed distant corruption. But in 2005 the Chinese government officially banned all "yidi baodao," or "reports from nonlocal places." Now, Chinese journalists have to stick close to home.

Foreign journalists in China face travel restrictions, but have often evaded them. The *New York Times*, London's *Guardian*, and other foreign publications have reported regularly from all over China. Some of their stories came from tips from Chinese journalists who were not allowed to report a story. The *South China Morning Post*, published in Hong Kong, frequently was able to break stories that Chinese papers were forbidden to report because their reporters could travel to cities and towns all over China. The *Oriental Daily News* of Hong Kong was a regular source of information about the mainland because of its contacts, and it frequently reported news that was blacked out by mainland media. *Apple Daily*, a popular, pro-democracy Chinese-language tabloid in Hong Kong that carried lots of news from mainland China, said its reporters were being denied visas for China because of its anti-corruption articles.

Exposing corruption

Stories exposing serious national problems and even corruption can be published in China if editors are careful in choosing the right targets and the right time. The official *People's Daily* led an attack in 2013 on air pollution that was choking Beijing and other Chinese cities, accusing officials of ignoring the problem as they pushed for industrial expansion. By then pollution was so bad that people were wearing masks for protection. In 2009 *Outlook* magazine exposed secret Beijing detention centers that provincial officials used to prevent citizens from bringing complaints to the central government. Xinhua spread the story across the nation, a clear sign that Beijing officials supported the exposé. Editors soon found that these stories boosted readership, but when the anti-corruption campaigns threaten to get out of control, Party leaders tell editors to cut back on the exposés. This pattern of government supporting anti-corruption exposés and then shutting them down has continued for decades. In 2003, for example, the *Southern Metropolitan Daily* reported the death in police custody of a graphic designer arrested because he lacked the proper identification. It became a national story, and within two months the Chinese government replaced regulations that allowed police to make such arrests. Soon after this, however, three senior editors of *Southern Metropolitan Daily* were charged with embezzlement, but many journalists believed they were being punished for pushing their criticism too far.

Even some bloggers have been able to expose corruption despite the risks. Zhu Ruifeng, a former migrant worker, posted, in January 2013, a secretly recorded video of a 57-year-old official having sex with an 18-year-old woman. The official went to prison for corruption while Zhu gained a national following. Zhu says he has six more similar videos and vowed to post them despite being questioned by police. "I dared them to throw me in jail," Zhu said. "Then watch how many human rights and journalism awards I win."[17]

Zhu's escape from any official retaliation is probably because his video was posted shortly after China's Communist Party leader Xi Jinping called for a crackdown on corruption at all levels. "Here on Chinese soil, it's almost impossible for citizen journalists like him to survive long term," said Zhan Jiang of Beijing's Foreign Studies University. In any case, later in 2013 the government announced a new campaign against what it called "malicious rumor-mongering online" and arrested hundreds of bloggers.[18]

Magazines

Of the more than 9,000 magazines published in China only about 25 percent are profitable. The rest are Party publications that government offices must subscribe to. Very profitable are "story magazines" for migrant workers. They are cheap, usually pocket-size, and are full of short, easy to read human interest articles. *Bosom Friend* specializes in love stories to attract the millions of lonely women who have moved to the cities in search of jobs. It also has its tragedies, such as the story headed: "Boss and His Secretary: A Game Ends in Blood."[19] *Reader* claims its circulation of over 10 million tops any magazine in China. It is similar to the American *Reader's Digest* with family stories and moral lessons. The biggest money-makers are fashion magazines, with advertisers paying high rates to reach their affluent readers. There are Chinese editions *of Elle, Cosmopolitan, Harper's Bazaar, Esquire, Men's Health,* and the British *HFM.* Most are jointly owned with foreign publishers with content left to European and American editors. Digital magazines are growing fast. Fashion magazines are most popular online and half the online readers do not buy the printed copy.[20]

Most of China's magazines stick with safe topics such as sports, fashion, entertainment, and accounting, but some have found that they are well placed to play the role of government critic with relative safety. *Caijing*, a business magazine published in Beijing, regularly exposed government as well as private corruption. While Hu Shuli was editor there were articles on stock market manipulation, corruption at government-owned banks, and government attempts to cover up the 2003 outbreak of SARS (Severe Acute Respiratory Syndrome). *Caijing* editor Hu actually got her start writing for the Communist Party's *Workers' Daily.* Even there, she wrote and got published stories about corrupt local officials. She joined journalists who demonstrated to support the 1989 student protests in Tiananmen Square, but found her paper would not publish anything on them. Shortly after, she became editor of *Caijing*. Hu exposed so many corrupt private and government officials that a profile called her "the most dangerous woman in China."[21] *Caijing* first reached a broad national audience with an exposé of backroom dealings by some of China's leading fund managers in 2000. Another major story involved accounting fraud at a blue-chip Chinese company. Only when the company came forth with a formal announcement of an internal investigation did the mainstream media run the story.

In China, even during times of relative media freedom, only a handful of media outlets will venture to report on corruption or other sensitive matters. The rest of the media follow after explicit government approval. Because of *Caijing*'s reporting it became required reading in the Chinese business community. But it was not just reporting on sensitive business stories that earned *Caijing* its reputation as one of the most important publications in China. When the World Health Organization reported in March 2003 that the SARS epidemic had crossed from Hong Kong to the mainland, *Caijing* leaped, ignoring government denials. *Caijing* produced four special weekly issues on SARS. The World Press Review in 2003 named Hu International Editor of the Year. From her early years on the more directly government-controlled *Workers' Daily*, however, Hu knew the limits on journalism in China. "I know how to measure the boundary lines," she said. "We go up to the line and we might even push it. But we never cross it."[22]

"*Caijing* is about as good as it gets in China," said Orville Schell, Dean of the Graduate School of Journalism at the University of California at Berkeley. "And, they've picked the perfect niche – business – which gives them the maximum latitude to do investigative work in China."[23] But the Chinese government finally yielded to pressure and Hu was forced out as editor.

A muckraker in the south

Any magazine or other media outlet located in Beijing is going to be closely watched by the state censors. Being distant from Beijing does give editors some advantages. *Southern Weekend*, 2,000 miles to the south in booming Guangdong province, has a national reputation for aggressive reporting and for strong opinions. *Southern Weekend* says it has to be aggressive to compete, especially with the Hong Kong media that are available in print and via television. Time and again, it has tested the limits of reporting and thus gained a national audience. A crisis came in 2011 when a new party propaganda chief in Guangdong province insisted on prior approval of all major articles and on all opinion pieces. When an editorial calling for greater respect for constitutional rights was censored, journalists at *Southern Weekend* threatened to strike. The situation drew worldwide attention, but the government promised greater editorial independence and the journalists called off the strike.

Another publication known for aggressive reporting on farm protests is *Freezing Point*, a supplement to the widely read *China Youth Daily*. The government shut down *Freezing Point* early in 2006. There were so many protests, however, that *Freezing Point* was allowed to start publishing again, but Chinese officials refused to reinstate *Freezing Point*'s nationally known editor, Li Datong. Li was already in trouble because six months earlier he had posted a letter on the publication's website criticizing the Propaganda Department for planning to dock reporters' salaries if they strayed from the Communist Party's line.

Even if journalists are unable to report stories in their own publication, the news often gets out anyway. When a flood in central China killed eighty miners, local officials tried to cover it up with bribes and threats. Local media were afraid to report it. Journalists who covered the story, however, quickly leaked the information to distant publications and Internet websites. The major Communist Party publications recognize that they will lose their readers if they do not do some hard reporting of their own. After the mine disaster news got out to the public, the *People's Daily* jumped in with a series of articles. But the Xinhua news agency ignored the story.

All the Chinese media ignore serious public protests, even when they turn violent and people are killed. The Chinese media were silent about a violent demonstration in December 2005, against construction of a power plant, which left twenty or more people dead. Four days later, Xinhua released a story reporting three deaths after villagers in the southern town "assaulted the police."[24]

China's Tabloid Press

Some Chinese newspapers still get government subsidies. These include the Party's flagship papers, *People's Daily* in Chinese and *China Daily* in English, both published in Beijing and circulated nationwide. Nearly 400 other, usually subsidized, Party newspapers are published by provincial and local governments. About 80 percent of the newspaper market is held by the urban tabloids. The Communist Party or the local government still owns the papers, but since the tabloids get no subsidies officials have difficulty controlling the editors. Editors can publish almost anything they think will attract readers and quickly adopted the same content that Western tabloids use to attract city readers: crime, sex, entertainment, features, color, short but graphic articles, and even some stories about corruption. Since most sales are by street vendors, editors provide such sensational headlines as "He Insulted Her; She Axed Him." The tabloids are generally evening papers, while the morning papers remain tightly government-controlled and contain official reports that interest few readers. As a result, the evening tabloids surged ahead in circulation and advertising revenue. Even the Party's flagship *People's Daily* lost 75 percent of its circulation. Trying to fight back, some Party morning papers mix official news with more of what the readers seem to want. In Shanghai the *Jiefang Daily* put the Party messages in a front section then added popular content, including society columns. The *Shanghai Daily* switched to a tabloid size and popular content and began making a profit. Tabloid editors are constantly frustrated with Xinhua, with its constant emphasis on "good news" in order to show a "harmonious China."[25] Some tabloids set up their own exchange networks to get news about crime, violence, and tragedy that they believe their readers want but Xinhua won't provide. Xinhua has its own dilemma. Since the government provides the subsidies that it lives on, the Party publications and not the tabloids have to be its priority. To survive, Xinhua must have "a mixture of party logic and market logic."[26]

Some journalists despair that the tabloids spell the death of "serious" journalism in China and suggest editors will not risk their economic success by challenging any but the most corrupt local officials. This is a "new opium for the masses," say some critics, who also charge that the low-paid tabloid journalists take bribes or charge fees to get stories into their newspapers. In 2009 ten journalists and forty-eight officials were charged with taking bribes to cover up a mine disaster.

A New Cultural Appeal

Perhaps the most dramatic example of a Chinese publication shifting from the government subsidy model to going after readers on its own is *China Culture Gazette*. It changed from a boring and money-losing Ministry of Culture magazine to a hot-selling industry leader, *Culture Weekend*. The secret was celebrity interviews and nudes. *Culture Weekend* even changed color from red to yellow. A "yellow" publication or film in China is X-rated. The ministry was furious, but the editor pointed out that the huge sales were the only thing that prevented the magazine from closing. *Culture Weekend* kept publishing, and other publications started providing a diet of girls in bikinis, movie stars, and pop singers. Again, editor Zhang Zuomin knew the limits: "I will not run anything antiparty in my paper," he said, "and I will not run pornography."[27]

Radio

The rapid rise in car ownership and the increased hours spent in commuting have boosted radio listening in China's cities. The Beijing Traffic program revenue jumped fifty times in ten years. Radio reaches 95 percent or more of the Chinese people. Much of it is the usual mix of music, weather, official news, and various special programs for farmers, women, children, and other groups. Some radio stations have their own staff for reporting local news, but most rely on Xinhua.

Competing with the tabloid press for the audience in China's cities is another Western import, talk radio. Talk radio is one of the few places where Chinese citizens can voice their opinions in public. It also sets up a different relationship between the media and the audience, since call-in listeners can often pick the topic for discussion. These programs generally focus on local issues (complaints about potholes, broken street lights, etc.), social issues (improper behavior on subways and buses), and the inevitable personal problems (inattentive husbands and unfaithful wives). Started to compete with radio stations in Hong Kong, the talk radio stations attracted far more listeners than the traditional stations that were filled with official propaganda and dreary programs. And talk radio hosts soon learned that some provocative dialogue on a sensitive issue could push up listenership in hurry. These hosts soon became local celebrities, and advertisers clamored to buy time on their programs. Programs to deal with special problems soon developed. Some hosts regularly helped dissatisfied customers get refunds from merchants; others collected complaints about the health system. Public officials, including city mayors, were invited on to answer citizen complaints. Late-night programs brought on physicians, psychologists, and others to deal with personal problems of callers. Among the most popular programs was *Secret Whispers*, a late-night show on

Shanghai Radio. The program tried to answer callers' questions about sex, a topic virtually ignored in both families and schools in China. A survey of callers found that, in Shanghai at least, sex and money were the most popular topics. One Shanghai talk show reportedly attracted 400 calls a minute. Inevitably, some callers want to talk about sensitive topics, such as government corruption or the gap between rich and poor in China. Since most shows are live, hosts have to be ready to redirect the discussion but still not discourage other callers. And some topics are just not open for discussion, at least not on China's radio stations: a Beijing host quickly cut off callers who wanted to talk about legalizing prostitution and easing the policy of one couple, one child. Program hosts fend off critics by arguing that their programs are educational and also frequently bring on guests who support official policies. The call-in radio programs suggest a different level of public participation in public issues in China. They are channels for public debate and discussion that are essentially beyond government control.

New Threats: The Internet and Cellphones

Perhaps even bigger threats to China's rulers are the Internet and cellphones. China has more than 640 million Internet users and more than 1.2 billion cellphones. They represent, in fact, an instant communication network. Internet cafés with rows of computers are found in China's cities. According to the *Beijing News*, China employs 2 million people to constantly monitor websites and scan tens of millions of messages posted daily looking for any sign of political or social unrest that could challenge its leadership.[28] Government tries to monitor messages that go to large groups, but the speed of cellphone messaging makes it very difficult. The Chinese authorities have been aggressive in their efforts to block and counter websites they consider unfriendly. They are especially on guard against the cult movement Falun Gong.

Most Chinese on the Internet are just looking for entertainment and chatting with friends. Internet servers in China are privately owned and are expected to look out for subversive activity. Baidu.com has the largest market share and has grown since Google left China in July 2010. It tried to attract more young users via Baidu Post Bar, an online community it calls the "water cooler" of the Internet. Students doing research papers routinely "Baidu it" to find the information they want. Baidu's video-sharing site has been censored by Chinese authorities for excessive sexual content and has had a daily poll to find the ten most beautiful women in China.

Other Internet search engines, all privately owned, are Alibaba, 40 percent owned by Yahoo and specializing in e-commerce; TenCent QQ, the most popular chatting tool for young people; Sina, the leading news site, although all its news comes from Xinhua or other official sources; Sohu, news and sports; and NetEase, an online games site. Also online are YouKou (like YouTube), Foufou (Twitter), and YuPoo (Flickr). The dominant social networking tool in China is Weixin, with 300 million "addicted" users.[29]

Despite their efforts, Chinese authorities find it impossible to monitor all websites. There are so many Internet messages to monitor that the censors reportedly only delete messages that seem to represent a serious threat. One indication of the problem is that even though China tries to suppress evidence of homosexuality in the country, one study reported 250 gay-themed websites in China.

But even though Chinese authorities are constantly alert to keep the Internet under control, they will encourage Internet use when it serves their purposes. The Internet has, for example, become an accepted channel for dissent, because it is much preferable to more threatening public demonstrations. The government has also ordered all government agencies to set up websites to receive complaints. The Ministry of Foreign Affairs website got 1.2 million complaints in three years, mostly saying that China was not acting strongly enough in world affairs. After many years of Western dominance, Chinese will rally to support the government against any perceived foreign threat. As C. C. Lee, a long-time China scholar, has pointed out, Party leaders will use the media to rally Chinese nationalism against any challenge to China's sovereignty or international status.[30]

"Policy-makers can't make decisions based on public opinion, but they can't ignore it either," said Li Minggang, Ministry of Foreign Affairs website director.[31] And even non-government websites can have a place under China's media policy at times. When China's Railway Ministry let a Japanese company bid to build a new Beijing–Shanghai express train, a Patriots' Alliance website sprang up to protest dealing with China's former enemy. Within ten days, its online petition had 87,320 protesting signatures, reflecting anti-Japanese feelings that remain strong more than sixty years after the end of Japan's World War II occupation. The Chinese government quickly rejected the Japanese proposal.

New Internet controls

Chinese authorities want to control the Internet just as they control all other media in China. They have had the "Great Firewall" (the Kung Fu Net to Chinese bloggers) in place for years to block unwanted Internet messages. In 2009 authorities proposed adding a "Green Wall" by requiring all new computers to be equipped with filtering software. This censorship plan was dropped only after massive resistance by Internet users. Twitter is particularly annoying to the censors because it is virtually impossible to monitor the millions of short messages, much less trace their origin. And Twitter is increasingly being used to organize online protests, as in the 2009 campaign that forced the government to release a waitress who had fatally stabbed a Party official as she resisted his advances. Microblogs, which are very difficult to censor or even monitor because the message is sent in fragments, are another threat to government control of the Internet. Leading Chinese microblogger Deng Fei of *Phoenix Weekly* exposed contaminated blood supplies in Henan Province. Reporters used microblogs to send the story of Chinese citizens blocked at the Beijing airport when they tried to present a petition to the government.[32]

The government has decreed that newspaper and magazine websites must "give priority" to news and commentary from official sources. The government ordered search engines Sohu and Sina, which had been posting private criticisms of the government in their chatrooms, to block such comments. "The foremost responsibility of news sites on the Internet," the regulations stated, "is to serve the people, serve socialism, guide public opinion in the right direction, and uphold the interests of the country and the public good."[33] Student bulletin boards were told to block access by off-campus computers. Despite student protests, bloggers were now required to register their real names. The new rules were seen as helping officials track down the authors of anti-government statements.

Students, of course, often find ways to outwit the Internet censors. When China banned Wikipedia, the online encyclopedia, a Chinese hacker in North Carolina, came up with a program called Freegate that links computers inside China with servers in the United States. At least temporarily, this made Wikipedia available via Chinese computers. Student use proxy servers to find information on almost everything including the Tiananmen Square demonstrations, but most are looking for entertainment. Some use "Verycd," also known as the "Electric Donkey," to reach blocked movies.

Chinese authorities keep trying to limit Internet access and have even tried some "Internet cops," Jingjing and Chacha. These animated icons are used in the southern city of Shenzhen, a hotbed of unauthorized Internet activity just across from Hong Kong. Xu Qian, one of the 100 staff of Shenzhen's Internet Surveillance Center, says of Jingjing, "He is just like a policeman, interactively moving along with you. Wherever you go, he is watching you."[34]

The Bloggers

Government officials have become increasingly annoyed with bloggers. They include individuals who have no connection to traditional media and suddenly appear and disappear before authorities can find out who they are. Li Xinde traveled around the country with a digital camera and a laptop computer looking into reports of corruption. He then posted his stories on his website and left town before local authorities could find him. There are millions of bloggers in China: one very popular one is "Aggressive Little Snake" whose "Dog Newspaper" won a German prize for best blog. Chinese officials strongly discourage public discussions of human rights, so the "Dog Newspaper" campaigns for the rights of canines.

Sex and politics

Bokee (Chinese for Blog) was once "Blog Central" in China with a staff of 200 servicing 2 million bloggers and many advertisers. One of Bokee's attractions was a sex diary by its own marketing director, Mu Zimel. It attracted millions until it was banned by the government. Another top Internet attraction was sex columnist Li Li on Sina.com. Her *Ashes of Love* book had huge preorders until the government banned it, along with her blog. Bokee has given up all of this, and in 2014 was an e-commerce site.

Chinese officials have always tried to keep explicit sexual material from the public, but over the centuries have failed. Mian Mian's 2003 novel *Candy*, promoted as "a blast of sex, drugs and rock 'n' roll" among modern China's youth, was banned by the government and as a result had a huge black market sale. She became a celebrity among Shanghai's young people. The Chinese government banned the film *Farewell My Concubine* and was embarrassed by its worldwide success. To the Chinese government, the film is doubly disturbing. It paints a stark picture of the turmoil of the 1966–76 Cultural Revolution and its main character is a homosexual Chinese opera star. Still, Chinese officials give great leeway to the top film producers in China, probably because they are well known to international audiences who can influence decisions that affect China. Meanwhile, Chinese filmmakers go to Hong Kong and elsewhere to escape the Beijing censors. But when there are no politics involved, Chinese censors seem to have become more willing to let sex into public view. Fashion magazines with scantily clad women on the covers plus "candid talk about sex" on the pages inside fill city newsstands throughout China. "We court the metrosexual," said Jin Jin, editor of *FHM* magazine.[35]

Future of the Media in China

Despite the sometimes anti-government bravado, however, there is little chance of any revolutionary change in China's media. The Tiananmen Square protests and their tragic end frightened many Chinese. They saw the abyss of civil war again opening up, and many Chinese believe radical political change is too dangerous. Editor Chen Xilin of *China Business Times* said of the student protesters who died: "Tragic, yes, but that's history. The new elite is a lot smarter, and one thing is certain about the future of China: it belongs to smart people."[36]

Still, journalists, including bloggers, "will continue to risk their jobs and even their lives digging out and telling the 'truth' – at least the 'truth' that journalists believe," said one former Chinese journalist.[37] But another writer suggests that much of this "investigative journalism" will be at lower levels of government and not a threat to the regime but may actually strengthen it by providing an appearance of an independent media.[38]

China's economic boom is muting the most serious discontent, and most people, especially the younger generation, see making a good living as more important than rapid political change. Some of the Tiananmen Square student protesters are now wearing business suits and are part of China's middle class. Even Mian Mian, denounced less than a decade ago as "a poster child for spiritual pollution" by the Chinese government, is fitting into the new China. Her latest novel, *Panda Sex*, uses the notoriously sex-shy bear as a symbol to suggest that getting ahead in life may be more important than either politics or sex. China's media leaders and foreign media moguls seem to agree on the political point, but sex is likely to continue to be a headache for Chinese censors, since newsstand sex sells well. China's media seem to be accepting a period of continued economic boom, but very gradual political change, in the country. But Chinese officials fear the Internet could push political change too rapidly and therefore see it as the big challenge to their rule and will increasingly try to control it. "Whether or not we can actively use and effectively manage the Internet," said China's former President Hu Jintao, "will affect national cultural information, security and the long-term stability of the state,"[39] A long-time American correspondent in China also sees the Internet as the "beating heart" of change in China.[40]

Because of China's economic success and growing international status and power, most Chinese accept the Communist Party's authoritarian rule and its control of the nation's media. China will change and its media may well lead the way, but the change will be slow. The economic boom and a cautious approach to political issues seem to be the compromise that most Chinese accept. Perhaps this compromise is symbolized by a best-selling music cassette, *Red Sun*. It features old hymns praising communist leader Mao Tse Tung set to soft rock rhythms.

Notes

1. David Barboza, "China Puts Best Face Forward in New English-Language Channel," *The New York Times,* July 2, 2010, A8.
2. Marshall Sahlins, "China U.," *The Nation*, November 18, 2013, 36–43.
3. Keith Bradsher and Paul Mozur, "China Clamps Down on Web, Pinching Companies Like Google," *The New York Times*, September 21, 2014, B1.
4. Yu Hua, "The Censorship Pendulum," *The New York Times*, February 5, 2014, 21.
5. Howard W. French, "Fashion Magazines Rush to Mold China's Sense of Style," *The New York Times*, October 3, 2005, A10.
6. Yan Lieshan, "When in Rome … A Few Thoughts on External Propaganda," *China Digital Times*, March 20, 2009.
7. Tsan-kuo Chang and Zixue Tai, "Freedom of the Press in the Eyes of the Dragon: A Matter of Chinese Relativism and Pragmatism," in *International Communication: Concepts and Cases*, K. Anokwa, C. A. Lin, and M. B. Salwen, eds. (Belmont, CA: Wadsworth, 2003), 24.
8. David Bandurski, "Goebbels in China?" China Media Project, Hong Kong University, December 5, 2011.
9. Chris Buckley, "China Warns Officials Against 'Dangerous' Western Values," *The New York Times*, May 14, 2013, A7.

10. John Jirik, "China's News Media and the Case of CCTV-9," in *International News in the Twenty-First Century*, C. Paterson and A. Sreberny, eds. (Eastleigh, UK: John Libbey/Luton Press, 2004), 133.

11. Geraldine Fabrikant, "Media Executives Court China, but Still Run into Obstacles," *The New York Times*, August 29, 2005, C1.

12. "China's New Faces," BBC World, http://news.bbc.co.uk, September 17, 2005.

13. Joseph Kahn, "China's State Secrets Will Guard One Less: Death Tolls," *The New York Times*, September 13, 2005, A5.

14. Wei Win and David Weaver, "Making Chinese Journalists for the Next Millennium," *Gazette*, 60(6), 1998, 513–529.

15. "China: The Media," Section 15 in *Library of Congress Country Studies*, October 3, 2005.

16. Jim Yardley, "Secrecy Veils China's Jailing of a Journalist," *The New York Times*, August 31, 2005, A1.

17. Andrew Jacobs, "Chinese Blogger Thrives as Muckraker," *The New York Times*, February 6, 2013.

18. Sui-Lee Wee, "China Holds Two Bloggers as it Expands Crackdown on Rumors," Reuters, October 17, 2013.

19. Li Pin, *Report on the Development of the Magazine Industry in China (No. 2)* (Beijing: Beijing Social Science Academic Press, 2007), 57.

20. Chen Gang, Chen Jinchao, Song Wenjie, and Zhou Shao, "Research on the Readers of e-Magazines," *New View of Advertising*, February 2008, 24.

21. "International Editor of the Year," *World Press Review*, October 2003, 20–21.

22. David Barboza, "Pushing (and Toeing) the Line in China," *The New York Times*, April 18, 2005, C3.

23. Barboza, "Pushing (and Toeing) the Line in China."

24. Howard W. French, "Beijing Casts Net of Silence over Protest," *The New York Times*, December 14, 2005, A3.

25. Charles W. Eliot, "Flows of News from the Middle Kingdom: An Analysis of International News Releases in Xinhua," in *The Global Dynamic of News: Studies in International News Coverage and News Agenda*, Abbas Malek and Anandam P. Kavoori, eds. (Stamford, CT: Ablex Publishing, 2000), 348.

26. Xin Xin, "A Developing Market in News: Xinhua News Agency and Chinese Newspapers," *Media, Culture and Society*, 28(1), 2006, 60.

27. Jianying Zha, *China Pop: How Soap Operas, Tabloids, and Bestsellers are Transforming a Culture* (New York: The New Press, 1995), 107.

28. "Two Million Monitoring Internet in China," Agence France-Presse, October 5, 2013.

29. David Barboza, "A Popular Chinese Social Networking App Blazes Its Own Path," *The New York Times*, January 20, 2014.

30. Chin-Chuan Lee, "The Global and the National of the Chinese Media: Discourses, Market Technology and Ideology," in *Chinese Media, Global Contexts*, Chin-Chuan Lee, ed. (London: RoutledgeCurzon, 2003), 1–31.

31. Charles Hutzler, "Yuppies in China Protest Via the Web – And Get Away With It," *The New York Times*, March 19, 2004, A4.

32. Ying Chan, "Chinese Journalists Circumvent Government's Tight Restrictions," *Nieman Reports*, 65(1), 2011, 53–55.

33. Joseph Kahn, "China Tightens its Restrictions for News Media on the Internet," *The New York Times*, September 26, 2005, A9.

34. Mure Dickie, "China's Virtual Cops Pinpoint Web Dissent," *Financial Times*, February 18, 2006, 3.

35. French, "Fashion Magazines Rush to Mold China's Sense of Style."

36. Zha, *China Pop*, 108.

37. Jingrong Tong, *Investigative Journalism in China* (New York: Continuum Press, 2011), 1.

38. Peter Lorentzen, "China's Strategic Censorship," *American Journal of Political Science*, 58(3), 2014, 402–414.

39. Mure Dickie, "China President Urges Party Officials to 'Purify' the Internet," *Financial Times*, January 26, 2007, 1.

40. Howard W. French, "China's Chess Match," *Columbia Journalism Review*, November/December 2010, 41–45.

10

Africa: The Mobile Continent

Africa is clearly the "mobile continent."

By 2014 two-thirds of households in Sub-Saharan Africa had at least one mobile phone. In Mauritania, on the edge of the Sahara, 96 percent of households had a mobile phone, while in Botswana, at the southern end of the continent, 87 percent of households had one (or more). On the west coast in Nigeria, Africa's most populous country, one or more cellphones could be found in at least 78 percent of homes. Across the continent in Kenya, 68 percent of households had at least one. Even people with little income have mobile phones. In South Africa, 50 percent of households below the poverty level have a mobile phone. The United Nations reported in 2013 that more people in the world have access to cellphones than to toilets, something undoubtedly true in Africa.[1]

Geography and Africa's colonial history are the main reasons for this remarkable mobile phone growth. Africa is a vast continent (11.7 million square miles/30.2 million square kilometers), second only to Asia in area and three times the size of Europe. Mountains and forests cover much of Sub-Saharan Africa, adding to travel and communications difficulties. Africa's large population (1.12 billion people) is, again, second only to Asia's. More than half of Africans are under age 20 and there will likely be 2.2 billion people in Sub-Saharan Africa by 2050.

Primarily because of its 100 years of European colonial rule, Africa is also a politically fractured continent of about fifty nations with some (e.g., Mauritania) sometimes placed geographically in Arab North Africa. Most of these countries exist as a legacy of colonial rule that created nations by chopping out a piece of the continent and putting up a European flag.

The World News Prism: Digital, Social and Interactive, Ninth Edition.
William A. Hachten and James F. Scotton.
© 2016 John Wiley & Sons, Inc. Published 2016 by John Wiley & Sons, Inc.

British and French flags flew over vast areas of Africa. Britain once ruled in eastern Africa from Egypt to South Africa. France ruled a huge land mass in western Africa, beginning at Dakar on the Atlantic Ocean and ending 3,000 miles to the east where it ran into the British-held Sudan. In addition, Portugal, Belgium, Spain, and later Italy took possession of other large areas of the "Dark Continent." Belgian Congo, in the heart of Africa, was as large as either Europe or the United States and seventy-five times the size of Belgium.

The political boundaries set by the European colonial powers paid little attention to traditional African nations and tribes. In East Africa the kingdom of Buganda was absorbed along with various tribal groups into British Uganda. In West Africa the British pushed together the major Yoruba, Ibo, and Hausa tribes along with hundreds of other smaller groups and created a nation called Nigeria. The other colonial powers did the same, simply drawing lines on a map and taking possession of the area. These national boundaries remained after independence, and African resistance to them led to many conflicts, the latest creating the new nation of South Sudan when the Africans there broke away from the largely Arab Sudan to the north. Also, some very peculiar smaller territories that were hardly viable as independent nations were created by colonial agreement. For example, the nation of Gambia exists because the British were able to control a sliver of land along the Gambia River 300 miles long and just 30 miles across (480 × 48 kilometers) at its widest point right in the middle of French-held Senegal. Gambia is the smallest nation in Africa, about twice the size of the state of Delaware.

European settlement was largely unsuccessful or repelled by the Africans except in South Africa, where the Europeans, descendants of Dutch and British settlers, didn't give up political control to the overwhelming majority (80 percent) of African citizens until 1994.

The vastness of Africa and the very fractured political structure made communication very difficult. First, the colonial powers saw no reason to connect with neighboring colonies of rival European nations. A telegraph message from Lagos, the capital of British colonial Nigeria, to the capital city of Cotonou in neighboring French Dahomey (now Benin), just 75 miles (120 kilometers) apart, had to go first to London, next to Paris and then back to Cotonou. Communication between African colonies and the European "home countries" was what colonial administrators saw as most important. Telegraph cables to London and Paris were laid along the African coasts and the mail service was remarkably fast. By 1960 an airmail letter from London or Paris could be delivered to an address in their African colonies in two or three days.

But even in the post-colonial period after World War II getting information across national borders in Africa was very difficult.

A Pan-African News Agency (PANA) was established in Dakar, Senegal, in 1983 to overcome this and to break the monopoly that Western news agencies held on African news, but political rivalries and budget problems shut it down in 1991. The United Nations has been trying to revive PANA. Babacar Fall, a Senegalese journalist directing PANA's new continental efforts, has noted the continuing problems of trying to get information from one country to another in Africa: "Forty-eight out of 52 African nations now belong to PANA," Fall said. "Most of them are using radio transmitting stations, which are totally dependent on the weather. Tropical storms and sandstorms can totally screw up transmissions . . . It can take three, five, even ten attempts to reach another African country by phone," he added, "And even where good telephone lines are available, the price is often prohibitively expensive."[2] PANA does have in Internet connection – it came just in 2014. But PANA's Internet hookup is available only five times per day. Fall voiced his frustration with the low priority given news even in a satellite and online age: "When you have news, it burns your hands . . . You've got to get it online very, very quickly because it's news."[3]

A New Continental News Vision

Fall's frustrations are echoed by journalists across Africa, but there are recent signs that a change may be coming. Across the continent from Dakar, in Nairobi, Kenya, a news organization from South Africa has established what it says can be a digital news and information portal for all of Sub-Saharan Africa. *M&G Africa*, was launched on May 1, 2014, by the *Mail & Globe* media group of South Africa. Charles Onyango-Obo, perhaps Africa's leading journalist, will lead a group of reporters and editors operating across the continent from a Nairobi office. Onyango-Obo, a journalist in Africa for more than twenty-five years, has been an editor in Uganda, Kenya, and South Africa and has a continental view of the future of communications in Africa. His focus will be on Africa's growing young population and he will reach them through their mobile phones.

"The aim is to focus on delivering quality African news and information via mobile to, primarily, a 30 to 40 year-old audience with a university education in both Africa and outside the continent," Onyango-Obo said. "The objective is to make *M&G* Africa's most trusted and diverse source of news on Africa."[4]

Onyango-Obo believes that *M&G*'s independence from government and even from UN support will enable it to avoid the political limits that have led the African public to mistrust the continent's own news media and often turn to Western news agencies, especially the BBC, to find out what is going on in Africa and even in their own countries. "With all the social tools we can muster, *M&G Africa* will be home to every African voice imaginable. (It will) tackle the continent's failures without fear and shine the light on its great possibilities intelligently," he said.[5]

Dependence on Western News Sources

It is because Africa's traditional media have generally avoided reporting the continent's failures – such as widespread corruption – that many Africans mistrust those media. Courageous print journalists frequently wind up in prison and government-controlled broadcasters avoid any news that would displease their employers. Independent broadcasters that have sprung up in recent years in Africa are often limited to music with all news to come only from the government news agency. The BBC and, to a lesser extent, the Voice of America have been the sources of trusted news for generations of Africans.

The BBC's overseas broadcasts started as the Empire Service in 1932 and its Africa Service grew strongly after World War II as the Common-wealth replaced the Empire. Several relay stations around and within Africa boosted the BBC's short-wave signal strength on the continent, and broad-casts in widely spoken Swahili and other African languages and in French and Portuguese as well as in English added to its audience. Besides having its own correspondents, mainly in larger cities such as Johannesburg, Lagos, and Nairobi, the BBC has also maintained a series of "Listening Posts" in Africa, collecting information by monitoring African broadcasts. The BBC news was considered so reliable that one Nigerian leader said he learned he had been ousted in a 1975 coup from a BBC broadcast he heard while at a conference in Uganda.[6] Now, thanks to satellites, BBC television and Internet programs are also received throughout Africa.

Africa's continued dependence on Western news agencies based in London, Paris, and New York even after political independence has irritated its leaders. These leaders believe Africa is ignored by these agencies unless there is ethnic violence or some disaster such as the 2014 Ebola epidemic. The Western media regularly picture Africa as impoverished, corrupt, and helpless, one study found. Myths and stereotypes are the basis of many reports on Africa.[7]

"I think there is a longstanding theme about ongoing famine and starvation, of chronic misgovernance, of Africa as a continent that needs to be saved," says Ethan Zuckerman, co-founder of Global Voices, an international community of citizen bloggers.[8] TMS Ruge, co-founder of the Ugandan Project Diaspora, said, "The more dire the situation, the more likely that [*New York Times* correspondent] Nicholas Kristof and [CNN's] Anderson Cooper will be deployed in their khaki pants." Ruge added that when Westerners hear about Uganda they first think of warlord Charles Kony and his army of kidnapped children because of one sensational 2012 YouTube video. Ruge said sensational stories about Africa have skewed the public's views to the point where Africa is considered hopeless by many. "That single perennial thread is so synonymous with the continent that it is hard for people to accept that there's another side of the story," he said.[9]

Even if Western journalists try to be unbiased, their reports are often seen by Africans as out of touch with the African reality. For example, African critics charged that Western media distorted the picture of South Africa's Nelson Mandela throughout his life, painting him at times as a communist agitator, and continued to misread his legacy even during his last days.[10]

In early 2014 a storm of protest erupted on social media over coverage by London's *Guardian* of the ongoing crisis in South Sudan. The report may have satisfied the *Guardian*'s Western audience, but not many African readers. Referring to the long-running struggle to make South Sudan a stable independent nation, one critic said:

> Most Western journalists who come to Africa believe they can get by because they speak English or even Swahili, but never really get down to the essence of what it means to be South Sudanese ...[11]

Africans have long complained that Western journalists who arrive at the airport are what they call "parachute journalists" who fly in and quickly fly out as soon as the crisis has passed. Even if the crisis continues, the journalists leave as soon as the story leaves the front pages of newspapers or the first ten minutes of the nightly news.

Internet and Social Media in Africa

It is because traditional communications (telephone, telegraph, and even postal services) have been so poor within most African countries that social media have spread so rapidly in recent years. Because computers were relatively expensive, however, it was not until cheap ($30 or less) smartphones appeared that the Internet started to grow rapidly in Africa. That growth in Africa was the fastest in the world between 2000 and 2012. In 2000 only 1 percent of households in Sub-Saharan Africa had access to the Internet; by 2012 it was 54 percent. In Kenya government officials categorized Internet growth as "staggering" when 300,000 Kenyans were using the Internet; by 2012 that figure had risen to more than 40 million.[12]

Internet Statistics for Africa

Nigeria, Africa's most populous country, leads all sub-Saharan countries in Internet users with 67 million (38 percent) of its 177 million people connected in 2014, according to Internet World Statistics. There was a 50 percent (22 million) increase in Nigeria's Internet users in just two years as inexpensive smartphones flooded the continent. Social media including email and Twitter have a strong presence throughout Africa, with older people as well as the young using them regularly. Studies find that when Africans go online, usually via their mobile phones, they are spending more time with social media such as Facebook, Twitter, and YouTube. Emails and seeking news seem less important, although older people still find email the easiest way to keep in touch with family and friends. Besides communicating with friends, younger users use social media heavily to access entertainment.

By 2014 there were more than 450 million cellphones in Sub-Saharan Africa. In five years those numbers will double, researchers predict, with 75 percent of the phones connected to the Internet. With the rapid growth of cellphones, especially smartphones, traditional government-operated land lines are falling into disuse. By 2014, 90 percent of all Sub-Saharan African telephone users were using mobiles.

Mobile Phone Use in Sub-Saharan Africa

"Africa is a mobile-only continent," said Toby Shapshak, a technology journalist and editor of the South Africa magazine, *Stuff.* "There never was a landline infrastructure to begin with, apart from urban areas." And the mobile phone is having a profound social impact across the continent, he added. "Better and faster Internet access means people can consume news via their mobiles – something that is especially important because so many African countries still control the major media outlets," Shapshak said.[13]

Business communication, often what attracts private investment, is also benefiting Africa because of the continent's huge leap into communication technology. "We are now in the middle of a mobile broadband revolution in Africa," said Fredrik Jejdling, in charge of African operations for the Swedish tech company Ericsson. "The rise of cheap smartphones will allow vast portions of the population –from middle classes in cities to small businesses in rural areas – access to mobile broadband."[14]

Kenya, although it has a much smaller economy than South Africa, may be taking the lead in technology investment because of its fast Internet growth and also its imaginative use of Internet and mobile phones. M-pesa (Mobile Money in Swahili) was started in 2007 primarily to serve the millions of Kenyans without bank accounts. M-pesa enables people to deposit or withdraw funds and pay bills with just a mobile phone. M-pesa has spread to other African countries and even to Afghanistan, and is used by millions of people who choose it because of convenience and very low fees. Although South Africa is by far the continent's largest economy, Kenya is rapidly catching up in the percentage of its population with Internet access.[15] Small businessmen such as fishermen on Lake Victoria and produce-sellers in Nairobi are using mobile phones to check market prices for their goods.

A 2011 Google study blamed South Africa's slowdown in Internet development on high broadband costs and a lag in government investment in infrastructure. An undersea fiber-optic cable being completed along Africa's eastern coast will provide more Internet access to some African countries, but it will not help meet South Africa's internal Internet needs.

The influence of government policy on the Internet can be seen clearly in Ethiopia. With the second-largest population in Africa (98 million), Ethiopia has barely entered the Internet age, and fewer than 2 million of its citizens have access to it. One reason, of course, is the geography of that vast and mountainous country, where providing any service is extremely expensive. Critics, however, primarily blame government policies that have all but blocked private firms from providing any Internet service in Ethiopia.[16]

Government officials in Africa have always been uneasy about media they did not control. Social media are, of course, much more difficult to control or even monitor than the traditional print or broadcast media. In

2012 the removal of fuel subsidies in Nigeria touched off mass protests that were organized primarily via Twitter. In 2011 a Nigerian organization called Enough Is Enough set up a mobile application to allow people to organize voting reports and watch for fraud.[17] In Kenya a group of tech-savvy people established the blog Mzalendo (Patriot in Swahili) to monitor parliament, developing a database that tracked MPs' votes and even their expense accounts. After violence broke out following Kenya's disputed December 2007 elections, another group set up the mobile phone network Ushahidi (Witness) to provide accurate information about the crisis that they said could not be found in newspapers or on television. Ushahidi carefully checked all information and was able to warn people about where the worst violence was occurring.[18]

In the Central African Republic, torn by Christian–Muslim violence in 2014, Human Rights Watch sent out a constant stream of Twitter messages documenting the violence there and warning the populace of atrocities by both rebels and government soldiers.[19] In Rwanda, where the government-controlled traditional media are at times reluctant to open up the wounds from that nation's genocide in 1994, social media posted photographs and testimonies of survivors as reminders of a past not to be forgotten. And social media can take control of a story and push it in a direction that government officials did not anticipate. What started as an article celebrating the ninetieth birthday of Kenya's former president Daniel arap Moi quickly turned into an online debate over whether he was the most corrupt public figure in that nation's short history.[20]

The role of social media in alerting the traditional media to wrongdoing by public officials has grown enormously in recent years. One study asserted that blogs and Twitter prompted journalists to investigate in up to 90 percent of investigations of public officials reported by the traditional media.[21]

Radio and Television

Radio and television broadcasting has been traditionally operated by governments in Africa starting in colonial times. Foreign television programs were seen as a threat to African leaders since they could show alternative lifestyles and the relative prosperity of Western countries. In South Africa the ruling white-controlled Nationalist Party kept television out of the country until 1976 because it feared its influence on the African population. Foreign radio broadcasts were impossible to keep out, so African governments were forced to give up their monopolies when their audiences were taken away by short-wave radio from the BBC and other outside broadcasters that proved more entertaining and was more trusted as a news source.[22] Independent television and radio are now found all over Sub-Saharan Africa. By 2014 there were over 1,500 TV channels broadcast to Africa via satellite. One company, Viewsat, transmits to seventy African TV channels and estimates it reaches about 20 million African households, mostly with entertainment and religious programs.

Before satellites Africans often turned to videotapes for entertainment, and some also watched anti-government videos smuggled across the border. Television production is very expensive, and few African countries can produce programs that attract strong audiences, especially since those audiences know that the government-operated stations are unlikely sources of any controversial news. Before satellites these government stations imported inexpensive videotapes to supplement their fare of English or French lessons and programs on health and traffic safety, plus arrivals and departures of the head of state. It was not unusual to see an old John Wayne film or *Mission: Impossible* TV series with French dubbed in or subtitled where necessary. Action films such as the Rambo series were very popular on African television, since their dialogue is sparse and often not essential for viewers to understand what is happening on the screen.

Radio, because it requires minimum investment by both broadcaster and listener, has historically been more important to African communication than television. Government-owned stations (usually AM rather than FM), plus overseas broadcasts by the BBC, Voice of America, Germany's Deutsch Welle, Radiodiffusion de la France Outre-Mer (RFOM), Radio Moscow, and a host of other countries, regularly reached Africans.

The BBC broadcast twenty-four hours a day, providing mostly news programs in multiple languages. The powerful Voice of the Gospel station in Addis Ababa, Ethiopia, could reach most of Africa with its religious programs. Started in 1963 by a Lutheran group in Norway, even its programs were reviewed by an Ethiopian censor, especially programs in the local Amharic language. When cheap transistor radios appeared in the 1950s, listener numbers boomed for all these broadcasters in Africa and around the world.

Governments, both colonial and, later, independent African, opposed private broadcasting although they were willing to allow some groups access to the airwaves. In Nigeria various civic and religious groups got broadcast time, and even students at the University of Lagos had a Sunday program.

That ended abruptly when the students decided to broadcast a play about the overthrow of the government, presenting it as a news broadcast similar to the *War of the Worlds* program in 1938 that panicked many New York area listeners. Soldiers stormed the studio and the students were arrested, though they were later released.

Community Radio

There are many community radio stations, sometimes called bush radio, across Africa. These low-powered stations reach out to communities with information about farming, health, education, and other local matters important to their listeners. The first bush radio station was apparently in South Africa, where a group of volunteers established one in late 1992 as an alternative voice to the media available under apartheid. The station was refused a license, so started broadcasting without one, reaching only audiences within a few miles of its Cape Town transmitter. The station was only on the air a short time before the police seized the transmitter and arrested the staff. The government spent a year prosecuting the case, but with the end of apartheid looming, it finally dropped all charges. The station, now broadcasting as an FM station and with a more powerful transmitter, calls itself "The mother of community radio in Africa." With a small staff plus volunteers, it is on air every day for twenty-four hours, broadcasting in Afrikaans, English, and Xhosa. It retains its activist and social role, with programs linked to many off-air social programs. English-learning programs, a campaign to raise awareness of HIV/AIDS, and even a childcare center for working mothers are just a few of its many activities. There are now close to 100 community radio stations in South Africa, all low-powered and designed to serve a small area. Similar stations are now found across Africa, but all suffer from a lack of funding.

Ghana has a network of three community radio stations (Radio Ada, Radio Peace, and Radio Progress). Radio Ada was the first to broadcast in 1998 from the capital, Accra, and claims there are 600,000 potential listeners within 40 miles (64 kilometers) of its transmitter. All of its programs are in Dangme, a local language. Community stations at times get involved in controversies that upset government officials. In Congo-Kinshasa a community radio station was closed when it broadcast information related to a teachers' strike.[23]

There were some private broadcasters allowed even in colonial Africa. In Rhodesia (now Zambia and Zimbabwe) Europeans formed broadcast clubs, set up a station, and started programs aimed at the local European audience. These soon ran into financial problems and closed down. The Portuguese issued licenses to commercial broadcasters in their colonies, and one station in Mozambique was so successful in attracting South African audiences to its music programs that the South African Broadcasting Corporation altered some program formats to compete. The idea that radio was a medium mainly for Europeans remained in most British African colonies right up to independence.

In contrast, radio in the French West African colonies was directed at Africans. Few programs were developed in Africa; instead transmitters merely relayed broadcasts from the French broadcasting schedule. The French believed their mission was to "civilize" the native peoples – that is, to make them more French – and eventually make them citizens of France. A small number of Africans did become "civilized": a Senegalese was elected to the French Chamber of Deputies in 1914 and a few others followed. The French colonial authorities expected, however, that their civilizing mission would keep them in power in Africa indefinitely.

The reluctance of African governments to issue radio licenses continued after independence. Radio reaches more people in Africa than any other medium. Many African nations are weak amalgamations of rival tribes, and governments may legitimately fear stirring up divisions in the population. Radio broadcasts in Rwanda have been at least partially blamed for stirring the tribal hatreds that killed at least half a million people in 1994. For that reason the commercial radio stations to be found all over Africa are often limited to only music programs. If they want to broadcast news, it must come from the government station. These independent commercial stations are very popular, attracting most of the radio advertising money and forcing government radio to change its programming and eliminate the long, dull speeches that politicians always want to provide. One loss has been the disappearance of education and development programs that the government stations provided. Some imaginative programming, however, has brought new life to such programs. In Tanzania a radio program about a promiscuous truck driver was used to spread messages about family planning and AIDS. In Senegal a radio program developed and primarily presented by children promotes equal rights for girls and boys. Both programs attracted large audiences and continue to be broadcast.

Independent radio stations, especially when linked to social media, can be a powerful political force. In Ghana, a West African nation of 26 million, President Jerry Rawlings gave up the government's monopoly of the air waves in 1995. After that more than forty FM stations cropped up around Ghana, broadcasting in English and African languages. The stations not only offered music but news broadcasts and even live talk shows. Ghanaians called in and told government officials and anyone else listening what was on their minds, ranging from potholes in the roads to poor schools and suspect politicians. The resulting national dialogue on FM radio enabled presidential challenger J. A. Kufuor to defeat Rawlings and oust his tired and corrupt party after twenty years in power. This was the first peaceful transition from one elected civilian government to another in Ghana's history. People spread the word via these FM stations that there was, indeed, something wrong with Ghana and it was time for a change. Kufuor won the vote in eight of Ghana's provinces, all with FM stations; Rawlings won only the two provinces without any FM stations. As one official said, "The minute people were able to talk freely – and anonymously – on the radio and ask what officials were up to was the beginning of accountability for government in Ghana.[24] Radio talk shows have been a barrier to all forms of government misdeeds or oppression, but other barriers are now available. Cellphones, owned by an estimated 350 million Africans in 2014, have become the way to reach huge numbers of citizens.

Print Media in Africa

Newspapers and magazines have increased their readership in most African countries in recent years, but the online challenge is beginning to appear. Many listed newspapers can only be found online. The cost of accessing online newspapers via a computer or smartphone is still too high for many Africans. This is a major reason for the print boom in countries like Kenya and South Africa. Also, readers can "rent" a publication from a vendor to lower the cost of even the relatively inexpensive print media.

Newspapers have been publishing in South Africa since 1800, but did not appear elsewhere on the continent until later. The earliest publications, often no more than a single sheet or small pamphlet, were directed toward European residents and were, of course, in European languages. The exceptions were missionary publications for Africans in Swahili, Luganda, Xhosa, and other African languages. Africans were trained to set type and before long started publishing their own newspapers, although lack of funds and resistance from government officials soon closed most of them. Many Africans who were to become national leaders were also journalists, persistently calling for fair treatment for Africans and later for independence. Jomo Kenyatta, the first president of Kenya after its 1963 independence, once edited a monthly newspaper; Nnamdi Azikiwe, founder and long-time editor of the *West African Pilot*, became independent Nigeria's first head of state in 1960. In South Africa the *Rand Daily Mail* and *The Drum* and small African publications fought apartheid for years but were eventually closed by the government.

In Kenya and in some other African countries the rapid rise in newspaper circulation in recent years is credited to the growing middle class. *The Nation*, published in Nairobi, circulates 250,000 copies daily and readership may be much higher since buyers often share their copies. The Nation company also publishes newspapers in Tanzania, Uganda, and Rwanda. The Nation group also publishes a Swahili daily, *Taifa Leo* (*The Nation Today*), and a weekly business magazine, *The East African*. The online *Nation* gets 3 million visitors each week.[25]

In South Africa in 2013 there were twenty-two dailies and twenty-five weekly newspapers, with tabloids specializing in sensationalism leading in circulation. *The Daily Sun* ("Your latest and loudest South African news") claims a circulation of 5.5 million. Notably, however, the *Mail & Guardian*, considered South Africa's leading political paper, publishes a print edition only weekly, focusing on its online audience.

Across the continent in Nigeria, newspaper circulation does not seem to be growing at nearly the rate found in Kenya. *The Punch*, published in Lagos, claims it is the "most widely read." The *Daily Times*, also published in Lagos, had the highest circulation in West Africa when the government purchased it in 1975. Since then it has declined steadily, and today can only claim to be the nation's "oldest newspaper." One study blames poor business management and the Internet for what it claims is "dwindling newspaper circulation in Nigeria."[26]

Media Control in Africa

The media have rarely been more than marginally free in Africa. Colonial rulers kept tight control over the media until African independence movements forced them out, either peacefully or violently. In the fifty years or so since independence swept through the continent the new African leaders have been only too ready and willing to use laws, some of them directly inherited from the colonialists they forced out, to control the media. Many of these governments are seeking new and stronger controls over the media, including the social media.

In South Africa, where the African media waged a decades-long fight to overcome the racist apartheid regime, the government is waging a concerted campaign against the media just two decades after Africans took political control of the country. As a result South Africa fell from thirty-eighth on the World Press Freedom rankings in 2010 to fifty-second by 2013. Journalists fear that the renewed government assaults on the media that are so prevalent elsewhere on the continent will grow in South Africa into widespread censorship.[27]

One example is a 2011 South African law calling for a prison sentence for any journalist reporting any information that a government agency classifies as "secret." In 2014 the government proposed a law to weaken the constitutional guarantees of freedom of speech and of the media that were enacted in 1997 by the ruling African National Congress (ANC) government under the leadership of President Nelson Mandela. The still-ruling ANC says the new law is needed to deter "foreign spies and their collaborators."[28] South Africa's media are certainly much freer to publish news and commentary than during the apartheid era (1948–94) when restrictions on information helped keep the minority white government in power. But that freedom is seen as being eroded by its African government.

African journalist Mohamed Keita says that, ironically, as Africa's economies are finally growing the attacks on media freedom are getting more intense. He suggests that because more African journalists have turned their attention to the growing problem of government corruption they are being persecuted, prosecuted, and imprisoned for their critical reporting. Keita places some blame on Western nations, who praise any African political leader who achieves some economic growth and maintains stability. If this includes total control of all national institutions including the media, the West seems to accept it. In contrast with the earlier post-colonial years, freedom of the press has a low priority on the Western agenda for Africa.

Keita also blames China, now Africa's largest trading partner. China has a large corps of journalists (all employed by the Chinese government) and press officers in Africa. Xinhua, the state news agency, has twenty bureaus in Africa, and China has a major television center in Nairobi and a print publication center in South Africa. In addition, China brings many African government press officers to Beijing for training in developing "truthful" reports about development and avoiding "negative" news.[29]

Governments everywhere in Africa are quick to move against "negative news," especially if it involves government officials. Uganda's leading independent TV station was banned from presidential events for showing President Yoweri Museveni sleeping in parliament. A government spokesman claimed the president was "meditating."[30]

Any item considered embarrassing to a top government official can bring a media crackdown. A year earlier two Ugandan newspapers were raided by police after they reported that the president planned to have his son succeed him.

Despite these actions, Uganda's media have been considered among the freest on the continent. At a 2013 inter-government meeting in Nairobi an Ethiopian official said the media in Uganda were "vibrant and free" overall despite "a bit of censorship." Ugandan journalists are certainly subject to government pressures, but as a Somali journalist at the conference pointed out, in his country "several journalists are killed in their homes or at work while others have survived explosions."[31] The Ethiopian official could also admire Uganda's media freedom if he compared it to the situation in his own country. Just a year earlier the Ethiopian courts convicted twenty-four journalists and opposition leaders for violating a 2009 anti-terrorism law which can bring heavy prison sentences. One of those convicted was Eskinder Nega Fanta, an independent journalist and blogger honored earlier with the prestigious PEN America press freedom award. Human Rights Watch counted at least eleven Ethiopian journalists jailed under the anti-terrorism law.

While organizations like the Committee to Protect Journalists (CPJ) give an overall picture of media freedom, Mohamed Keita, CPJ's Africa coordinator, also keeps a careful record country by country of the struggles of individual African journalists as they try to cover their communities. All over the continent, whether in East Africa, West Africa, or Southern Africa, Keita reports journalists are under attack, with some being killed. In Ethiopia five more publications were added in 2014 to a long list of banned publications, and nine journalists and bloggers were charged with "terrorism." In neighboring Eritrea, once a part of Ethiopia, Keita noted the complete lack of an independent media with the government in control of almost all information.

In West Africa's Burkina Faso journalist Lohé Issa Konaté was imprisoned for alleging there was corruption in the Public Prosecutor's office. In

2014 the African Human Rights Court finally placed some of the blame for the murder of four people in Burkina Faso, including prominent editor Norbert Zongo, sixteen years earlier on the government. The bodies were found in the burned wreckage of their vehicle along a rural road. Zongo and his colleagues had been investigating alleged corruption within the presidential guard unit. In Burundi in Central Africa a radio reporter was shot when he questioned police at what he alleged was an unlawful police "tax roadblock." In Southern Africa, Zimbabwe lawyer Beatrice Mtetwa, known for her defense of journalists against government charges, was imprisoned for a week for "obstructing the course of justice." Later acquitted, she suggested that the government used the false charges to slow down her work defending journalists in Zimbabwe.

Self-censorship is perhaps the strongest control that government imposes on African journalists since they know that arrest, prosecution, prison, and even assassination can be the result of even a careless error in a story. In 2012 the Rwandan community radio announcer Epaphrodite Habarugira mixed up the words for "victim" and "survivor" in Kinyarwanda, a local language, in a story about ceremonies marking the anniversary of the 1994 genocide tragedy there. Colleagues said it was clearly just a slip of the tongue, but he was arrested and spent three months in prison until a court released him. Even student journalists can be targeted by police. Student Idriss Gasana was charged with trying to "deceive the intelligence services" when his article claimed he was kidnapped by police when he went to a police station to get information for an article. After three days in jail in he "confessed" to fabricating the story and was released. Once out of jail, Gasana said the kidnap story was true and the confession was coerced. Police arrested him again and he spent thirty more days in jail.

Zimbabwe has a new constitution guaranteeing press freedom but, as in so many African countries, it is sometimes carefully limited by government. Riot police broke up a gathering of Zimbabwe journalists at a rally on World Press Freedom Day in 2014, although they were later allowed to hold their rally. The Minister of Information blamed the problems on "miscommunication."[32]

The Future of Communication in Africa

Although print is doing well in some growing economies such as Kenya and South Africa, like the rest of the world Africa is moving more and more toward the Internet. There is a rapid growth in mobile phones all over the continent, and as soon as smartphone prices come down sufficiently it is likely that more Africans will move online to get their news and even the sensational gossip provided by the tabloid press. Given the "staggering" growth of the social media in Africa, these changes are soon to come all over the continent. The only thing that could block or slow this growth is government attempts to control information, as in South Africa and Ethiopia, and failure to provide support for needed technological infrastructure. Regardless of government action or inaction, however, Africa is clearly becoming the "mobile continent" and is on the move toward bringing all Africans into the Information Age.

Notes

1. Yue Wang, "More People Have Cell Phones Than Toilets, U.N. Study Shows," *Time*, March 25, 2013.
2. Quoted in Jeff Greenwald, "Wiring Africa," *WIRED*, September 7, 2014.
3. Greenwald, "Wiring Africa."
4. "*Mail & Guardian* Launches Pan-African Platform, M&G Africa," *Mail & Guardian*, May 20, 2014.
5. "*Mail & Guardian* Launches Pan-African Platform."
6. He was General Yakubu Gowon. See Nowa Omolgul, "Military Rebellion of July 2, 1975," Dawodu.com.
7. Ezekiel Makunike, "Out of Africa: Western Media Stereotypes Shape Images," Center for Media Literacy. http:// www.medialit.org (retrieved September 12, 2014).
8. Nadra Kareem Nittle, "Critiquing Western Media Coverage of Africa," Maynard Institute, April 4, 2012.
9. Nittle, "Critiquing Western Media Coverage of Africa."
10. Danny Schechter, "How the Western Media Distorts the Historical Legacy of Nelson Mandela," *Global Research*, July 1, 2013.
11. Nanjala Nyabola, "Why Do Western Media Get Africa Wrong?" Al Jazeera, January 2, 2014.
12. Joel Macharia, "Internet Access Is No Longer a Luxury," *AfricaRenewal*, April 2014.
13. Tony Shapshak, "Africa Is Not Just a Mobile-First Continent – It's Mobile Only," *CNN Tech*, October 4, 2012.
14. Fredrik Jejdling, "We Look for Ways to Leverage Our Global Expertise." http://mobileworldmag.com (retrieved September 16, 2014).

15. Duncan McLeod, "SA Losing to Kenya in Tech Race," *TECHCENTRAL*, June 9, 2013.

16. Jacey Fortin, "Missed Connections: As African Tech Hubs Flourish, Is Ethiopian Government Stifling Telecommunications?," *International Business Times*, November 15, 2013.

17. "Tracking Social Media: Tracking Social Media Centre and the 2011 Nigerian Elections." http://yaraduacentre.org/files/tracking.pdf (retrieved, September 8, 2014).

18. "Ushahidi: From Crisis Mapping Kenya to Mapping the Globe." *TAVAANA*. https://tavaana.org/en (retrieved September 1, 2014).

19. Christine Hauser, "Social Media Dispatches: Death and Destruction in Central Africa," *The New York Times*, February 11, 2014.

20. "From School Milk to Nayo Bus to Torture Chambers: Kenyans Relive Moi's Legacy on Social Media," *The Star*, September 2, 2014.

21. Andrew Gunn and Jennifer MacDonald, "It Started with a Tweet: How Social Media is Shaping the News," *Brunswick Review*, 4, Summer 2011.

22. Christi van der Westhuizen, "South Africa Confronting Choices about Free Expression," *Xindex*, August 7, 2013.

23. "Congo Kinshasa: DRC Radio Station Shut Down, Accused of Inciting Teachers to Strike," International Freedom of Expression Clearing House (Toronto). http://www.ifex.org/ (retrieved September 16, 2014).

24. Thomas Friedman, "Low Tech Democracy," *The New York Times*, May 1, 2001, A27.

25. "Paper Kingdom: East Africa's News Business," *The Economist*, January 19, 2013.

26. "The Solution to the Dwindling Newspaper Circulation in Nigeria," WOWEffect, 2010.

27. Julie Reid, "Analysis: South African Media on World Press Freedom Day 2014," *Daily Maverick*, April 24, 2014.

28. David Smith, "ANC's Secrecy Bill Seen as an Assault on South African Press Freedom," *Guardian*, June 6, 2012.

29. Mohamed Keita, "Africa's Free Press Problem," *The New York Times*, April 15, 2012.

30. David Smith, "Uganda TV Station Banned after Showing President Asleep in Parliament," *Guardian*, June 19, 2014.

31. Cecilia Okoth, "Uganda Leads Region in Press Freedom," Cecilia Okoth, *New Vision*, September 25, 2013.

32. Keita, "Africa's Free Press Problem."

11

The Middle East: Media in the Midst of Turmoil

The Middle East is changing fast. In recent years, the region has witnessed several uprisings and revolutions leading to political change. In some countries the change has been more pervasive than in others and was more than political in nature; it also affected social and even psychological aspects of people's lives. The media systems in the Middle East have been part of this change and have been credited as a major factor behind the change. The rise of social media has contributed to the change in this part of the world and is credited as a major catalyst in promoting political and social change.

A few months before the wave of uprisings took over parts of the Middle East, a study identified three main "Big Bang" changes that have rocked media institutions in the region in the last twenty-five years. Those were the introduction of the Cable News Network (CNN) to the Middle East in 1991, ushering in an era of satellite television; the launch of Al Jazeera in 1996; and the introduction of the Internet in 1993.[1]

It is important to note that most media outlets in the Middle East are government-owned and controlled. The exceptions are in Lebanon, Iran, and Israel, and to a lesser extent, in Egypt and Saudi Arabia. Before 1991, when CNN and satellite television were introduced to this part of the world, there were hardly any privately owned media outlets in most of the Middle East and most media were monotone, basically echoing the voice of the government. Newsworthiness was never the main factor in how news items were structured on a news bulletin. Instead, the bulletin started with the meetings of the president or head of state on that day, followed by news of the prime minister, followed by senior state ministers and officials. There

The World News Prism: Digital, Social and Interactive, Ninth Edition.
William A. Hachten and James F. Scotton.
© 2016 John Wiley & Sons, Inc. Published 2016 by John Wiley & Sons, Inc.

was also no "television journalism" as we know it today. The news bulletin basically consisted of an anchor reading the news off some scattered pieces of paper, with footage of the president or state officials on the screen. Universal standards of journalism and newsworthiness were sacrificed for political protocol that left the news mundane and devoid of real content.

CNN and Satellite Television

This dull picture suddenly changed with the introduction of CNN in 1991, ushering in what was then the media revolution of satellite television. CNN became a phenomenon in the Arab world when it was introduced to Egypt and a few other Arab countries during the 1991 Gulf War. With the catchy slogan, "History as it Happens," CNN became an instant hit and found its way into the homes of Arabs who were suddenly transferred from the dull, mundane style of news they had to a war broadcast live on television. The effects were strong and instantaneous on viewers as well as on governments. Viewers had access, for the first time, to good-quality television journalism beamed into their living rooms, complete with sound effects, graphics, maps, statistics, and background information. This also meant that governments in the Middle East had to change their old ways of broadcasting to cope with this new phenomenon. Government television was no longer the sole source of news and information for the Middle Eastern viewer, and hiding information was no longer easy for governments. The first reaction of several Middle Eastern broadcasters was to try to imitate the CNN style of reporting in both content and format. They started producing, or at least attempting to produce, news in inverted pyramid style, and started introducing graphics and sound effects into the news bulletins. Although news about the head of state remained relatively high on these bulletins, a change could definitely be seen.

But perhaps the more important change was in officials' attitudes, as the repressive governments of the Middle East realized it would very difficult to "conceal" information from their citizens any more. The age of the open skies was ushered in through satellite television technology, and people had an option to seek news from different sources. This was a major change, as before that time Middle Eastern governments had taken it for granted that, if they didn't inform their citizens through government television, there was very little chance of them finding out what they were missing.[2] What they were missing was sometimes as major as a war. When Iraq invaded

Kuwait in 1991, Saudi Arabian television hid the news for three days. Saudi citizens found out from CNN and from US Armed Forces Television, which was beaming to the US forces that were stationed in the Gulf as part of the conflict. The advent of CNN basically ended the possibility that something like that could happen again and introduced the Middle East to the concept of a 24/7 news channel that was capable of holding its viewers' interest.

As direct broadcast satellite technology was becoming more popular, a huge market was opening up for governments and investors alike. The most popular content was Egyptian drama, both movies and serials. The first Arab satellite station in 1990 was the Egyptian Space Channel (now called Al Masriya, or The Egyptian). It was followed by Nile TV International, also out of Egypt, which to this day broadcasts in English, French, and Hebrew.

The affluent Gulf states established several networks, including the Saudi Middle East Broadcasting Centre (MBC). MBC started in September 1991 and tried to produce CNN-style news in addition to drama and entertainment. The network remains one of the biggest in the Middle East, with several channels dedicated mostly to Western movies and entertainment. It recently launched MBC Masr, focusing on news and entertainment from Egypt.

The second major network out of Saudi Arabia is Sheikh Saleh Kamel's Arab Radio and Television (ART), which started in 1994 and is composed of over twenty specialized entertainment channels, now operating on a subscription basis. The channels do not offer news programming, but instead specialize in a vast selection of entertainment programs, including Arabic serials, Arabic movies and entertainment, music, sports, and Western movies and sitcoms. Transmitted from a huge production center in Italy, ART also has a production center in Cairo's Media Production City as well as in several other Arab cities.

A third large Saudi network is Orbit, also subscription-based and operating from Italy. Orbit has more than sixty channels, including Western channels to suit every taste. In addition, it has a variety of Arabic channels, including one that airs a popular daily talk show *Al Qahira Al Youm* (*Cairo Today*).

Every Middle Eastern country soon felt the need for at least one satellite channel to broadcast its views and cultural programs to the world. The United Arab Emirates has a solid group of channels, airing mostly Western entertainment as well as some local and Arab drama. Lebanon also has popular entertainment channels, including the Lebanese Broadcasting Company (LBC) and Future Television.

Al Jazeera

Al Jazeera was launched in 1996 as the first Arabic-speaking 24/7 news channel. Based in the tiny Arab nation of Qatar, it has played a major role in bringing professional journalism to the Middle East, although its own journalistic standards have suffered recently because of severe bias toward the Muslim Brotherhood.

Al Jazeera was established by the Qatari emir, Sheikh Hamid bin Khalifa Al-Thani, who had overthrown his elderly father less than a year before in a peaceful coup. He announced he wanted to modernize Qatar and that he was abolishing censorship and the Ministry of Information, two unprecedented steps in the Arab world. He launched Al Jazeera (The Island) with a government gift of $137 million that was supposed to sustain the channel for five years. Al Jazeera inherited a BBC-trained staff that was about to launch a BBC Arabic channel as part of Orbit when plans fell through because the Saudi regime insisted on some censorship. That crew was hired to launch Al Jazeera, and so the Arab Middle East finally had its own Arabic-speaking 24/7 professional news channel.

Al Jazeera has attracted viewers but not advertisers, and remains dependent on the Qatari government for funding. This has created a problem in terms of its editorial independence. Mamoun Fandy has said it was "very difficult" for the channel to claim independence given that it receives an annual gift of over $300 million from the Qatari government and that some royal family members and senior government officials are amongst its highest-ranking officials.[3] This issue came to the light when the Muslim Brotherhood took power in Egypt in June 2012, but was heightened a year later when the army ousted President Mohamed Morsi, closely aligned with the Brotherhood. Al Jazeera lost much of its credibility when it broadcast massive anti-Morsi demonstrations describing them as pro-Morsi.

There is no denying, though, that Al Jazeera took public discourse in the Middle East to a different level. The level of professional journalism it practiced up until 2012 set the bar for television journalism in the Arab Middle East, and brought many issues that were previously taboo to the discussion table. But since its inception, controversial Qatari issues were have also been taboo, and the channel clearly reflects Qatar's foreign policy. While the channel regularly and openly criticizes *some* Arab leaders and features many controversial topics, Qatari leaders and Qatari issues are rarely discussed and comments on countries and their leaders are always closely related to Qatar's foreign policy at any given time.

Soon after Al Jazeera's launch, its main competitor, Al Arabiya, followed. Al Arabiya is a Saudi channel owned by the MBC group. However, this channel is also sometimes viewed as politicized as it closely follows the US political agenda. President Obama made his first media appearance in the Arab world on Al Arabiya just days after his inauguration. Al Arabiya does not have an English-language service, unlike Al Jazeera, which launched its Al Jazeera International channel in 2005. Both channels have elaborate Web portals in English and in Arabic.

The Evening Talk Show

Talk shows are a relatively new genre in the Middle East. They were first introduced to the region through CNN's *Crossfire*, then Al Jazeera followed suit with *The Opposite Direction*. The talk show genre represented an idea of wide appeal to the Arab Middle East, a place where citizens mostly only receive information from their governments through the media. The talk show represented debate and diversity of opinion, and as such created a new forum for exchange of ideas if only through the in-studio guests. The Egyptian satellite channel followed with its own talk show, which featured a news segment, followed by several segments of guests moderated by a presenter. It did not follow the *Crossfire* format, but it still provided more diversity of opinion and managed to escape the "shouting match" phenomenon which was characteristic of Al Jazeera's *The Opposite Direction*. What made it engaging for viewers, though, was the idea of participation through phone calls, and later through social media. This provided a wide window of opportunity for citizens who wanted to engage with the programs to express their opinions. Such simple examples of citizen participation, where the average viewer feels his or her voice is being heard, have added much value to the media scene in the Middle East. There are several talk shows competing for viewers' attention on major networks, including Orbit and several private Egyptian channels. These shows gained attention following the string of uprisings that started in the Arab world in 2011. Viewers are glued to their television screens for hours, zapping their remote controls between channels to watch segments of their favorite shows. Talk show presenters are paid millions of dollars a year, and regular talk show guests become instant celebrities.

Bassem Youssef and Political Satire

Bassem Youssef is a cardiac surgeon turned political satirist who has become something of a phenomenon in the Arab world. Dubbed the Jon Stewart of Egypt, Youssef's political satire career started when, a couple of months into Egypt's 2011 revolution, he started recording a half-hour political satire show in his own laundry room and posted it on YouTube. The show was amateurishly produced but well written and executed, and within a few months Youssef had attracted millions of viewers. The show, which mostly addressed the hypocrisy of Egyptian state television at the time in covering the events of the revolution, was an instant success and filled an important gap in political satire in the region. A few months later, Youssef landed a contract with private channel OnTV for *Al Bernameg* (*The Program*), with a budget of half a million dollars. The following year, Youssef moved to the CBC channel and his show was recorded with a live audience in a downtown Cairo theater. The show became a platform for criticizing politicians, the Muslim Brotherhood, the media, and the president, and proved very popular among audiences in the Arab world. Youssef's YouTube channel became the top subscribed-to channel in Egypt.

Youssef's satire show deserves attention for many reasons, including the fact that it was the first program to have started online and then converted to a television phenomenon. Several Egyptian groups and regimes have targeted Youssef for his outspoken critique of their policies. Early into his second season, lawsuits had already started against him, mostly for "defamation." In January 2013, he was investigated for "insulting the President," at the time Mohamed Morsi. In March, an arrest warrant was issued against Youssef for "insulting Islam and the President, and disturbing public peace," a move which advocates viewed as a dangerous sign of opposition to freedom of expression. He was released on bail of EGP 15,000 (about $2,200). True to his style, Youssef showed up to court in a huge black hat, modeled after the one Morsi wore as part of his academic regalia while receiving an honorary doctorate degree in Pakistan a month earlier. Youssef tweeted as he awaited the start of the investigation, "The officers and the lawyers of the public prosecutor's office want to take pictures with me. Is this the reason for the summons?"

Youssef has become a media celebrity and was featured repeatedly on many international media outlets including *Time* magazine, *The New York Times*, the *Guardian*, CNN, and the BBC. He became good friends with

Jon Stewart and appeared several times on his show. Stewart also appeared as a guest on Youssef's show, and wrote the entry when Youssef was ranked thirty-ninth on *Time*'s 2013 list of the 100 most influential people in the world.[4] Youssef was also awarded the 2013 International Press Freedom Award of the Committee to Protect Journalists, and received the award from Jon Stewart.[5]

Youssef took some time off after the end of his second season of *Al Bernameg*, during which period the army ousted Mohamed Morsi. He returned to CBC in October 2013 with an episode that apparently upset everyone in power. He criticized the failings of the Muslim Brotherhood regime which he said had led to its downfall, but also criticized the army-backed government and the tone of adulation and glorification of the army's commander, General Abdel Fattah El Sisi. He asserted that Egyptians needed to be careful not to replace religious fascism with another type of fascism in the name of national security and fighting terrorism. At the end of a comic musical sketch, one of his aides said that El Sisi had carried out a military coup, a scene which ended with Youssef shutting the aide's mouth with his hands and escorting him off stage to music. The next day, CBC issued a statement distancing itself from the episode and said it was "keen on not using phrases and innuendos that may lead to mocking national sentiment or symbols of the Egyptian state."[6] The following week, Youssef's show was canceled a few minutes before it was due to go on air. Negotiations with CBC failed, and he left the channel to join MBC Masr. Youssef's program was again blocked, supposedly temporarily, during the 2014 presidential elections. However, he announced in June 2014 that he was permanently ending the show out of fear that the political climate in Egypt would not tolerate his sarcasm.

The Internet and Social Media

The last few years have been characterized by a huge surge in Internet use in the Arab world, particularly in the countries that have witnessed revolutions or uprisings. Generally speaking, Internet use has risen sharply in the Middle East since the turn of the millennium, with user numbers increasing from 3.2 million in 2000 to over 90 million by July 2012, with a penetration rate of over 40 percent, higher than the 34 percent world average. The region has witnessed a growth rate of 2,640 percent during these twelve years, almost five times the overall world average growth rate. The greatest Internet penetration is in Qatar, where 86 percent of the population has Internet access, followed by Bahrain at 77 percent, Kuwait at 74 percent, and the United Arab Emirates at 71 percent. These are followed by Israel at 70 percent (with 57 percent in Palestine). Even in Iran and Saudi Arabia, where Internet use is controlled and sometimes dangerous, about half of the population is online.[7]

Some of these numbers are worth a closer look. For example, Internet use in Tunisia during the last six years increased from 9 percent to over 39 percent. In Libya, it increased from 6 percent in 2010 to 17 percent in 2012, while in Egypt, it rose from 21 percent in 2010 to over 44 percent in 2013. The increase in Internet use, especially in countries that have witnessed uprisings or revolutions, was accompanied by a sharp increase in the use of social media, particularly Facebook and Twitter. In Egypt for example, there were 4 million Facebook users when the revolution started in January 2011, but by 2014 there were 17 million.

The Internet and social media have helped bring about a wave of uprisings in the Arab world. While revolutions cannot be credited solely to social media, the new online forms of expression have certainly acted as a catalyst and accelerated a process that started many years before their advent. Social media "played a vital role as a democratic model. . . . [Their] inclusive space indirectly taught lessons in democracy to a wide sector of Egyptian youth that was not necessarily politically inclined. When the right moment arrived, they were ready to join the revolt."[8] Many youth of the Arab world, who were used to being talked at by everyone in authority (including their parents), suddenly found a space that they can truly call their own, even if it was virtual. A new public sphere became available for information exchange and horizontal discussions, including political discussions. Young people could finally talk to each other rather than be talked at vertically in a one-way monologue.

Another way the Internet helped in accelerating activism and revolt in the Arab world was to show people that they were not alone in their struggles and/or dismay. Rather, they were joined by hundreds of thousands, if not millions, who suffered the same problems and could not find a way to have a voice or to organize. Social media played a major role in creating political awareness, luring youth to political discussions they would not have ventured into before. When the right moment came, they were the main tool for organizing and providing timely information and advice. Egypt's revolution started on January 25, 2011. It was posted as an event on Facebook eleven days before, where people were literally clicking that they were "attending" the revolution.

Some have argued that Facebook unconsciously helped create a democratic atmosphere in some Arab countries through providing a space for political (and other) discussions. Facebook also showed dismayed citizens that they were not alone through the power of horizontal rather than vertical communication. On Facebook, any young person is the ruler of his or her domain. On their individual Facebook pages, these individuals are the center of attention. Their "friends" are there to see what they post and read and comment on what they write. This could be visualized as a circle of "friends" where only the individual is inside the circle. But in order to play the social media game, the person at the center has at some point to click on a friend's name to interact with them, and at that point that friend becomes the center of the circle and the person clicking moves to the periphery. That interactive state where one is listened to but eventually has to listen provides the core of the horizontal communication model that the youth in the Arab world lacked. Facebook and other social media helped by showing young people, particularly those who were not politically oriented before, that their voices counted.[9]

The role of social media in political participation started with their very basic form, blogs. Blogging became popular in the Middle East around the mid-2000s as it provided a forum for activists on the ground to portray their activism to audiences that otherwise would never have heard of them. The authoritarian media system in the Middle East meant that only what the government approved of made it through. Political blogging started to become popular, and a few bloggers became stars. With followings of 50,000–70,000 people, a blogger's reach was increasing to match that of major daily newspapers. Among those early bloggers were Alaa Abdel Fattah and his wife Manal Hassan, who created one of Egypt's earliest and most popular blogs, "Manal and Alaa's Bit Bucket." Acting also as a blog aggregator for major bloggers in the Arab world, they documented their offline activism and posted credible information on protests and political movements, election monitoring and rigging, and police brutality. The blog was awarded the Special Award from Reporters Without Borders in the international Deutsche Welle's 2005 Weblog Awards (Best of Blogs) contest, where it was cited as an instrumental information source for the country's human rights and democratic reform movement. Abdel Fattah was detained four times by the authorities and kept in jail for up to two months. Even jail, however, does not silence most bloggers. Abdel Fattah managed to write several notes from jail that his supporters posted on the Internet. A few were even published in a major daily newspaper. The crackdown on bloggers and online dissidents in repressive countries is clear testimony to their potential impact and to the headache that they constitute to these authoritarian regimes.

Wael Abbas is another Egyptian award-winning blogger. Abbas received the 2007 Knight International Journalism Award of the International Center for Journalists for "raising the standards of media excellence" in his country. This was the first time that a blogger, rather than a traditional journalist, had won this prestigious journalism award. CNN in 2007 named Abbas Middle East Person of the Year. He (along with others, including Malek Mostafa) has been instrumental in bringing to light videos of election rigging and police brutality in Egypt, topics that were taboo before bloggers exposed them. As a result, the Egyptian government brought three police officers to court on charges of police brutality for the first time in Egypt's history, where they were convicted and sentenced to three years in jail.

Blogger efforts were aided by the introduction of YouTube in 2005, which made it possible to actually "show" evidence of violations in different arenas, and made it easier for bloggers to win the trust of their audiences. At a time when small political movements were being formed (for example, the National Coalition for Change, also known as Kefaya [Enough] in Egypt), YouTube helped bring visibility to their efforts. It is one thing to hear that thirty people made a stand outside the Journalists Syndicate and shouted "Down with Hosni Mubarak," but it's a totally different thing to see a video of it.

Blogging exploded in the Middle East, with nearly half a million bloggers by 2009, the majority in Egypt. Outside of Egypt, other political bloggers were getting noticed. In Tunisia, Sami Ben Gharbia's efforts offline and online forced him to live as a political refugee in the Netherlands from 1998 until the fall of President Zein El Abidine Bin Ali in 2011. In 2004, Ben Gharbia co-founded a major collective blog and aggregator, Nawaat (Core). The portal was established to provide a voice to Tunisian dissidents. Nawaat played an important role in the months before and during the Tunisian revolution, providing information on security online and advice on how to organize, and exposing the atrocities of the regime. The website has won several important awards, including the Reporters Without Borders Netizen Award. Other bloggers active within Nawaat included co-founder Riadh Guerfali (known as Astrubal), Malek Khadhraoui, and Lilia Weslaty. They have all fought the Bin Ali regime, frequently using the Internet as their main tool. Astrubal is a Tunisian lawyer and human rights activist, has been active online since the introduction of the Internet in the early 1990s. Astrubal's special concern with issues of freedom of expression was recognized in 2011 by an award from Reporters Without Borders.[10] Lilia Weslaty is a young Tunisian journalist also active online before the revolution, posting anonymous short videos exposing the regime.[11]

Some important blogs by youthful critics have come out of some very repressive countries, such as Saudi Arabia. Fouad al-Farhan blogs in Arabic about political reform in Saudi Arabia and the Arab world. He blogs under his real name, one of only a few Saudi bloggers willing to take this risk. Al-Farhan was arrested in 2007 and held without charge for four months. While in jail he slipped out a message, posted on his blog by friends, revealing that he was promised release if he apologized for his online activism, a deal which he refused.[12]

Ahmed Al Omran is another pioneer Saudi blogger: he operates the popular English-language blog Saudi Jeans. The blog started in 2004 as a social blog and within a few months delved into politics. Al Omran is a multimedia journalist with a Master's degree from the Graduate School of Journalism at Columbia University in New York, His blog was one of the first out of Saudi Arabia, which is why he has been dubbed "the Saudi blogfather." He focuses on issues of freedom of expression, plurality, and human rights, especially women's rights.

Saudi female activist Manal al-Sharif has been at the forefront of a campaign defying the ban on women driving in the kingdom. Al-Sharif co-started a campaign called "Women2Drive," using a Facebook page as the main advocacy tool. She and other women drove their cars and posted videos of their driving on YouTube. As a result, she and many other women were briefly detained by the authorities. Al-Sharif was named one of the Top 100 global thinkers by *Foreign Policy* magazine in 2011. *Time* magazine also named her one of the 100 most influential people in 2012. She received a prize for Creative Dissent at the Oslo Freedom Forum in the same year.

Indeed, female bloggers in the Arab Middle East have established themselves on the scene. In addition to the blogs created by Saudi Arabia's Manal al-Sharif, Egypt's Manal Hassan, and Tunisia's Lilia Weslaty, interesting and important blogs have been created and maintained by Mona Elfarra in Palestine, Razan Ghazzawi in Syria, Zeinobia and Baheya ya Masr in Egypt, Lina Ben Mhenni in Tunisia, and Loujain Al Hathloul and Arab Lady in Saudi Arabia, to name just a few.

Even online activists were surprised by how far they could go and how much they could accomplish. One key moment was April 6, 2008 in Egypt, when a female blogger named Esraa Abdel Fattah created a Facebook page in support of striking workers in the industrial city of Al Mahalla Al Kobra. More than 70,000 Egyptians joined the page, an unprecedented figure at the time. This marked the initiation of the April 6 Youth Movement, later to play a major role in organizing the revolution.[13] "The Internet is our battle-field," said Ahmed Maher, the movement's coordinator.[14] Abdel Fattah was detained for two weeks in 2008, and Maher has been detained several times. He and two other prominent activists received three-year jail sentences for organizing an unauthorized protest.

No discussion of the impact of social media on political participation in the Arab Middle East would be complete without mentioning the "We Are All Khaled Said" page on Facebook. Khaled Said was a young Egyptian beaten to death by police informants outside an Internet café in Alexandria in 2010. This Facebook page, run by Google marketing executive Wael Ghonim and his friends, appeared shortly after his death, and asked a growing audience to silently protest his murder by standing in black shirts with their backs to the street. The demonstrations soon spread to every part of Egypt, with more people joining daily. The page is credited with hosting a massive demonstration on January 25, 2011, Egypt's annual Police Day. The site provided exact times and locations, and information on what to wear and what to do, as well as emergency contact numbers. In the months preceding that day, the administrators of the page gave Egyptians a little taste of democracy by asking them to vote for the best places in which to demonstrate. Thousands of responses were tabulated and posted. This was one small act that showed participants that their vote counted and that they could actually have a say in decisions. It also gave credibility to the page, and helped generate a massive response when the revolution "event" was posted.

Governments in the Middle East are increasingly taking notice of the threat posed to their repressive regimes by online activists. Their reactions vary from monitoring email communication, social media, and websites to detaining and torturing activists, sometimes to death. Some governments are more repressive than others. Saudi Arabia may have the most elaborate Internet filtering process, centralizing all Internet messages via one government control point, and monitoring Internet content through US-made software called SmartFilter.[15] The kingdom is proud of its filtering and claims it is necessary to "protect Saudi youth" from evil Western influence. The Saudis block websites concerned with pornography, drugs, and gambling, but also those discussing politics, sex education or sexual orientation, human rights, including women's rights and children's rights, online privacy tools, religious conversion, non-monotheistic religions, and sometimes even websites discussing any other version of Islam but the fundamentalist Wahabi version that is dominant in Saudi Arabia.[16] Also blocked are websites containing images of "provocative" attire or naked body parts. As a result, many medical websites are blocked if they contain pictures of body parts or words such as "sex" or "breast" (even as in "breast cancer").[17]

Another Middle Eastern country with pervasive Internet filtering is Iran, which became much harsher in its Internet control after the 2009 elections and the riots that followed. All Internet traffic in and out of Iran goes through one government-controlled portal. However, as in Saudi Arabia or any other repressive country, tech-savvy users can use proxy servers to access blocked websites anonymously. In 2006 twenty Iranian female journalists founded the website Change for Equality after the closure of all women's print magazines. The website received the Reporters Without Borders first Netizen Award in 2010. There are over 70,000 active blogs in Iran, a country that severely punishes online dissidents. Four Internet activists have been sentenced to death for "anti-government agitation," "misleading the youth," "threatening morality," "publishing false information," and "insulting Islam." In addition, blogger Sattar Beheshti died in police custody and Iranian bloggers Hossein Derakhshan and Sakhi Righi each received a twenty-year prison sentence, the longest ever for a blogger. Reporters Without Borders deemed Iran "the world's biggest prison for journalists." The Iranian regime demonizes new media, claiming that they are the West's tools for destroying Iranian youth.[18]

Bahrain has also been cracking down on Internet activists. The government has successfully implemented a media blackout on the uprising that started in 2011, making it difficult for the outside world to know what was happening. The only outlet for activists is the Internet, hence the crackdown. There are some avid users of social media, particularly Twitter, in Bahrain. These include blogger Zainab Alkhawaja, jailed in 2014; her sister Maryam Alkhawaja who blogs from exile in Denmark; and human rights defender Nabeel Rajab, also jailed. One of the country's pioneer bloggers, Ali Abdulemam, was arrested and tortured in September 2010 for his activism. After his release in 2011, he went into hiding shortly before he and twenty other activists were tried before a military court. He was sentenced to fifteen years in prison in absentia. In 2013 Abdulemam fled and the United Kingdom granted him political asylum.[19]

Syria is another staunch enemy of the Internet. The country stepped up its already harsh crackdown on Internet freedoms with the start of the uprising and subsequent clashes in 2011. In a country where plainclothes police officers roam Internet cafés and a blogger received a nine-month prison sentence for forwarding a political joke, the Internet remains an important tool for sending out messages despite the risks.[20]

In Jordan, the government imposed strict online censorship in June 2013, blocking more than 300 news websites. In October, a letter to King Abdullah II of Jordan signed by twenty-two human rights organizations expressed concern over online censorship and new media "policies that effectively silence independent voices of information."[21]

Although a complete shutdown of the Internet can have disastrous economic and business consequences, Syria on several occasions has blocked access to the network in parts of the country. But perhaps the biggest crackdown came in Egypt, when the Mubarak regime shut down the Internet in the entire country for five days during the initial eighteen days of demonstrations that led to his downfall. Egypt does not block websites although, as noted earlier, the country has targeted online activists. Blogger Maikel Nabil was tried before a military court and given a three-year prison sentence for a blog he wrote in March 2011 entitled "The Army and the People Were Never One Hand." He was pardoned after spending ten months in jail. Former parliamentarian and professor of political science Amr Hamzawy was accused of "insulting the judiciary" in a tweet he wrote commenting on a court case. In June 2014 the Ministry of Interior issued a request for proposals for software that would monitor online and social networks. The software would monitor popular social networks such as Facebook, Twitter, and YouTube as well as private messaging and telephone applications such as WhatsApp, Skype, and Viber.

The Print Media

There are countless publications in the Middle East, mainly in Arabic but also in English, French, and several other languages including Farsi, Hebrew, and Turkish. Newspapers vary enormously throughout the Middle East, ranging from Lebanon's free dailies in Arabic, English, and French to Iran's tightly controlled publications, mainly in Farsi.

William Rugh has classified the Arab press into four categories. The Mobilization Press, represented by Libya, Syria, Sudan, and pre-2003 Iraq, is characterized by tight control and the use of media to propagate government messages and state positions. The Loyalist Press in Bahrain, Palestine, Oman, Qatar, Saudi Arabia, and the UAE is characterized by a system where private media may exist, but they still support the regime and provide little if any criticism of the system, thereby adding no real diversity of opinion. The Transitional Press is found in Egypt, Jordan, Algeria, and Tunisia, where journalists strive for slightly more freedom and attempt to criticize the government, although significant control is still prevalent. More plurality is found in countries with a Diverse Press system, primarily Lebanon, followed by Morocco, Yemen, and Kuwait.[22]

The remarkably diverse society of Lebanon is credited with giving it the freest press in the Middle East, despite also giving it internal political strife and a greater bias on the part of each faction of the media. The press is largely divided among different political and/or religious factions, with each representing the voice of its particular community in Lebanon's political strife.[23] Lebanon had its first weekly newspaper, *Hadiqat al-Akhbar* (*The News Garden*), by 1858. The four leading Lebanese dailies are in Arabic, followed by the French *Orient de Jour* and the English *Daily Star*. Lebanon's newspapers are free of government control but political party subsidies and ties to various sects tend to restrict their independence.[24]

In nearby Jordan, there is little direct government editorial intervention, although the media environment is getting more repressive and editors often practice "self-censorship" to avoid potential lawsuits. Recent media laws have made newspapers and news websites legally responsible not only for their content but for their readers' comments. Jordan was the only Muslim country where two newspapers reprinted some of the Danish cartoons of the Prophet Muhammad that set off riots in several cities worldwide. However, the two editors were detained and at least one of them was fired.[25]

A major barrier to publishing throughout the Arab world is licensing laws. The publications, the printing presses, and even most journalists require licenses from the government. Private media licenses are rarely granted in most Arab countries, and when granted are only for businessmen closely connected to the government. Some choose to publish in neighboring countries such as Cyprus, and fly the printed copies back to their own country. They then face another problem, as usually a censor has to approve each issue of this "foreign" publication. Media laws are always vague, and while theoretically granting freedom of expression, usually leave much room for censorship. Editors also exercise self-censorship to avoid high-cost problems with the authorities. The laws usually restrict defamation of royal families, presidents, ministers, and other government officials, thereby greatly restricting criticism of the regime.

Sometimes self-censorship goes to extremes as editors try to please those in power. Egypt's *Al-Ahram* (*The Pyramid*) newspaper was established in 1875, and is one of the most influential newspapers in the Arab world. In September 2010, the government newspaper published a doctored photograph showing Mubarak at the head of a group of Middle East leaders and US President Barack Obama at the White House. In the original picture, Obama was leading the group with Mubarak at the back. A blogger caught the photo manipulation and alerted the public via social media. *Al-Ahram's* response was that the picture is an "expressionist" portrayal of the role of Mubarak as a leader. In 2013 a front-page story by the newspaper's editor in chief implied that the United States was a partner in an alleged conspiracy with the Muslim Brotherhood to "sabotage" Egypt. In reaction, the former US ambassador had to issue a public response, where she called the story "outrageous, fictitious, and thoroughly unprofessional." Ambassador Anne Patterson added, "This article isn't bad journalism; it isn't journalism at all. It is fiction."[26]

Al-Ahram is unfortunately typical of many government newspapers in the Middle East. Readers are faced with continual rhetoric glorifying the head of the country, as the press calls him a "father," a "leader," and a "savior," or, as *Al-Ahram* said of Mubarak, "the most trusted leader in the world."[27] On the other hand, on January 26, 2011, the day following the start of Egypt's revolution, *Al-Ahram's* main story covered a protest in Lebanon. And on February 3 the paper's banner headline said, "Millions March to Support Mubarak Nationwide." Mubarak stepped down on February 11, and the next day *Al-Ahram* totally changed its tune. The banner headline said, "The People Have Toppled the Regime." The same newspaper that glorified Mubarak and then, very briefly, the people of Egypt, soon started glorifying the Supreme Council of Armed Forces and its leader at the time, General Hussein Tantawi.[28]

The Future

The Middle East is changing fast. The most pervasive change is the spread of the Internet and social media, and that is likely to continue with different platforms and different applications that serve new functions. The question is to what extent these media can help foster democratic change in the region.

The last few years have shown that despite the plethora of media outlets in some countries, pluralism is not always the outcome. Governments in the Middle East are so in control of the media that they are making it very difficult for anyone to sing a different tune on traditional media from what governments want. Fortunately, the Internet provides the ultimate exception. From Cairo to Tehran, online activists are finding ways to create new content, in new formats, and trying to spread it to as many people as possible, even beyond the boundaries of the Internet. A few examples: in Egypt, Mosireen (Determined), a group of independent filmmakers and activists, has vowed to document the revolution and provide a challenging narrative to the conforming traditional media. They publish videos provided by anyone who has a camera or a mobile phone and who has managed to film an incident related to the revolution. The extensive library of revolution footage on their website is available to the public. They also offer their expertise by providing training, technical support, equipment, or a place for others to work.[29]

Online news portals by young journalists are also developing throughout the Middle East. In Tunisia, Nawaat is exposing issues related to human rights in Arabic and French. In Jordan, Ammon News has established itself as a credible source in Arabic and in English. In Egypt, Mada Masr is a news portal run by a group of young journalists who refuse to follow the restrictive editorial policies of one of the country's daily newspapers. They resigned and started their own online project. Such outlets are gaining more followers and more credibility every day.

There is much reason to be hopeful for the Middle East region both in terms of the media and in terms of political and social change, despite the regimes' continued attempts to crack down on freedoms. For one thing, the region has a young population, with young people comprising over half of the population of most countries. These are motivated tech-savvy individuals who have tasted a bit of freedom over the last few years and are trying to achieve a dream of a better life for their countries. Such change is irreversible. It might take longer to achieve democracy than these people had originally thought, and it might cost them more sacrifices and more lives, but it is the inevitable light at the end of the tunnel. Media institutions and policies are part of the core system of any country, and so change is inevitable there too. The catch is that major reform requires political will, which seems to be non-existent at the moment. However, the Internet and new media are making it more possible for youth to create little cracks in the system. The question is how big the cracks are, and when the tsunami will hit. Probably only then will a major reform of the traditional media sectors in these countries be possible.

Notes

1. Rasha Abdulla, "The Changing Middle East Media over the Past 20 Years: Opportunities and Challenges," in *The Changing Middle East*, B. Korany, ed. (Cairo: The American University in Cairo Press, 2010).

2. Rasha Abdulla, "An Overview of Media Developments in Egypt: Does the Internet Make a Difference?," *Global Media Journal – Mediterranean Edition*, 1(1), 2006, 88–100.

3. Mamoun Fandy, *(Un)Civil War of Words: Media and Politics in the Arab World* (London: Praeger, 2007), 47.

4. Bassem Youssef, "TIME 100," April 23, 2013.

5. CPJ Annual Press Awards 2013.

6. Patrick Kingsley, "Egyptian Satirist Bassem Youssef Upsets All Sides on Return to TV," *Guardian*. October 28, 2013.

7. Internet World Statistics 2012; www.internetworldstats.com/stats.htm.

8. Rasha Abdulla, "The Revolution Will Be Tweeted," *Cairo Review*, 1(3), 2011.

9. Abdulla, "The Revolution Will Be Tweeted."

10. Abdulla, "The Revolution Will Be Tweeted."

11. http://www.nawaat.org.

12. Faiza Ambah, "Dissident Saudi Blogger Is Arrested," *Washington Post*, January 1, 2008.

13. Abdulla, "The Revolution Will Be Tweeted."

14. Heba Saleh, "Arab Dissent Finds Voice in Cyberspace," *Financial Times*, July 2, 2009.

15. Rasha Abdulla, *The Internet in the Arab World: Egypt and Beyond* (New York: Peter Lang, 2007); Rasha Abdulla, *Policing the Internet in the Arab World*, Emirates Occasional Papers (Abu Dhabi, UAE: Emirates Center for Strategic Study and Research, 2009).

16. Open Net Initiative, "Internet Filtering in Saudi Arabia," 2009. https://opennet.net/research/profiles/saudi-arabia (retrieved January 3, 2014).

17. Abdulla, *Policing the Internet in the Arab World*; Abdulla, *The Internet in the Arab World*.

18. "Iran," Reporters Without Borders, 2013.

19. Peter Beaumont, "Bahrain Online Founder Ali Abdulemam Breaks Silence after Escape to UK," *Guardian*, May 10, 2013.

20. "Syria," Reporters Without Borders, 2013.

21. "International Free Expression Groups Call for an End to Internet Censorship in Jordan," Reporters Without Borders, October 7, 2013.

22. William Rugh, *Arab Mass Media: Newspapers, Radio, and Television in Arab Politics* (New York: Praeger, 2004).

23. Rugh, *Arab Mass Media.*

24. Ami Ayalon, *The Press in the Arab Middle East: A History* (New York: Oxford University Press, 1995), 73–106.

25. "Two Jordan Editors are Arrested," BBC News, February 4, 2006.

26. Ambassador Patterson's Letter to Al Ahram Newspaper, Embassy of the United States of America, August 28, 2013; http://egypt.usembassy.gov/pr-082913.html.

27. "Mubarak Is the Most Trusted Leader in the World," *Al-Ahram*, June 18, 2008, 1.

28. Kam McGrath, "Egypt: State Media has New Bosses, Old Habits," Inter Press Service, August 7, 2011.

29. http://www.mosireen.org.

12

Reporters Abroad:
Paid, Free, and Harassed

The craft of gathering foreign news by journalists stationed overseas has been undergoing substantial changes in recent years. Because of financial cost-cutting and new technologies, less news is reported from abroad and by very different methods. The foreign correspondent – that widely traveled and glamorous specialist of journalism – is becoming a different breed of reporter from the old days of the Cold War. The public today seems less interested in foreign news, and editors and broadcasters are giving them a lot less of it. Yet, on the other hand, as we have seen, the Internet and new media tell a different story: great amounts of news and useful public information are readily available to users of computers and social media.

In the brief two centuries of global news reporting, changes in news are linked to changes in the technology of news gathering. In the nineteenth century, news was collected by reporters who later used telephones, and then the telegraph – hence, the "telegraph editor" long a mainstay on newspapers. For news from abroad, the press relied on journalists' letters carried by ships – hence the "foreign correspondent" who resided in a foreign capital – a term that has persisted long after news began arriving via international telephones and comsats and now the Internet. With instantaneous two-way global communication the foreign correspondent and his "foreign bureau" have become anachronisms. News gathering today is more and more a cooperative and collaborative enterprise with more reliance on "other" non-professional media to initially gather news. And as mentioned, global media still get much of their news from print-on-paper journals.

The World News Prism: Digital, Social and Interactive, Ninth Edition.
William A. Hachten and James F. Scotton.
© 2016 John Wiley & Sons, Inc. Published 2016 by John Wiley & Sons, Inc.

During the decade before 9/11, the news media were somewhat indifferent to foreign news at a time when ethnic conflicts killed millions and globalization touched most American communities. During the 1970s, network television devoted 45 percent of its total coverage to international news. By 1995, foreign news represented only 13.5 percent of total coverage. Budgets and staff were cut, bureaus closed, and the media emphasized shifts to economic and entertainment/trivia concerns.

Yet serious journalists and editors have long argued that foreign news is important and should be reported thoroughly and well. Many of the best and brightest journalists have spent part of their career in what must be among the most demanding jobs in journalism. Transnational news gathering is an exacting occupation for the professional newsmen and newswomen who put together the various stories, reports, rumors, and educated guesses that make up the daily international news file. To them, theirs is a difficult, dangerous, and badly misunderstood enterprise. They understand its shortcomings and difficulties far better, they believe, than politically motivated critics or cost-conscious media owners.

In a real sense, the world's ability to learn the news about itself depends on what gets into the news flow in the fifteen or twenty open societies with highly developed media systems. After an important story appears, for example, in New York, London, Paris, Berlin, or Tokyo, it immediately starts flowing through the arteries of the world's news system and will be widely reported elsewhere – but not everywhere, and certainly not every story; the majority of non-Western governments act as gatekeepers, screening news in and out of their nations. These political controls, as well as poverty and illiteracy, deprive the great majority of the world's peoples from learning even the barest outline of major current events. But any major story that "breaks" in the West has at least the possibility of being reported throughout the world. To the few thousand foreign correspondents, the world's nations are strung out on a continuum, from "free" or open at one end to "not free" or closed at the other, and with many variations in between. To illustrate, the Associated Press has little difficulty gathering news in open Sweden, because several newspapers there take AP services and share their own news and photos with the agency. In addition, AP correspondents can use other Swedish media as sources and can develop their own stories or easily gain access to public officials.

Sudan, like other developing nations, offers a different kind of challenge. AP has no clients in Sudan, largely because the Sudan News Agency lacks the hard currency to buy the Comsat-beamed AP world service. The local media are subject to official controls, and AP cannot justify the expense of maintaining a full-time correspondent in Khartoum. Therefore, AP "covers" Sudan by using a local stringer (a part-timer who is paid for what news is used). Periodically, AP may send a staff correspondent to Sudan to do background or round-up stories. At other times, AP may try to report on events in Sudan from Nairobi, in neighboring Kenya. Yet as recent events in Sudan have illustrated, the world knew too little about a state that condoned, if not encouraged, genocide against its own people. Despite the efforts of a few hardy reporters who managed to get into Darfur to report the atrocities against helpless civilians, the United Nations has still not taken effective action to halt the genocide.

At the "not free" end of the continuum are a few countries that for years barred all foreign journalists and news agencies. In the Cold War days, when something important happened in Tirana, Albania, for instance, AP and the world usually found out about it belatedly from a government-controlled Albanian radio broadcast monitored abroad, or from travelers or diplomats leaving the country. Albania has since opened, and Western analysts were surprised that Albanian refugees knew about the collapse of communism, which they learned about by listening carefully to English broadcasts on the BBC and the Voice of America (VOA). Much news of the turmoil in Africa is often reported from the safety of neighboring countries.

A foreign correspondent often defines a country as free or not free according to how much difficulty he or she has in reporting events there. This may sound narrow and self-serving, but it has validity: the freedom of access that a foreign reporter enjoys is usually directly related to the amount of independence and access enjoyed by local journalists themselves. If local journalists are harassed or news media are controlled by a particular government, so, very likely, will be the foreign journalists. With the availability of impressive gadgets used by today's foreign correspondents – satellite telephones, videophones, laptop computers, social media, Twitter, Facebook, and even reliable phone lines (or better yet cellphones), and faxes – the reporter abroad is able to do his or her job better. An important recent gadget is the video telephone so widely used in Afghanistan. Even so, collecting news throughout the world is still an erratic and imperfect process. Some significant events are either not reported or reported long after the fact. Certain areas of the world, such as Central Africa, rarely get into the world news flow.

In the dangerous and confusing post-Cold War world, foreign reporters and news organizations went through an identity crisis over what is news. As

John Walcott of *Newsweek* said, "The Cold War provided us with a coherent global road map, in terms of what to cover and how to cover it."[1] The press is not used to reacting to a world full of conflicts and violent encounters that, as George Kennan put it, offer no "great and all absorbing focal points for American policy."[2] The war on terrorism provided for some nations a focus for global news comparable to that of the Cold War.

A key challenge is disagreements between journalists and government officials over the very nature of news. To journalists, news is the first, fragmentary, and incomplete report of a significant event or happening that editors think will be of interest or importance to their readers or listeners. To many government officials, news is "positive" information that reflects favorably on their nation (and hence themselves) and serves their country's general interests and goals. Yet those same leaders want to know all that is happening elsewhere that affects their own interests and countries. An AP man once said that news is what a government official wants to read about somewhere else, whereas propaganda is what the official wants the world to read about his or her country. Politicians and government leaders in every nation attempt to manage or manipulate the news so that it favors their causes, their programs, their image. Any major news story is perceived differently by the press in almost every country for these reasons. Media everywhere tend to have a "bias of nationalism" that affects the way a story is reported. What has been called "journalism as politics" permeates foreign news in subtle ways. Moreover, the maxim "all news is local" has validity because editors usually respond more fully to what happens nearby or what affects local interests.

Certainly, before 9/11 the news media, especially television and news magazines, had been paying less attention to foreign news. Always expensive to cover, the consensus in the news business had been that you can expect international news to turn a profit only when it is really domestic news in a foreign setting, such as a US military intervention, when it is "our boys" who are "over there," as in Afghanistan or Iraq. Even among Western nations, there can be profound differences on issues such as free speech and access to news versus the right to privacy. In February 2010, an Italian court ruled that Google had violated Italian privacy law by allowing users to post a video on one of its services. The ruling raised the issue of how much responsibility Google has for offensive material that it passively distributes. But it also called attention to the profound European commitment to privacy which runs headlong into the American concept of free expression. This standoff could restrict the flow of information on the Internet to everyone. Because of World War II experiences, the right of privacy is to Europeans a basic human right. Free press advocates usually support the view of Walter Cronkite that the press should be free to go where it wants, to see, hear, and photograph what it believes to be in the public interest. That view is basic to the American/British press practices and is being gradually accepted by media around the world. International journalism seems to be groping for uniformity of law to protect journalists and the public interest.

CBS News, long famed for its international coverage, once maintained twenty-four foreign bureaus. By 2005, it had reporters in only four overseas cities: London, Moscow, Tel Aviv, and Tokyo. Dan Rather told a group of Harvard students, "Don't kid yourself. The trend line in American journalism is away from, not toward, increased foreign coverage. Foreign coverage requires the most space and the most air time because you are dealing with complicated situations, in which you have to explain a lot. And then there's always somebody around who says people don't give a damn about this stuff anyway … 'If you have to do something foreign, Dan, for heaven's sake, keep it short.'"[3] Tom Fenton, a former CBS reporter, recently wrote that foreign news is down 70 to 80 percent since the early 1980s, supplemented by "junk news" and "tabloidism." Meanwhile, the all-news cable channels – once our great hope – degenerate to celebrity and commentary formulas, offering little credible reporting. One of the most alarming comments in Fenton's book is as follows: "In the three months leading up to September 11, the phrase 'Al Qaeda' was never mentioned on any of the three evening news broadcasts – not once. I, and scores of my fellow American foreign correspondents, had been tracking stories about Al Qaeda and its allies for more than a decade. But we rarely reported what we knew on network news – because, much of the time, our bosses didn't consider such developments newsworthy."[4] Fenton said CBS relies increasingly on information supplied by video wire services and overseas broadcasters. It is television's equivalent of outsourcing.

In 2009 CBS News announced that it had formed a partnership with GlobalPost, a foreign news website that would provide CBS with reporting from its seventy affiliated correspondents in fifty countries. CBS suggested that the alliance with GlobalPost for which the network would pay a monthly undisclosed fee was really an expansion of CBS News' efforts to cover the rest of the world. Others saw it as indicative of the continued decline of the news organization's proud traditions associated with such greats as Edward R. Murrow, Walter Cronkite, and Eric Sevareid.

Meanwhile a rival, ABC News, has gone through several downsizing stints. In April 2010, the news unit of the Disney Company completed one of the most drastic rounds of budget cuts and firings at a television news operation – roughly one-quarter of the staff, over 100 people, were laid off. Then in September 2010, David Westin, the ABC news chief, resigned after fourteen years. ABC News, long a solid second to NBC News, found it hard to compete without a cable outlet such as MSNBC, and was unable to increase revenue, share labor, and reduce costs. Television journalists were stunned by these developments, and the capability of television news to cover global news seemed seriously diminished.[5]

Changing Correspondents

"What is commonly referred to as the world flow of information," AP correspondent Mort Rosenblum wrote, "is more a series of trickles and spurts. News is moved across borders by a surprisingly thin network of correspondents. . . . The smaller countries are squeezed into rapid trips during lulls between major stories in the larger countries." Rosenblum quoted a comment from a Latin American academic that "news breaks in South America along the direct line of the international airline route."[6] In some places it may seem that way, and yet the total flood of daily news reports from abroad is immense. One study estimated that the big four agencies send out about 33 million words a day, with 17 million from AP, 11 million from UPI, 3.4 million from AFP, and 1.5 million from Reuters. Among the smaller agencies, DPA of Germany was set at 115,000, ANSA of Italy at 300,000, and EFE of Spain at 500,000.

Considering the demand for foreign news and the difficulties of reporting from far-flung places, there are probably too few correspondents stationed overseas. Rising costs and inflation have made maintenance of a staffer overseas quite expensive. Estimates for maintaining a newspaper bureau overseas (that is, at least one reporter) for a year range from $150,000 to $250,000, and the costs keep going up. A television bureau can cost more than $1 million a year. It is not surprising, therefore, that many news media rely on the news agencies for their foreign news. In most countries, that means the Associated Press and Reuters. High costs help explain the drop in overseas television bureaus and the loss of regular staffers in overseas bureaus. The void has been filled to some extent by freelancers or independent part-time journalists. Perhaps more important is the increased amount of news coming from diverse Internet sources not really connected to regular news outlets. This includes, of course, the vast number of social media "amateurs" who contribute bits of information that can round out a news story.

Western journalists, such as AP and other news agencies, are using more and more "locals" – nationals of countries they cover. Foreign journalists are not only less expensive, but often have a grasp of local languages and knowledge of their own countries that US journalists cannot match. Journalist Scott Schuster attributed the trend to a global acceptance of English as a media language and the global influence of American journalistic methods: "American influence is most profound among broadcasters, and foreign broadcast journalists need only to turn on their television sets to receive lessons on how to do the news American-style," he said. Schuster goes on:

> American methods of news production are being adopted all across Western Europe and in many third world countries. . . . During the coming decade journalistic styles in both print and broadcast media are likely to experience continuing international homogenization. The nationality of the reporter will no longer be an issue. Brits will cover Britain. Ghanaians will cover Ghana, and a large number of American journalists will become "foreign correspondents" – covering America for foreign media.[7]

Increasingly, to deal with rising costs and tighter budgets, news media are relying on stringers or freelancers. A study by Stephen Hess of the Brookings Institution of 404 foreign correspondents working for US news media found that 26 percent are freelancers. Moreover, many of these are underemployed, with 40 percent saying they do other work as well. All suffer the usual fate of freelancers: low pay, no benefits, and a precarious relationship with their employers.[8] Hess found six types of stringers: "spouses" of other correspondents; "experts," who know languages and the area; "adventurers," like Oriana Fallaci; "flingers," a person on a fling who might start a serious career; "ideologues" or "sympathizers," who are often British; and the "residents," who are often longtime residents and write occasional stories.

A significant change has been the increasing number of women among foreign correspondents, especially today as war reporters. Before 1970, their numbers were small, although there had been a few famous names: Dorothy Thompson, Martha Gellhorn, Marguerite Higgins, and Gloria Emerson. Hess found that, by the 1970s, about 16 percent of new foreign reporters were women; this doubled during the 1980s to about 33 percent. This ratio of two men for every woman was also found in Washington media as well as in US journalism generally. In the past, some women correspondents have earned outstanding reputations, including Caryle Murphy and Robin Wright of the *Washington Post*, syndicated columnist Georgie Ann Geyer, and Elaine Sciolino of the *New York Times*. Christiane Amanpour of CNN became a kind of celebrity because of her aggressive and frankly partisan reporting of such stories as the first Iraq War, civil upheaval in Africa, the civil war in Bosnia, and wars in Afghanistan and Iraq. A significant number of women have been covering the wars for Western media. National Public Radio (NPR) is a major source of reliable news from the world's hot spots and many of its capable reporters are women. Foreign correspondents today are better educated, know more foreign languages, and have higher-status backgrounds than their predecessors. In 2014, during the wars or armed clashes in Syria, Iraq, and Ukraine, numerous women reporters, very competent but not well known, dominated US television screens with daily reports from Baghdad, Damascus, and Kiev.

When not reporting a war, the networks increasingly seem to be relying on news film supplied by the syndicates, Reuters Television, APTV News, and other foreign broadcasters for international coverage. These less costly ways of collecting news have undermined the credibility of some foreign news. A few years ago, if you saw a foreign news story on NBC News, chances are that it was reported by an NBC reporter at the scene, with film shot by an NBC crew. Now, you cannot be sure. The networks are relying more on less expensive, and often less experienced, freelancers and independent contractors whose products are rarely identified on the air, leaving the impression that the story was reported by network staffers. This practice gives rise to a growing concern about quality control. "By the time the tape gets on the air, nobody has the foggiest idea who made it and whether the pictures were staged," contended Tom Wolzien, a former NBC news executive.[9]

More loss of authenticity results when US network correspondents, based in London, add voice-overs to stories they did not cover. Bert Quint, former CBS correspondent said, "There's no reason to believe the person [doing the voice-over] because odds are he or she was not within 3,000 miles of where the story occurred."[10]

For readers and listeners, serious questions have been raised about the quantity and quality of foreign news. The debate tends to be circular. AP and other agencies have long maintained that their services gather ample amounts of foreign news, but that their newspaper and broadcast clients do not use very much of it. The media clients in turn argue that their readers and viewers are not very much interested in foreign news. Yet critics say that Americans are uninformed about the world because their news media report so little about it. The widespread shock and fear felt by many Americans after the September 11 terror attacks was in part related to their lack of knowledge about terrorism and the Middle East. Certainly the generalization that the majority of the public, with access to the world's most pervasive media, are ill informed about world affairs has substance. A panel at Columbia's School of Journalism criticized the audience:

> There is a crisis in international news reporting in the United States – and not one that should simply be blamed on the reporters, the gatekeepers, or the owners. We know there is stagnation, and even shrinkage, in the number of international stories in the media and the number of correspondents in the field for most US media outlets. But the primary reason for this decline is an audience that expresses less and less interest in the international stories that do appear. What we're increasingly missing, as a culture, is connective tissue to bind us to the rest of the world.[11]

Foreigners traveling in the American heartland are uniformly impressed by the lack of world news in local media and the ignorance shown by most Americans about the outside world. By contrast, the average German, Dane, or Israeli knows more global news because his or her media carry more. Part of the problem is that Americans, like Russians and Chinese, have a continental outlook, living as they do in the midst of a vast land mass that encourages a self-centered, isolationist view of the world. With two friendly neighbors and protected by two oceans, Americans are slow to recognize their interdependence with others. The shock of 9/11 may have modified that mindset, but only temporarily.

The public's interest in foreign news has its ups and downs, depending on the perceived impact of any current crisis on their lives. During the Vietnam War, much concern was focused on happenings in Southeast Asia, but not in Latin America or Africa, where news coverage dropped off. After Vietnam, foreign concerns receded as the nation became enthralled by Watergate and its aftermath. But after the rapid increases and then decreases in the price of foreign oil, the Soviet incursion into Afghanistan, continuing Arab–Israeli conflict, and a rising level of terrorism directed against Americans, the average American's interest in (if not knowledge of) foreign news, especially that of the Middle East, clearly increased. Then, during the summer of 1990, after Iraq invaded Kuwait and American forces were moved into Saudi Arabia before war began in January 1991, American and European interest in and anxiety about the Persian Gulf soared.

In 1998, the nation's prosperity and the continuing story about President Clinton's personal problems pushed foreign news off the nation's news agenda. The continuing crises in the former Yugoslavia, Iraq, and Israel and the teetering Asian and Russian economies did not go away; they just seemed less urgent and less visible. By mid-1998, nuclear tests by India and Pakistan and the possibility of war in South Asia brought a heightened interest in foreign news. The aerial war over Kosovo and Serbia led by America and NATO held the spotlight while it lasted. But the terror attacks of 9/11 have brought an abrupt, if temporary, change in Americans' attitude toward the outside world. Many were clearly frightened and saw themselves as vulnerable to the perils faced by Israelis and many Europeans. This, together with the world economic crisis, global warming, and so on, has added to anxieties.

Some critics believed that television had profoundly affected the public's news perceptions. Neil Postman believes television projects a "peek-a-boo" world, "where now this event, now that, pops into view for a moment, then vanishes again. It is a world without much sense or coherence. . . . Americans know of a lot of things but about almost nothing. Someone is considered well informed who simply knows that a plane was hijacked or that there was an earthquake in Mexico City."[12] But despite ignorance of the world, there is a growing recognition that perhaps the term "foreign news" is a misnomer and that in our interdependent world we are potentially affected by any event almost anywhere. Failing overseas economies can threaten the US stock market and prosperity. American workers who lose jobs in manufacturing due to cheap foreign imports, or farmers unable to sell wheat abroad due to the overvalued dollar, are becoming more knowledgeable about world economic trends. And the Iraq and Afghan wars and other turmoil reminded Westerners of their dependence on Middle Eastern oil and the lack of a conservation policy to deal with that dependence. Since 9/11, many Americans for the first time have believed they could die in a terrorist attack.

The reporting of foreign news has been criticized as being too crisis-oriented. An ABC News poll found that among viewers polled, 55 percent agreed, "Television news only does stories about foreign countries when there's a war or some other violent crisis going on."[13] Media critic Hodding Carter said the networks "concentrate on showing kids throwing rocks at troops or guns going off or planes bombing or rubble falling. These are the repetitive images that block out the complexities." In addition, he cited the "extraordinary lack of continuity and perspective, which is the shadow of all television news."[14] Inevitably, much of what happens in the world will go unnoted. Wherever he or she may be, the average person obviously does not have the time or interest to follow all the news from everywhere. As one editor asked, "Who wants to read about Zaire if there is nothing going on there?" Gerald Long of Reuters explained more fully: "The prevalent school of journalism throughout the world is a 'journalism of exception.' In other words, you don't report that everything is fine in Pakistan. You report that there has been an air crash."[15] This approach contributes to an inevitable imbalance and distortion of reality.

The journalism of exception – reporting civil unrest, the coup d'état, the train wreck, the drought – is at the root of much hostility and antagonism toward Western reporting. Journalists who work abroad say it is difficult to gain access to many parts of the world, particularly Africa, the Middle East, and Asia. Americans who often hold domestic journalists and broadcasters in low esteem, especially on cable television, are mostly uninformed about the dangers of practicing journalists in the Middle East and other trouble spots in the world. Journalists had particular difficulty in reporting the eight-year conflict between Iran and Iraq and the prolonged civil war involving Serbia, Bosnia, Croatia, and Kosovo. In its early stages, the war in Afghanistan was dangerous and challenging to report. Before 9/11, in India, the foreign cable networks, CNN and the BBC's World Service television, became a target for Indian politicians looking for scapegoats to blame for secessionist movements, religious strife, and natural disasters. India's own television network, Doordarshan, owned and controlled by the government, is well known for delaying and sanitizing news broadcasts. CNN and the BBC came to India in 1991 while reporting the first Gulf War and later aggressively reported the razing of the Babri Mosque in late 1993 by Hindu fundamentalists, which led to national riots in which 1,800 died. In response, Indian political leaders of both left and right demanded strong action against the networks. However, when things go in favor of the politicians, they praise foreign coverage.[16]

A major point of contention, as mentioned, is that most governments believe the press, including foreign reporters, should serve the host country's national aims, whereas the Western press believes it must decide for itself what news to report. And each foreign reporter will report his or her version of events, as colored by the culture and traditions of his own national media.

Physical and Psychological Dangers

Foreign correspondents often risk their lives to cover wars, civil unrest, and other forms of violence. Within unstable nations, journalists, both foreign and domestic, are often singled out as targets for arrest, beatings, or assassination. Sometimes they are just in the wrong place at the wrong time.

One difficulty in protecting journalists abroad is that there are now different kinds of journalists, for example, "citizen journalists" who provide news not otherwise available, and sometimes their identity cannot be revealed. In 2010, a George Polk award was given for the brief video reports of the violent death of an Iranian woman during election protests in Tehran in 2009. The thirty-seven-second video of the death became a symbol of Iranian opposition and was viewed worldwide. The prestigious Polk Award committee said it wanted to acknowledge the role of ordinary citizens in disseminating words and images in times of turmoil when professional journalists faced restrictions, as they did in Iran. It was the first Polk Award given anonymously.

Another new breed is the inexperienced reporters from lesser-known media who run afoul of autocratic regimes. Two young American women, Laura Ling and Euna Lee, were working on a story about North Korean refugees when they were arrested by North Korean border guards. Later, they were sentenced to twelve years in a labor prison, setting off diplomatic efforts to win their release. They were not working for a well-known news organization but for an obscure television channel, Current Television, which lacked the clout to bring pressure on their captors. The Committee to Protect Journalists (CPJ) found that in 2008 at least fifty-six of the jailed journalists worked for online organizations and that forty-five of that total were freelancers.[17] The admirable CPJ keeps track of such violence, and reported in 2014 that since 1992 some 1,059 journalists had been killed worldwide. The countries with the most deaths were: 1. Iraq, 163; 2. Philippines, 76; 3. Syria, 64; 4. Algeria, 60; 5. Russia, 56; 6. Pakistan, 54; 7. Somalia, 45; 8. Colombia, 45; 9. India, 32; 10. Mexico, 30; 11. Brazil, 29; 12. Afghanistan, 26; 13. Turkey, 21; 14. Sri Lanka, 19; 15. Bosnia, 15.[18]

In twenty-four cases since 1995, journalists were kidnapped by militants or government forces and some were subsequently killed. In August 2014 journalist James Foley, kidnapped in Syria nearly two years earlier, was beheaded by the radical group ISIS, who threatened more such murders unless the United States withdrew entirely from Iraq. Several weeks later a second American, freelance journalist Steven J. Sotloff, was killed by ISIS in the same way as Foley with the beheading also shown on a video. Great indignation followed in world media. The kidnapping and murder of *Wall Street Journal* reporter Daniel Pearl in 2002 was an earlier example of this terrible phenomenon. In several cases, notably in Algeria and Turkey, journalists have simply "disappeared" after being taken into government custody.

Among the many killed in Russia, some died covering the war with Chechnya, but at least eleven reporters have been murdered in contract-style killings in the four years since President Putin took power. Paul Klebnikov, the American-born editor of *Forbes Russia*, was gunned down outside his office in Moscow in July 2004.

In June 2014, another egregious suppression occurred in Egypt when three reporters for Al Jazeera's English-language network were each given seven-year prison sentences for their reports about Egypt. One was an Australian and one a Canadian citizen, and all had excellent reputations. The charges were considered specious by many Western nations, but the new Egyptian president was determined to stamp out all dissent and even unfriendly news. Numerous Western nations protested the verdicts. At the time, more than a dozen journalists were in jail among the 16,000 in custody for political reasons. More than 7,000 Egyptians had been killed during recent political protests.[19]

Finally, it should be said that the Western practice of "journalism of exception" continues to rankle critics of the press everywhere. In America, many feel that the media report far too much negative news. But as Daniel Patrick Moynihan once said, "It is the mark of a democracy that its press is filled with bad news. When one comes to a country where the press is filled with good news, one can be pretty sure that the jails are filled with good men." The reporting of modern wars – their own wars – has presented special challenges to American and British news media and to reporters who cover them. That problem is discussed in the next chapter.

Notes

1. Leon Hadar, "Covering the New World Disorder," *Columbia Journalism Review*, July/August 1994, 27.
2. Hadar, "Covering the New World Disorder."

3. Stephen Hess, *International News & Foreign Correspondents* (Washington, DC: Brookings Institution, 1996), 61.

4. Tom Fenton, *Bad News: The Decline of Reporting, the Business of News and the Danger to Us All* (New York: HarperCollins, 2005), 4.

5. Brian Stelter, "Job Cuts at ABC News Leave Workers Stunned and Downcast," *The New York Times*, May 1, 2010, B2.

6. Mort Rosenblum, *Who Stole the News?* (New York: Wiley, 1993), 20.

7. Scott Schuster, "Foreign Competition Hits the News," *Columbia Journalism Review*, May/June 1988, 45.

8. Stephen Hess, "The Cheaper Solution," *American Journalism Review*, April 1994, 27.

9. Hess, "The Cheaper Solution," 100.

10. Hess, "The Cheaper Solution," 100.

11. "World News: Truth or Consequences," *Columbia Journalism Review*, January/February 1995, 4.

12. Sally Bedell Smith, "How New Technologies are Starting to Change the Nation's Viewing Habits," *The New York Times*, October 9, 1985, A10.

13. Sally Bedell Smith, "Why TV News Can't Be a Complete View of the World," *The New York Times*, August 8, 1982, entertainment section, 1.

14. Smith, "Why TV News Can't Be a Complete View."

15. Rosemary Righter, *Whose News? Politics, the Press and the Third World* (New York: Times Books, 1978), 70.

16. Arthur J. Pais, "Anger in India," *Columbia Journalism Review*, May/June 1993, 17.

17. Brian Stelter, "A World at Risk for a New Style of Journalism," *The New York Times*, June 15, 2009, B1.

18. Press Freedom Online Committee to Protect Journalists, 2014.

19. David Kirkpatrick, "Egypt Convicts 3 Journalists," *The New York Times*, June 24, 2014, 1.

13

Reporting War

In 2014 the Middle East and southern Europe became much more contentious and violence-prone regions of clashes and warfare. As the civil war in Syria simmered and dragged on, violent Sunni militants calling themselves ISIS or ISIL spread across the northern border into Iraq, overrunning several cities and threatening to split Iraq into three regions: Sunni, Shiite, and Kurdish. Baghdad, dominated by Shiites, had the potential support of Iran.

Then, in July 2014, the long-standing feud between Israel and Hamas, the Palestinian militant group that dominates the Gaza Strip, broke out again, with rockets showered into Israel, which retaliated with aerial bombings of Gaza. The next phase was a ground attack led by Israeli tanks, producing heavy casualties in Gaza. Warfare in the Holy Land had to share front pages and television news broadcasts with warfare in eastern Ukraine, where rebels, supposedly armed and clearly supported by Russia, waged a low-grade civil war. Then, on July 17, 2014, the world was shocked to learn that a Malaysian airliner with 298 passengers and crew had crashed near the Russian border with Ukraine, killing all on board. Russia denied any involvement, but evidence and intelligence suggested the plane was shot down by a surface-to-air missile traced to Russia. The airline disaster reignited the dispute between the United States and other NATO nations with President Putin of Russia over the independence of Ukraine.

As a sideshow, Libya became ungovernable due to fighting among factions in that North African nation. These current and recent wars required journalists to not only report the ongoing violent events on the ground but

The World News Prism: Digital, Social and Interactive, Ninth Edition.
William A. Hachten and James F. Scotton.
© 2016 John Wiley & Sons, Inc. Published 2016 by John Wiley & Sons, Inc.

also to explain the political and strategic meaning of the hostilities. Much of this violence had roots in earlier wars and crises that had been going on for years.

Four recent wars – the 1991 first Gulf War, the aerial war over Serbia and Kosovo, the winding down in Iraq, and the continuing seven-year-plus struggle in Afghanistan – have dramatically altered the ways that armed conflicts are reported to the world. Although long-standing frictions and suspicions persist between the press and military officials, the use of new communication technologies has altered journalism, for better or worse. The wars themselves have changed – from short, intensive clashes, to asymmetrical struggles against terrorist guerrillas, to drawn-out counter-insurgency efforts involving nation-building to win hearts and minds. The West has relearned a basic tenet. Wars are much easier to get into than to get out of.

In the brief Gulf War, television, and especially CNN, turned much of the world into a global community witnessing a televised real-time war, as the brief conflict evolved from armed confrontation to spectacular aerial bombardment and finally to lightning ground warfare. The war became the biggest global news story in years, and telling it utilized the full resources of US and European news media as well as much of the international news system. More than 1,600 print and broadcast journalists were on hand to report it.

The 1999 NATO bombing campaign against Serbia, whose ground forces were mauling Kosovo civilians, was a new kind of war: an effort, mainly by US air power, to bomb a nation into submission without deploying ground troops or even incurring casualties. As in the first Gulf War, the press accused the military of withholding news and of "spinning" combat reports for political and strategic reasons. The seventy-eight days of NATO bombing finally forced Yugoslavian dictator Slobodan Milosevic to yield and permit 16,000 NATO soldiers to chase the fleeing Serbian forces out of Kosovo and thus bring relief to the battered ethnic Albanians. In that last war of the twentieth century, global news coverage was greatly facilitated by the satellite telephone, twenty-four-hour cable TV coverage, and, for the first time, the Internet.

During the opening months of the war against the Taliban in Afghanistan, press and military relationships were still evolving. The Bush administration made it clear that the press would receive less access to combat-related information than in previous conflicts. Yet the news media, in the United States and elsewhere, poured out a steady torrent of news, speculation, commentary, and pictures about this many-faceted conflict. The world of 2001 was more completely "wired" for 24/7 coverage, and journalists from many nations flocked to the region. The Iraq War, launched with great fanfare in spring 2003, at first dominated the world's front pages and television screens as the United States and its coalition forces quickly overwhelmed the army of Saddam Hussein and captured Baghdad. Then, when the blitzkrieg morphed into a tortuous insurgency with no end in sight, most of the world paid less and less attention. But for journalists still in Iraq, reporting became increasingly dangerous and difficult.

The role of the news media in reporting and explaining Iraq has gone through changes. Wars, particularly when they involve Western powers, are always at the top of the news agendas for foreign nations. And as the world becomes more interconnected by global communications, many more people in more places are paying close attention through the news media. But after seven years, as the Iraq War had finally wound down and most (but not all) combat troops had departed, most of the journalists had left as well. The public too had largely lost interest.

Many journalists traveled to Afghanistan, where the United States under a new president, Barack Obama, had deployed 150,000 more troops in order to counter the growing influence of the Taliban. By the end of 2010, relations between the military and the press were at a low ebb; Western leaders and the informed publics were increasingly dubious that the war was winnable. With the strategic emphasis on counter-insurgency, the news was less and less about combat and more about the politics and diplomacy of dealing with an erratic Afghan president presiding over a corrupt government. And the old mutual suspicions between the press and the military persisted.

Background of Press Controls

How did relations between American journalists and the US military become so abrasive? In World War I, some 500 American correspondents covered the conflict for newspapers, magazines, and press associations in France and, unlike British and French reporters, they were free to go to the front line without military escorts. Still, everything written by such star reporters as Richard Harding Davis, Will Irwin, or Floyd Gibbons was passed through military censors. Details about specific battles, numbers of casualties, and names of units could be released only after being mentioned in official communiqués.

US military censorship followed the same general pattern in World War II, with the added feature of controlling radio broadcasts. In far-flung combat "theaters," reporters were generally free to move about and join military units but were always subject to censorship. About 500 full-time American reporters were abroad at any one time, and provided coverage that many considered the best ever seen. Relations between the military and reporters were mutually trusting and supportive. Despite occasional conflicts over withheld information, everyone seemed to be on the same team. During the Korean War, the press–government relations were pretty much the same.

The change began in the 1960s with the Vietnam War, when relations soured and reached their lowest ebb. Reporters and camera crews, working within military guidelines, were given free access without field censorship to roam Vietnam; some called it the best-reported war in history. Yet many in the US military believed critical press reporting contributed to the American defeat by over-stressing negative aspects, including graphic pictures of the dead and wounded, highlighting scandals such as the My Lai massacre, and misinterpreting key events.

Reporters felt that the US military had misled and lied to them in Vietnam and that officials consistently painted a much rosier picture of the war than the facts justified. Given the record of deception, the press, it was argued, was correct in being skeptical of the military. A view prevailed within the military that the free rein given reporters in Vietnam led to reporting that seriously damaged morale and turned American public opinion against its own troops. If news or information is a weapon, then, the generals argued, it should be controlled as part of the war effort.

The brief war in 1982 between Britain and Argentina over the Falkland Islands in the South Atlantic provided a model for the Pentagon on how to manage the press during wartime. Only British reporters were permitted to accompany the task force and they had to accept censorship. The reporters would be "expected to help in leading and steadying public opinion in times of national stress or crisis," the Ministry of Defence said. After the war was over the British press detailed losses, mishaps, and failures of British forces previously blocked by censorship.

For the United States the war news issue surfaced again on October 25, 1983, when US forces invaded the tiny Caribbean island of Grenada. Only after two days of rigorous protests from the press were some journalists finally flown in with a military escort. By the end of one week, with the fighting winding down, 150 reporters were ferried to the island and allowed to stay overnight. Walter Cronkite of CBS said the Reagan administration had seriously erred, arguing, "This is our foreign policy and we have a right to know what is happening and there can be no excuse in denying the people that right."[1] But as in the later Gulf War, opinion polls showed that the public supported the ban on press coverage.

Similar problems arose in 1989 when US forces invaded Panama.

The First War with Saddam Hussein

Global television came into its own as CNN and other broadcasters reported a war as it was happening, or as it appeared to be happening – a "real-time" war. After hostilities began early on January 17, 1991, reporters described antiaircraft tracers in the night sky of Baghdad and flashes of bomb explosions on the horizon. On succeeding nights, viewers were provided with live video reports from Tel Aviv and Riyadh of Scud missiles, some apparently intercepted by Patriot missiles, exploding against the night sky, and of television reporters donning gas masks on camera. The press talked of the "CNN effect" – millions were anchored hour after hour to their television sets lest they miss the latest dramatic development. Restaurants, cinemas, hotels, and gaming establishments all suffered business losses. Ratings for CNN soared five to ten times their prewar levels.[2] The first Gulf War was a worldwide media event of astonishing proportions. Global television had never had a larger or more interested audience for such a sustained period of time. Television became the first and principal source of news for most people, as well as a major source of military and political intelligence for both sides. CNN telecasts, including military briefings, were viewed in Baghdad as they were being received in Riyadh or Washington, DC – as well as in other non-Western countries.

But information was tightly controlled; one observer called it "the illusion of news." For its own self-defined security reasons, the military often held back or distorted the news it did release. In the opening days of the war, much was made of the "smart bombs" that hit their targets with about 90 percent accuracy. After the war, the US Air Force admitted that smart bombs made up only 7 percent of all US explosives dropped on Iraq and Kuwait. The Air Force later said that 70 percent of the 88,500 tons of bombs dropped on Kuwait and Iraq missed their targets.[3]

Peter Jennings of ABC News reminded viewers that much of what was revealed in the opening days of war was speculation, mixed with some hard facts and some rumors in the rushing river of information. But whether they were getting hard news or not, many millions of viewers stayed by their television sets. Public opinion polls showed that the overwhelming majority of Americans supported both the war and the military's efforts to control news; further, some thought there should be more controls on press reporting. A *Los Angeles Times* Mirror poll found that half of the respondents considered themselves obsessed with war news, but nearly 80 percent felt that the military was "telling as much as it can." About the same proportion thought that military censorship might be a "good idea."

But after the brief war, many in the press felt that the traditional right of US reporters to accompany their combat forces and report news of war had been severely circumscribed. Michael Getler of the *Washington Post* wrote, "The Pentagon and U.S. Army Central Command conducted what is probably the most thorough and consistent wartime control of American reporters in modern times – a set of restrictions that in its totality and mind-set seemed to go beyond World War II, Korea, and Vietnam."[4]

President George H. W. Bush and the Pentagon followed a deliberate policy of blocking negative and unflattering news from the US public lest it weaken support for the war. Long after the conflict, the public learned that some Iraqi soldiers had been buried alive in trenches by US plows and earthmovers and that the military had waited months to tell the families of thirty-three dead soldiers that their loved ones had been killed by friendly fire. Not until a year after the war did the public learn that key weapons such as the stealth bomber and the Cruise missile had struck only about half of their targets, compared with the 85 to 90 percent rate claimed by the Pentagon at the time.[5] American casualties were reported, but there were few pictures of dead and wounded. Details of tactical failures and mishaps in the bombing campaign were not released, nor was the information that at least twenty-four female soldiers had been sexually assaulted by American servicemen.

But the shooting war itself was quite a media spectacle, which started just as the evening news programs were beginning at 6.30 p.m. Eastern Standard Time (January 16, 1991 in the United States; January 17 in the Middle East). The networks and CNN interrupted their prepared news shows to report that aerial bombing had begun in Baghdad. Then followed one of most memorable nights in television history: the opening phases of a major conflict reported in real time by reporters in Iraq, Saudi Arabia, and Washington.

CNN stole the show that night, as three CNN correspondents, John Holliman, Peter Arnett, and Bernard Shaw, gave vivid eyewitness descriptions of the US air attack from the windows of their Baghdad hotel room. As in old-time radio, reporters relied on words, not video, that first night. Other networks reported the fireworks, but CNN, with its previously arranged leased lines, stayed on the longest after the lines were cut for the other networks. The next day, General Colin Powell jokingly said that the Pentagon was relying on CNN for military information. The second night gave prime-time viewers another long, absorbing evening, when CNN and NBC reporters in Tel Aviv reported live as Scud missiles landed. Reporters, often wearing gas masks, provided raw and unevaluated information. At one point, NBC reported dramatically that nerve gas had been detected in one Scud attack. Tom Brokaw described the situation for some minutes, but, after the report proved false, NBC apologized. For the first three days, people everywhere stayed glued to television and radio sets, including short-wave receivers. Networks expanded to near twenty-four-hour coverage for the first thirty-six hours, and even the daytime soap operas were preempted briefly for war coverage. There was not that much to report at that point, and the same facts, theories, and speculations were repeated again and again. Nevertheless, the mesmerized public stayed tuned.

If the war had gone badly, the press would have had difficulty reporting the negative aspects. With more than 1,600 reporters in the theater, only about 100 could be accommodated by the pools to report on the American force of 500,000. As the ground war neared, the large press corps became increasingly restive and frustrated at this lack of access.

The response of some reporters was to "freelance" – to avoid the pools and go off on their own. Malcolm Browne reported, "Some reporters were hiding out in U.S. Marine or Army field units, given GI uniforms and gear to look inconspicuous, enjoying the affection (and protection) of the units they're trying to cover – concealed by the officers and troops from the handful of press-hating commanders who strive to keep the battlefield free of wandering journalists."[6] Browne noted that nearly all reporters who tried to reach front-line US troops were arrested at one time or another (including reporters for the *New York Times*, *Washington Post*, Associated Press, and Cox papers), and were sometimes held in field jails for up to twelve hours and threatened with revocation of their press credentials.

The Triumph of Twenty-Four-Hour Global News

During the American Civil War, in 1861–65, the demand for news was so great that US newspapers went to seven-day publication for the first time. During the 1963 Kennedy assassination, live television emerged as the preeminent medium for reporting breaking news. This story positioned ABC, CBS, and NBC as major news gatherers, but as still reaching essentially US audiences.

During the forty-two-day first Gulf War, CNN established the importance of a twenty-four-hour news network with true global reach. The concept has certainly changed the international news system, especially during times of international crisis and conflict. The three major US networks were shaken by CNN's success. After CNN's historic scoop on the first night of the war, a number of independent television stations, radio stations, and even several network affiliates relied on CNN in the crisis. Although the three networks had more talented and experienced reporters, they could not compete with CNN either in time on the air or in the vast audiences CNN reached in about 100 countries. The success of CNN encouraged similar services, such as the BBC's World Service television.

The first Gulf War certainly conditioned viewers everywhere to keep their television sets tuned to CNN (or its later cable imitators) during times of high crisis. Newsrooms from Milwaukee to Cairo to Shanghai routinely keep a television set tuned to CNN or the BBC for the first report of any global crisis. Perhaps the news business today places too much emphasis on immediate and fast-breaking news "as it happens." Video shots of F15s roaring off runways, of "smart bombs" scoring direct hits, of Tomahawk missiles flying through Baghdad, and of tank formations rolling through the desert made memorable viewing. But after the fog of war had cleared, the press and the public found that the war was not quite what they thought it was.

The tragic events in the volatile Middle East also reminded the public that wars and political crises are complex and intricate processes that can still best be reported and explained by the printed word. The best and most complete reporting of the first Gulf War came ultimately from print media, which rounded out the picture and provided the context and perspective necessary for full understanding. During the first several weeks after the ceasefire, it was the print reporters, not television, who dug out and filled in the details of what actually happened during the air campaign and the brief ground war – details that the military on both sides had so effectively screened from public view.

From all indications, the US military as well as the first Bush administration were pleased with the results of their media policy and would do the same thing again. But among American and British journalists there was a general conclusion that the press had been unduly and even illegally denied access to information about the war.

After the first Gulf War, a report that called military restrictions in the war "real censorship" that confirmed "the worst fears of reporters in a democracy" was delivered to Defense Secretary Dick Cheney. It was signed by seventeen news executives representing the four networks, AP and UPI, and major newspapers and news magazines. The report bitterly complained that the restrictions placed on reporters by the Pentagon were intended to promote a sanitized view of the war. The war was called the first in the twentieth century to restrict all official coverage to pools. "By controlling what reporters saw and when they saw it, the military exerted great power to shape and manage the news," the report said. Also criticized were the use of military escorts and "unwarranted delays in transmitting copy."[7] After more than eight months of talks with news executives, in May 1992 the Pentagon issued a set of principles intended to guarantee that journalists would have greater access to future military operations than they had in the first Gulf War. However, news media and the government could not agree on whether there should be any official "security review" of news reports before they are published or broadcast. The statement affirmed that "open and independent reporting will be the principal means of coverage of U.S. military operations." The guidelines limited the role of military escorts and said that "press pools are not to serve as the standard means of covering operations."[8]

The incursion of US Marines into Somalia in December 1992 was intended to provide military protection to the relief organizations trying to feed starving Somalis caught in the crossfire of warring clans. Under these conditions, the Pentagon decided to place no restraints on the media. Howard Kurtz called what happened the most embarrassing moment ever in media–military relations: "the infamous night in December 1992 when Navy SEALS hitting the beach in Somalia were surrounded by a small army of reporters and photographers who blinded them with television lights, clamored for interviews, and generally acted like obnoxious adolescents. That sorry performance, turning a humanitarian mission to aid starving Africans into a Felliniesque photo op, underscored what the Pentagon had been saying for years: that the press simply could not discipline itself, that reporters would blithely endanger the safety of American troops for the sake of journalistic drama."[9] It was not one of the news medias' finer days.

David Hackworth of *Newsweek* wrote, "To lurch from thought control to no control is plain stupid. When the press corps beats the Marine Corps to the beach, everyone loses."[10] The Pentagon wanted full coverage of Somalia, so no controls were placed on the press, and what resulted was a confused circus. There are those, however, who suspected that the Pentagon deliberately orchestrated the fiasco to make the media look bad. Somalia raised the question of whether the media, by its heavy barrage of pictures and stories of starving Somalis, had pushed President Bush during his last days in office to send troops on their humanitarian mission. The answer is unclear, but Bush did react by committing US armed forces to a limited and supposedly feasible assignment of famine relief. When the Somalia assignment expanded in the early Clinton administration to include warlord hunting, it provoked a devastating firefight in the streets of Mogadishu. When eighteen US soldiers were killed and the pictures shown on US television, the American public was unprepared to accept casualties when vital US interests were not at stake. The White House soon announced that the United States was getting out of Somalia.

James Hoge, editor of *Foreign Affairs*, commented, "From its understanding of Vietnam came the military's subsequent emphasis on quick solutions, limited media access and selective release of 'smart' weapons imagery. The public, however, will not remain dazzled when interventions become difficult. As in Vietnam, public attitudes ultimately hinge on questions about the rightness, purpose and costs of policy – not television images."[11]

NATO's Air War over Yugoslavia

After NATO bombs started falling on Serbia and Kosovo in 1999, military relations with the press deteriorated abruptly. Critics protested that the lack of detailed after-action reports – routinely provided in earlier conflicts – made it impossible to assess NATO's claims that it was steadily dismantling Milosevic's war-making powers. At both the Pentagon and Brussels NATO headquarters, spokespersons stubbornly refused to provide specific information about bombing sorties. These policies were considered even less forthcoming than in the first Gulf War, which the press had considered overly restrictive.

Yet the war was reported and, in some basic ways, differently from others. After being forced to watch seventy-eight days of bombing through the lenses of official video cameras, some 2,700 journalists had a chance to see for themselves when NATO troops rolled into Kosovo in June 1999. According to editors, the key device for putting together information into coherent stories was the satellite telephone and, more broadly, satellite communications. The satellite uplink was the key information medium for the air war. "Instantaneous communication has changed everything," said Andrew Rosenthal, foreign editor of the *New York Times*. "The ability of a reporter on the Macedonian border to call a reporter on the Albanian border or to call a reporter in Brussels or Washington instantly made a huge difference. Newspapers were able to put together groups of reporters to do joint efforts in a way that was previously impossible," he said.[12]

For television, the same satellite technology allowed a profusion of images to be transmitted at great speed. Whether the vivid video showed the fate of Kosovar refugees or fleeing Serbian troops, the emotional impact of television was great indeed. Some thought such reportage helped to justify the humanitarian aspects of the hostilities and convinced otherwise dubious viewers to support the NATO effort. For the first time, the Internet was a player in war reporting, providing a plethora of websites (that is, blogs) presenting war issues and other information from diverse viewpoints – Serbian, Albanian, Republican, Democratic – and ranging from the in-depth reporting of the BBC to the erratic sensationalism of Belgrade news outlets. As a result, some observers thought that the sum total of these trends amounted to sharper, speedier coverage. David Halberstam wrote: "Despite all the restrictions and just God-awful limitations and dangers, there were enough different people in different places to give you the dimensions you needed."[13]

Even though CNN had more competition this time – BBC World Service, MSNBC, and Fox – than in the first Gulf War, the Atlanta cable network emerged from the Yugoslav conflict in a much-enhanced *international* role for its news dissemination as a global twenty-four-hour cable news channel. During the first Gulf War, some 10 million households outside the United States had access to CNN. In the Yugoslav war, the number had jumped to 150 million households. Still the air war in Yugoslavia demonstrated that the democracies of America and NATO were unwilling to be candid and forthcoming with reliable information to their own peoples while engaged in hostile actions against other states.

Chasing the Taliban in Afghanistan

The world's press – mainly Americans and Europeans – geared up to cover the war in Afghanistan with essentially the same technologies as well as limited access to the battlefields. Global audiences were now larger and the news flow was much heavier. One reason was that reporters could now report news from war zones in real time even though they might have less to tell. Because the military sharply limits access and thus what reporters can know, the war reporter is not in a position to decide what is appropriate and safe to report. Basically, the military today is very uneasy with new media technology. The old battlefield censorship is no longer feasible because reporters carry their means of transmission (that is, satellite phones and videophones) with them. More and more, reporters are kept away from troops and military organizations. As a result, much of what is considered "war coverage" has originated in the Pentagon press briefing room. Today, the global audience is accustomed to getting its news quickly and often. People will check their favorite websites four or five times a day, or tune in to twenty-four-hour cable stations for the latest developments.

As mentioned earlier, the Afghanistan War may go down in history as our first "videophone war." The videophone, basically a camera plugged into a satellite phone, enabled television news crews to venture out to remote and dangerous areas of Afghanistan, untethered to the cumbersome satellite uplinks that can weigh over a ton. The videophone costs about $8,000 and can fit into two briefcases. With the videophone and a car battery, a reporter is ready to roll. Videophone reporting has been criticized for being "too sketchy" or almost "indecipherable." But the technology will only improve over time and it does get the television reporter closer to the battlefield.

But what the press has gained in time and convenience, it has lost in access to the military itself. For families of servicemen and women, this was not considered a good precedent. News about casualties caused by "friendly fire" and other battlefield mishaps tend not to be reported if there are no reporters on the ground. The press has been likened to an uncle representing the family. They go to the front line and say, "Well, how is Johnny doing? What's going on here? Who's running this operation? Are there needless frontal assaults?" Walter Cronkite, the longtime CBS News anchor, has said that there is another reason people should care about how the military operates: "We must know what they are doing in our name."[14] The journalists' concerns have not yet aroused similar concern from the public. As noted in a recent survey by the Pew Research Center, half of the respondents said the military should have more control over war news than news media have.

During the opening weeks of the Afghan War, almost all significant information was released from the Pentagon, far from the battlefields, and much of it was considered dated and vague. The extremely restrictive policy toward release of information was set by Defense Secretary Rumsfeld, who said that the nature of the war against terrorism made the constraints necessary. Rumsfeld several times stated that defense officials who leaked information might be in violation of federal criminal law. Later, after President Obama ordered a renewed effort in Afghanistan, press–military relations were improved. But there was less reporting of American soldiers living in peril and more about the political corruptions of President Karzai and the difficult diplomatic relationship with neighboring Pakistan, which was accused of harboring and even aiding Taliban terrorists and leaders of the still elusive Al Qaeda. The Afghan War had become the longest in US history; public interest and support had clearly declined. This disillusionment was clearly reflected in Western media.

The Second War against Saddam's Iraq

The invasion of Iraq and the toppling of Saddam Hussein's regime were quickly accomplished by coalition forces – mainly American and some British – in the spring of 2003. Around the world, millions watched the unfolding of this, the most heavily televised war in history. As in the 1991 Iraq War, hundreds of journalists and photographers used new and refined communications gadgets – videophones, cellphones, Internet, and email – to flood the world with words and images.

Combat journalism has changed, as has warfare itself. Technology has markedly changed how wars are waged and for how long. Reporters utilize new tools to gather news and send it out faster than ever. In Iraq, the typical television war correspondent found he needed the following essential carry-along gear that weighed about seventy-six pounds: a digital video camera, five pounds; microphones, cables, and batteries, ten pounds; camera tripod, ten pounds; two satellite phones, twenty pounds each; laptop computer, six pounds; and night scope lens, five pounds.

Reporters in Iraq were comfortable with their technology as never before. Television reporters carried hand-held video cameras and print journalists traded their seventy-pound videophones of 1991 for handy models that can be held against an ear. High-speed Internet lines in the desert meant that journalists could make a connection almost anywhere. One reporter said that today's digital devices enable a reporter to provide a more intimate and multi-faceted view of the war than had ever been seen before. The high quality and diverse nature of the reporting reflected this.

The most important policy innovation of the war was the Pentagon's unexpected decision that journalists be "embedded" with the military units fighting their way across Iraq. For the first time since World War II, and on a scale never seen in military history, some 600 reporters, photographers, and television crew members – about 100 of them from foreign and international news organizations, including the Arab satellite news network Al Jazeera, had access to troops in combat. Embedding was considered the greatest innovation (and improvement) in press–military relations in many years. The results of the experiment were generally positive. The viewing public had a front-row seat during the invasion, with the "embedders" providing a steady stream of news reports, anecdotes, and human interest stories, along with dramatic and vivid video and photos about the military they accompanied.

One observer, Rem Rieder, commented, "Now that the fighting has stopped, it's clear that the great embedding experience was a home run as far as the news media – and the American public – are concerned. Six hundred journalists had a first-hand view of the combat. That's a far cry from the first Gulf war when reporters were at the mercy of government briefers and that misbegotten press pool."[15] But there were negative aspects to embedding. Some critics saw the reporters as tools of the military – only turning out good news. And it was dangerous duty – several correspondents were killed, including David Bloom of NBC News and Michael Kelly of the *Atlantic Monthly*.

Another important dimension was the role of transnational satellite networks in the Arab world. They became important sources of war news in Arabic, and were in fact challenging the hegemony of the British and US media. Al Jazeera then reached about 45 million viewers, and broadcast a very different version of the conflict than CNN or the BBC World Service. The Arab networks were accused of sending inaccurate and biased information. But many millions of Arabs were now receiving news and views in Arabic that differed from that sent out by their own closed national media systems.

How good was the televised reporting of the brief shooting war? At their best, reporters managed to humanize the war without becoming cheerleaders for the military. News organizations went to great expense to provide thorough coverage. But critics questioned how clear and complete the coverage was. One journalist said the war was too big a canvas to capture on the small screen of television. Yet at the same time there was so much television coverage that sometimes viewers became confused. The effectiveness of television was limited by the limitations of the medium itself – the mismatch between words and images. Vivid pictures from one fixed position in a battle of no consequence could overwhelm any context provided by a voice-over correspondent.

Embedded reporters could not report visually a key aspect of the ground war – that incessant bombing attacks had worn away Iraqi ground forces before battles began. And sometimes, reporters were too downbeat about the invasion's early setbacks.

Insurgency and Counter-Insurgency

After the fall of Baghdad, the war changed into another unexpected phase – a deadly and persistent guerrilla war waged against the occupying forces, and at times the Iraqi public itself. Attacks against US and coalition forces, usually as roadside bombings of cars and trucks or seemingly random suicide bomb attacks in crowded urban areas, took a steady toll of soldiers and civilians during the following two and a half years. The more serious media stayed on and maintained full coverage of the confused and discouraging events in Iraq. By 2005, many journalists had left Iraq – from a total of 2,000, at one time numbers were down to 200.

For the reporters, life became much more dangerous. One reporter said it was like being under house arrest and not able to do your job. Just leaving their hotel meant facing the chance of being kidnapped or shot. Increasingly, reporters relied more and more on Iraqi stringers or "fixers" to go out and gather information. Some reporters began to share their bylines with Iraqi colleagues. Every day was a gamble; ten Iraqi fixers were killed; Reuters lost three cameramen; and in all thirty-five Iraqi journalists were killed. Being pinned down this way, many reporters felt they were getting only part of the story. They said the war looked different on the other side and they were not able to report it.

One of the best, Dexter Filkins of the *New York Times*, said the "business of reporting in Iraq has become a terribly truncated affair, an enterprise clipped and limited by the violence all around. . . . Even in areas of the capital thought to be relatively safe, very few reporters are still brazen enough to get out of a car, walk around and stop people at random. It can be done, but you better move fast."[16] Ironically, it appeared that being embedded with troops at the front was the safest place to be. But not always: Filkins spent two weeks with a US Marine company during the siege of Fallujah. In some of the deadliest urban warfare since World War II, 25 percent of the Marines Filkins was with were killed during sixteen hours of continuous conflict. About this experience in Iraq, Filkins said the "list of hits and near misses was long enough to chill the hardiest war correspondent: we have been shot at, kidnapped, blindfolded, held at gunpoint, detained, threatened, beaten, and chased."[17]

An American freelancer, Steven C. Vincent, was abducted and shot dead in the port city of Basra in August 2005. It was believed that Vincent was targeted for writing about the rise of conservative Shiite Islam and the corruption of the Iraqi police in Basra. Vincent was one of nineteen correspondents killed in attacks in which they were the apparent targets. Soon after, on September 29, 2005, an Iraqi journalist and photographer working for the *New York Times* (as did Vincent) in Basra was found dead after being abducted from his home by a group of armed men. Like Vincent, Fakher Haider had been reporting about the rising violence among Basra's rival Shiite militias, which had apparently infiltrated the police.

Reporting the drawn-out insurgency in Iraq certainly contrasts sharply from riding along with combat troops as they quickly and decisively overwhelmed the army of Saddam Hussein in 2003. As public interest waned, more and more media pulled out their reporters and relied more on local Iraqi newsmen to cover the news. NBC News, with the largest US evening news audience, appeared to rely heavily on one veteran reporter, who reported all the major stories in Iraq even though he was no longer stationed full-time in Baghdad but just flew in and out frequently. There was a large turnover of reporters, including many women, who shuttled back and forth. There have been few journalistic celebrities, as there were in Korea and Vietnam, such as Homer Bigart, Marguerite Higgins, and David Halberstam, all highly regarded and well known. The best-regarded reporter today is Dexter Filkins, who wrote Pulitzer Prize-winning stories about the Marines' battle at Fallujah as well as superior interpretive reporting from Afghanistan. There seem to be fewer scoops and more sharing of news. The US public often learned about Afghanistan from the BBC and Independent Television News from the UK on US public television. Nevertheless, on the Internet a good deal of war news appeared but somehow seems less distinctive and authoritative than similar reports on the front pages of the *New York Times* and *Washington Post*.

But the public and the media, while losing hope for a successful ending and withdrawal of troops from the Near East, has not, as it did in Korea and Vietnam, lost its support for troops overseas. The press assiduously reports all casualties and reminds the public to heed the needs of the returning soldiers.

First Amendment Concerns

From Grenada to Panama to Kosovo and, recently, to Afghanistan and Iraq, the press has been barred from fully covering wars or military incursions that it has historically and traditionally reported. This is important because the US Supreme Court has ruled that the press, in order to inform the public, has a First Amendment right to those places that "historically" and "traditionally" it has had the right to cover, such as trials and town meetings. The Supreme Court has also ruled that the press has a First Amendment right to be present at all "public" events. Certainly, an invasion lasting more than several hours or a full-scale war is a public event.

Perhaps the press's constitutional rationale for war coverage was best expressed by Justice Hugo Black in the Pentagon Papers case:

> The Government's power to censor the press was abolished so that the press would remain forever free to censure the Government. The press was protected so that it could bare the secrets of government and inform the people. Only a free and unrestrained press can effectively expose deception in government. And paramount among the responsibilities of a free press is the duty to prevent any part of the government from deceiving the people and sending them off to distant lands to die of foreign fevers and foreign shot and shell.[18]

The press has no "right" to report sensitive military information that could aid an enemy, nor would it want to do so; but, we believe, it does have a right to be there, to keep a watchful eye on the military, just as it does on the proceedings of a criminal trial. When wars go badly, as they often can – with incompetent leadership, confused tactics, and unnecessary "friendly fire" casualties – it is essential that the press, as the independent representative of the public and of the forces themselves, be there to report, at the time or later, what occurred. The peoples of Iraq and Afghanistan had no independent press reporting back to them about the military disasters and political incompetence that led to the battlefield deaths of thousands of their young men – a basic difference between a democracy and a dictatorship.

This view is not shared by Professor Jane Kirtley, who has argued that no First Amendment right of access to military operations exists. She wrote,

"The message from the court is clear: with no constitutional right to accompany troops the press should be grateful for whatever access the military decides to allow."[19]

Thus, apparently, the Supreme Court of the United States is unlikely to come to the defense of the US press in this matter. Perhaps the best hope of the press is to protest and complain until a significant portion of the public supports their own right to know. In the first Gulf War, it was apparent that the American news media and their owners did not complain loudly and vehemently enough about the pool and censorship restrictions before the bombs started dropping. The more open policy of embedding troops with combat units in the second Gulf War may have been a result of press pressures for more openness. Also, of course, it was very good public relations by the Pentagon to do so.

Few Americans were willing to second-guess the military policy of harsh controls over war news. A sitting president is not likely to modify such restrictions of free expression in wartime until forced to do so by political pressures. Yet it is imperative for the press to keep pushing for greater access to news relating to the military.

Ironically, the greatly expanded capability of global television and the Internet to report instantly on any new information in a modern war provides perhaps the major rationale for governments to control and censor war news. And when American or British journalists are denied access to war news, the rest of the world is denied access as well.

Notes

1. "Media Access to Grenada Stirs Controversy," *AP Log*, October 31, 1991, 1.
2. "Tourism Shaken by CNN Effect," *The New York Times*, January 28, 1992, A8.
3. Tom Wicker, "An Unknown Casualty," *The New York Times*, March 20, 1991, A15.
4. Michael Getler, "The Gulf War 'Good News' Policy is a Dangerous Precedent," *The Washington Post National Weekly Edition*, March 25–31, 1991, 24.
5. Howard Kurtz, *Media Circus* (New York: Times Books, 1993), 215.
6. Malcom Browne, "The Military vs. The Press," *The New York Times Magazine*, March 3, 1991, 45.
7. Jason DeParle, "17 News Executives Criticize U.S. for 'Censorship' of Gulf Coverage," *The New York Times*, July 3, 1991, A4.
8. Robert Pear, "Military Revises Rules to Assure Reporters Access to Battle Areas," *The New York Times*, May 2, 1992, A8.

9. Kurtz, *Media Circus*, 214.

10. David Hackworth, "Learning How to Cover a War," *Newsweek*, December 21, 1992, 32.

11. James F. Hoge, Jr., "Media Pervasiveness," *Foreign Affairs*, July/August 1994, 139–140.

12. Felicity Barringer, "A New War Drew on New Methods to Cover It," *The New York Times*, June 21, 1999, C1.

13. Barringer, "A New War."

14. Kim Campbell, "Today's War Reporting: It's Digital But Dangerous," *Christian Science Monitor*, December 4, 2001, online edition: http://www.csmonitor.com/2001/1204/p2s2-ussc.html (retrieved February 11, 2015).

15. Rem Rieder, "In the Zone," *American Journalism Review*, May/June 2003, 6.

16. Dexter Filkins, "Get Me Rewrite. Now. Bullets are Falling," *The New York Times*, October 10, 2004, 1.

17. Filkins, "Get Me Rewrite."

18. *New York Times* v. *United States*, 403 U.S. 713, 717 (1971).

19. Jane Kirtley, "Accompanying the Troops," *American Journalism Review*, April/May 2005, 60.

14

Public Diplomacy and Propaganda

Most media systems are usually under the control of the nation in which they operate. The free press model (United States, Britain, France, etc.) espouses the concept that the press must be free of government restraints to serve its constitutional mandate to report the news. The controlled press model (China, Russia under Putin, North Korea, various Arab nations, etc.) sees press restraints as legitimate and necessary for the government to function.

Further, with today's digital media, the Internet has become the choke-point vital to media freedom. And these globally competitive nations, both free and controlled, rely on public diplomacy to achieve their goals. (Public diplomacy is defined as a nation's open efforts to influence other governments and their publics.)

Public diplomacy and propaganda have much in common with the armed forces: in peacetime, they are somewhat ignored and diminished, but during time of war these activities are mobilized by governments to join the fray and to win the "hearts and minds" of both followers and adversaries. In modern times, government-sponsored short-wave radio, which reaches many millions almost anywhere on the globe, has been a preferred medium in political warfare – in World War II, the Cold War (including the Korean and Vietnam wars), and other international crises. And now, since 9/11, along with international television and the Internet it has come to the fore in the war on terrorism. For Western governments, the tools, strategies, and messages of political warfare had been neglected,

The World News Prism: Digital, Social and Interactive, Ninth Edition.
William A. Hachten and James F. Scotton.
© 2016 John Wiley & Sons, Inc. Published 2016 by John Wiley & Sons, Inc.

but were quickly being sharpened for the conflict in Afghanistan, Syria, and Iraq with the additional tools of satellite television and the Internet.

Under the Obama administration, America's efforts to influence world opinion have come into sharper focus. Secretary of State Hillary Clinton has declared Internet freedom to be a plank of American foreign policy.[1] An attack on one nation's computer network "can be an attack on all." She warned that the United States would defend itself from cyber attacks. Internet freedom was in effect placed alongside freedom of expression and the press as a policy value essential to democratic states. Further, the current State Department, while still communicating by traditional diplomatic methods, has been also using the Internet and various social media, especially Twitter, Flickr, Facebook, YouTube, etc., to communicate directly to non-Americans around the world. This policy initiative had the effect of drawing a line in the sand between the open nations of the West and the authoritarian-leaning states like China, Russia under Putin, Saudi Arabia, Iran, Vietnam, and Malaysia – all of which are trying to control or repress the Internet and its progeny.

Although the looming frictions on the Internet are a global phenomenon, the focal point for the clash of ideas and propaganda is still found in the Middle East cauldron, especially Iran, Iraq, Syria, Afghanistan, Pakistan, and the perennial standoff in Palestine and Israel.

Our "Truth" vs. Your "Propaganda"

Since the end of the Cold War in 1989 and before September 2001, global broadcasting over short-wave radio had not diminished in volume but had less impact than global television. On any given evening, an Arab in a café in Algiers, a Peruvian llama herder in a shelter in the Andes, or an African in a Ghanaian village can share a common communication experience. By merely flicking on a short-wave radio receiver and twisting the dials, each will hear the same polyglot cacophony of sounds detailing the news, unfolding diverse feature programs, and playing all sorts of music. The variety of languages spoken is immense, but each listener can, with little difficulty, find a program he or she understands. Nowhere is the prism of international communication more apparent. In short-wave radio broadcasting, one person's "truth" or news is another person's "propaganda," and vice versa. And again, one person's music is another's "noise." Transnational radio (now supplemented by global television, the Internet, and AM radio) is reaching large audiences. Cellphones are also a major conveyor of what is sometimes called public diplomacy.

For more than forty years, public diplomacy (a government's overt efforts to influence other governments and their publics) and short-wave radio were dominated by the great East–West struggle called the Cold War, which in effect ended in 1990 with the reunification of Germany and the withdrawal of Soviet troops from central Europe. But public diplomacy and propaganda wars continued on other polemical battlefields: in the Persian Gulf after Iraq invaded Kuwait; in the tragic and protracted struggle among Serbs, Croats, and Bosnian Muslims in the former Yugoslavia; in the Israeli–Palestinian struggle; and in clashes over human rights in China.

With the globalization of the economy, international frictions were for a time more concerned with economic competition and business contentions between nations, rather than with political and ideological differences. Concerns about incipient war in, say, the Korean peninsula, in Kashmir, or in the Middle East were partially replaced by worries about the flagging economies in Indonesia, Japan, or Argentina, and how these trends might undermine more stable economies of the West. For a time, political espionage was replaced by economic espionage and concerns about the global pirating of videos, movies, CDs, and computer software. For example, 90 percent of the software used on China's computers is reported to have been pirated. The privacy issue has been pushed aside by national security concerns raised by international terrorism.

Much of the torrent of messages constantly washing over the globe is not neutral or "disinterested" information (that is, news) but "purposive" communication – words, sounds, and images intended to influence people's perceptions and opinions. A great deal of what refracts through the prism of international radio is purposive and is often called "propaganda"; that is, the systematic use of words or symbols to influence the attitudes or behaviors of others. *Propaganda* is a loaded term, a pejorative epithet subjectively defined as a "persuasive statement I don't like." No one – journalist, broadcaster, writer, or educator – wants to be called a propagandist. Transnational communicators put on their ideological blinkers when they insist, "We deal in information or truth. They deal in propaganda."

International political communication (IPC), a cumbersome term though it is, is a useful and neutral expression encompassing such terms as public diplomacy, overseas information programs, cultural exchanges, and even propaganda activities and political warfare. A useful definition for IPC is as follows: the political effects that newspapers, broadcasting, film, exchanges of persons, cultural exchanges, and other means of international communication can achieve.

Without doubt, the overseas impact of private US communications is far greater than that of US public diplomacy, but the actual influence is difficult to assess. As we have seen, Western pop culture has certainly contributed to political change in eastern Europe in recent years. Unintended effects sometimes can be more profound than those caused intentionally.

The international news media of all nations play a significant role in international political communication. The privately owned media organizations of the West serve their own commercial purposes by distributing and selling news and entertainment around the globe without intentional political aims. Yet at the same time, the news media transmit a good deal of purposive official information – that is, propaganda – because all governments work hard at getting their versions of news and events into the world's news media. Much of the news from official sources in national capitals is intended to serve foreign-policy goals. News and propaganda are not mutually exclusive categories. The media serve the purposes of public diplomacy when they carry a story of President Obama's views of Iraq or Afghanistan. Yet what a US president or British prime minister says is always "news." A continuing problem for professional journalists is that of separating legitimate news from self-serving official "interpretations" of the news, whatever the source. Nevertheless, the two are often identical.

News media of authoritarian nations, less independent of official controls, often serve as unquestioning conduits of political communication from their own governments. Editors in Beijing, Moscow, or Tehran usually face no professional dilemmas over whether to carry stories supporting their governments' foreign policies. Less developed nations are mostly on the receiving end of public diplomacy, because most lack the communication capability to compete effectively on a global basis.

International Radio Broadcasting

In this day of direct-broadcast satellites, global television, and the Internet, the powerful and pervasive medium of international radio broadcasting, long capable of carrying messages around the world almost instantaneously, is still important in the poor nations of the South. According to audience surveys, listening on short-wave radio continues to increase. A BBC study found that 143 million people tune in weekly, and according to sales figures, there are about 600 million short-wave radios around the globe – half in Asia and Africa. That is indeed mass communication, beamed mainly at the most populous and poorest nations.

In the 1930s, political leaders such as Nazi Germany's Joseph Goebbels talked of international radio as a "limitless medium" and saw it as a powerful instrument of international diplomacy, persuasion, and even coercion. For more than half a century, transnational radio has been just that – a key instrument of international political communication as well as many other things. The medium enjoyed a rapid and diverse expansion and by the late 1930s was being used by national governments, religious organizations, commercial advertisers, domestic broadcasters, and educators to carry their messages across national borders.

As the twentieth century was closing, the total number of national broadcasters rose to more than 150, and the number of hours broadcast was almost double that of the 1960s.[2] Short radio messages are sent from transmitters directly throughout the world to receiving sets, but international radio's growth and diversity continue today with the utilization by national broadcasters of local AM and FM with signals sent down by satellites. The BBC does this with 800 stations around the world, 200 of them in the United States. But most people in affluent nations do not listen much to international radio and so are unaware of how pervasive it is: 1,600 short-wave stations, the voices of 160 countries. These stations offer a choice of some sixty or more language services, broadcasting for a total of 100 hours a day or more. The formats are equally diverse: newscasts, talks, interviews, editorial comment, press reviews, documentaries, and a good deal of music. News on the hour, every hour about domestic and foreign events is a common feature, but other informational programs try to reflect the broader cultural, social, and economic aspects of particular nations through dramas, music, sports events, and religious services. Today, international broadcasters often have websites as well to transmit their messages over the Internet.

Here, we are concerned with the largest international broadcasting operators. Currently, in order of numbers of weekly listeners, they are Britain, the United States, Germany, and France. The BBC World Service broadcasts in forty-three languages to 149 million listeners weekly. The Voice of America broadcasts in fifty-three languages to about 86 million weekly. Deutsche Welle goes out in thirty-five languages and uses 1,700 journalists. Radio France International uses eighteen languages to reach about 30 million weekly.[3] The most widely used languages, in descending order of usage, are English, Russian, Mandarin Chinese, Arabic, Spanish, French,

Japanese, Indonesian, Portuguese, German, Italian, Persian (Farsi), Swahili, Hindi, Hausa, and Korean.

A significant portion of international political rivalries and frictions are refracted through the prism of international broadcasting: the nationalistic and ethnic animosities in the post-Cold War world; the Arab-versus-Israeli tensions as well as those between moderate and radical Arab regimes; the North–South disputes between rich and poor nations; plus dozens of smaller regional controversies and disagreements between neighboring nations. More recently, increasing concerns about terrorism have dominated. Any major global crisis will be widely reported, analyzed, and commented upon on short-wave radio.

As the Cold War was winding down, Radio Moscow and its related Soviet broadcasters were on the air 2,257 hours weekly during 1988.[4] The United States countered with sixteen hours daily of Russian-language VOA broadcasts into the Soviet Union, while US-backed Radio Free Europe broadcast into eastern Europe, and Radio Liberty broadcast in non-Russian languages to various parts of the Soviet Union. In 1988, the United States was broadcasting globally 2,360 hours weekly; China, 1,517 hours weekly; the United Kingdom, 756 hours; and India, 444 hours.[5] By June 1994, after the demise of the Cold War, the United States had dropped to 2,000 hours weekly and Russia to 1,400 hours; China was steady at 1,600 hours, the UK was up to about 1,800 hours, and India was steady at 500 hours.

Amid the cacophony of sometimes strident and pejorative voices clashing over the international airwaves, it is important to remember that international radio also is a substantial news source for many millions, but nowhere is the truism that one person's news is another person's propaganda more apparent. Listeners can twist the dials to find a version of world events that suits their own needs and worldviews; this is especially true for people living under autocracies that lack popular support. News on international radio may often be acrimonious and self-serving, but without question it provides a diversity of news and views for untold millions. The importance of short-wave news is demonstrated, for example, when a political crisis or attempted coup occurs in an African nation. At such times, local broadcasters usually go off the air, and local residents habitually tune in to the BBC or the VOA to learn what is really happening in their own country.

With so much of what fills the night air (when reception is best) perceived by many as propaganda, the credibility of an international station's news and commentaries is crucial for its reputation among foreign listeners. The international broadcaster that has long enjoyed the best reputation for believability and objectivity is the World Service of the BBC. As a public corporation, the domestic BBC radio is financed by license fees paid by each British household with a radio or television set. The BBC World Service is not funded by license fees; instead, it receives about $160 million annually in parliamentary grants-in-aid. The government, in consultation with the service, has the final decision over which languages are broadcast, but editorial control of the programs rests entirely with the BBC. The World Service broadcasts in English and forty-four other languages and, according to its research, reaches 143 million regular listeners in a week. Of those, 122 million listen directly, whereas about 27 million, with some overlap, listen to re-broadcasts on local stations. Of the total audience, 35 million listen in English. The World Service receives about half a million letters a year; the total in 1996 was 671,002. The language used in most letters was English, with 119,897, followed by Hindi, 107,602; Burmese, 103,602; Tamil, 86,102; and Arabic, 38,303.

During Britain's brief war with Argentina over the Falkland Islands, Prime Minister Margaret Thatcher bitterly criticized the BBC for not sufficiently supporting the British war effort. Some saw this as evidence of the BBC's independence – the independence that draws so many listeners to the BBC during times of crisis.

Shortly after the BBC World Service announced the start of the Gulf War in January 1991, it expanded its Arabic-language radio broadcasts to fourteen hours a day, five hours longer than before the crisis.[6] Today, an estimated 10 million Arabs from North Africa to the Persian Gulf listen in, a far larger number than listen to either the Voice of America or Radio Moscow. The BBC is implementing an ambitious news and information expansion for the Arab world. In 2008, it started a new Arabic-language TV channel, BBC Arabic TV, which started broadcasting twelve hours daily to the Middle East, Persian Gulf region, and North Africa, and later introduced around-the-clock programming, operating with a $50 million annual budget. Arab critics wondered whether the BBC could succeed in a region where Britain is sometimes viewed with animosity. But the World Service has beamed radio to the region in Arabic since the 1930s and has long since established BBC's credibility.[7]

Another powerful voice in the region is the BBC's Persian-language TV service, on the air since 2009 and reaching an audience of 6 to 8 million Iranians – a powerful fraction of Iranian viewers in a population of 70 million. The Iranian government has singled out several foreign newscasts as biased; CNN''s English broadcasts, Voice of America, and the BBC. But the BBC's

Persian service was considered the main threat. As always with the BBC, broadcasters strive for political independence and impartiality. The Persian channel also goes to Persian-speakers in Afghanistan and Tajikistan and has an annual budget of $25 million.

US Activities in Public Diplomacy

In the past, US activities in public diplomacy shared many similarities with those of the United Kingdom, but with some important differences. The United States Information Agency (USIA) was one of the key organizations, working closely with but separately from the State Department. The Voice of America began broadcasting in 1942 and was largely under the aegis of the USIA. During the Cold War, the VOA's efforts were supplemented by Radio Free Europe, which broadcast 555 hours weekly in European languages to eastern Europe, and by Radio Liberty, which broadcast 462 hours weekly in Russian and fourteen other languages (but not English) to the Soviet Union.

The USIA, usually operating with a budget of about $900 million, employed about 12,000 people between Washington and some 275 US Information Service (USIS) posts in 110 countries. Typically, a USIS post worked under a US ambassador and included a public library. USIS personnel cooperated with local media by providing news and related material, holding exhibits, running language courses, giving seminars of various kinds, and arranging visits and cultural exchanges of both Americans and local people. However, on October 1, 1999, the USIA was abolished and the State Department absorbed most of its activities.

The VOA, and the now-disbanded USIA, both suffered from an identity crisis: were they objective news and cultural organizations reflecting the diversity of American life and culture, or were they arms of the State Department, vigorously advocating US foreign policy objectives? (This dispute has arisen again during the war against terrorism.) Past managerial participation by such well-known journalists as Edward R. Murrow, Carl Rowan, and John Chancellor suggested the former. At other times, as during the Vietnam War and the Reagan administration, the latter role has been stressed. Under Reagan, the VOA was accused of repeatedly compromising its news integrity by broadcasting misleading and biased reports.[8]

Another policy issue debated within public diplomacy circles is audience targeting, revolving around the question of who the United States is trying to influence. If it is the ruling elites of the world's nations, then the person-to-person efforts of diplomatic posts and various cultural and educational exchanges seem called for. If the target is the mass public, then expanded and more aggressive radio broadcasting seems appropriate.

After 1981, the USIA undertook the development of a government television network called Worldnet, with the potential of linking sixty overseas television systems to USIA headquarters in Washington. In addition to producing cultural and public affairs programs for local overseas networks, Worldnet employed satellite links for two-way televised news conferences between foreign journalists and American public figures. Part of the programming in its first years included a two-hour program of news and features to Europe, five days a week. During the first Gulf War crisis, President George H. W. Bush used Worldnet to address foreign publics.

Another Reagan project was Radio Marti, a VOA-linked facility patterned after Radio Free Europe to broadcast news and commentary specifically to Cuba. Named for a Cuban independence hero, the radio station went on the air in May 1985, broadcasting news, entertainment, and sports in Spanish for fourteen hours daily from studios in Washington and a 50,000-watt AM transmitter in the Florida Keys. A Television Marti service was later added and has since been more controversial. Opponents argued that since Cubans regularly listen to non-jammed US radio and television stations from Miami, the new service was unnecessary.

Public Diplomacy after the Cold War

The dramatic and unexpected ending of the Cold War during 1989–90 and the accompanying demise of communist regimes in eastern Europe profoundly altered public diplomacy, because East–West rivalries had so long dominated the propaganda wars. Most agreed that the West had "won" the Cold War. However, there was not the same certitude about many aspects of the victory. Foreign radio broadcasting by the VOA, Radio Free Europe, and Radio Liberty, as well as the BBC and the other Western broadcasters, had proved far more effective than most Western experts had supposed. In 1990, journalist Morton Kondracke commented, "If ever there was an American foreign policy success story, it's in international broadcasting. By the testimony of everyone from Václav Havel (of Czechoslovakia) to Lech Wałęsa (of Poland) to ordinary people in the streets of Bucharest and Beijing, democracy would not be what (and where) it is today without the two U.S. foreign broadcast networks, the Voice of America and Radio Free Europe/Radio Liberty."[9]

Michael Nelson, in his book *War of the Black Heavens: The Battles of Western Broadcasting in the Cold War*,[10] argues that the Western radio programs presented a compelling message of the good life that undermined communist regimes and connected listeners with the cultures of Europe and North America. Nelson believes that radio, not diplomacy or the global economy, raised the Iron Curtain.

Despite their Cold War successes, US planners talked of consolidating the US radio services as well as cutting back on their budgets because they no longer seemed needed. But due to the uncertainty of economic reforms and political instability in Russia, unrest in the former Soviet republics, and unresolved crises in the Balkans, the survival of both Radio Liberty (RL) and Radio Free Europe (RFE) seemed necessary. President Václav Havel of the Czech Republic and the new democratically elected leaders of Poland and Hungary all pleaded that the stations be saved, because they considered those broadcasts irreplaceable. The administration and Congress agreed to continue funding the stations. So, with pared-down budgets, RFE and RL moved to Prague in 1995 from Munich, where they had been since the CIA established them in 1951.

The success of RFE and RL during the Cold War led to proposals in Congress for a similar broadcaster to beam news and persuasive communications into China, ruled by a communist government and beset with human rights problems. The VOA and the BBC had played a key role during the Tiananmen Square events in 1989, by providing the only Mandarin-language news reports not controlled by China's government that were received throughout the Chinese hinterland, where most Chinese live.

Congress agreed in early 1994 to establish a new radio service, Radio Free Asia, to beam news and other programming to mainland China, Burma, Cambodia, Laos, North Korea, and Vietnam – all essentially authoritarian nations with serious human rights problems. The new station was modeled after RFE and RL, with grants set at $30 million a year. Radio Free Asia got off to a shaky start in September 1996. Neighboring countries loudly opposed it and it was resented by other international broadcasters. Most Chinese who listen to radio broadcasts are devoted to the BBC, the VOA, and Radio France International, all of which had bolstered their Asian broadcasting in the two previous years.

By early 2001, Tibet and China's western deserts were the scene of a radio battle for the hearts and minds of restive minorities in the region. The VOA was transmitting in two Tibetan dialects, and Radio Free Asia had eight hours daily of Tibetan broadcasting. Other foreign broadcasters represented Muslim separatists and Saudi religious programming. Beijing was fighting back by expanding programming in local languages and extending Chinese radio into remote corners of Tibet and the Muslim region of Xinjiang. Further, the Chinese were building facilities to jam foreign broadcasts. The jamming was called China's new Great Wall, and part of the effort to rein in the restive western province, with its threat of Muslim fundamentalism and terrorism.

On April 30, 1993, President Clinton signed the International Broadcasting Act, establishing the International Broadcasting Bureau, which for the first time combined all US government international broadcasting services under a Broadcasting Board of Governors. The board oversees the operation of the VOA, Worldnet television service, and Radio and TV Marti to Cuba, as well as Radio Free Europe/Radio Liberty and Radio Free Asia. These services transmit nearly 2,000 hours a week in sixty languages. No one knows how much money is wasted due to duplication. No one knows how many people are listening. The VOA says surveys show 65 million, but that figure could be 86 million. RFE/RL may have 20 million "listeners," defined as persons who tune in one or more times a week.[11]

US global broadcasting employs about 3,500 people. Besides the shortwave audience, millions more listen to VOA programs placed on local AM and FM stations around the world. The VOA's original programming, all of it produced in studios in Washington, DC, totals almost 700 hours a week. Most programs concern news and news-related topics. Music programs, from jazz to rock, classical to country, are popular.

Radio Free Europe/Radio Liberty broadcasts primarily from Prague more than 500 hours weekly in twenty-three languages. Its programs target central Europe, Russia, and the various republics of the former USSR, several of them near Afghanistan.

In 1994 the VOA began distributing, via the Internet, its newswire and selected newscasts and program audio files in nineteen languages, along with VOA frequency and satellite information. The VOA launched a web page on the Internet in May 1996. (The BBC World Service offers similar information on the Internet.) Using a network of fourteen relay stations worldwide, the VOA transmits its programs to its global audience via satellite, short wave, and medium wave. The connection is instantaneous, so listeners may never realize that the signal passes through several different channels before it reaches their receiver.

Since 9/11, there has been concern that the abolition of the United States Information Agency in 1999 diminished the nation's ability to conduct public diplomacy. On a per capita basis, France and many other countries, including Spain, spend more money on public diplomacy than does the United States. Yet public diplomacy is needed by a nation at war.

After the Soviets withdrew from Afghanistan in 1989, the United States began losing interest in Pakistan. After budget cuts, five American cultural centers there were either closed or greatly reduced in scope. Pakistan was only one of many countries where the United States cut its public diplomacy programs in the early and mid-1990s. Across the Arab world, where anti-Western propaganda is a staple, the Voice of America broadcasts are barely audible and reach less than 2 percent of the population in the twenty-two countries targeted. The budget in 2001, which allotted $370 billion for the military, gave $22 billion for all nonmilitary spending abroad, including foreign aid grants, VOA and radio projects, and budgets of the State Department, which has absorbed the USIA functions. Funding for foreign exchanges such as the Fulbright grants, measured in constant dollars, fell by nearly a third from 1993 to 2000. But policymakers in Washington are listening again to advocates of increased cultural exchange and public diplomacy.[12]

In 1994, when public diplomacy was being dismantled, historian Walter Laqueur warned:

> No specialized expertise is needed to realize that, far from being on the verge of a new order, the world has entered a period of great disorder. This refers to all kinds of regional conflicts as well as to the proliferation of the means of mass destruction, all of which makes nuclear war in the not-too-distant future a distinct possibility. It also refers to a potential second coming of fascism and communism and anti-Western onslaughts by other forces. . . . Cultural diplomacy, in the widest sense, has increased in importance, whereas traditional diplomacy and military power (especially of the high technology variety) are of limited use in coping with most of these dangers.[13]

The "long thin war" against terrorism has no end in sight. Without question, public diplomacy and propaganda have important roles to play; and very likely Congress will substantially strengthen various facets of the United States public efforts – the VOA and more targeted broadcasting, cultural exchanges, and more person-to-person contacts with foreign nationals overseas.

A key question for policymakers in times of war is whether the Voice of America should be a propaganda tool, pushing hard for American policy objectives, or whether it should be a reliable source of accurate, unbiased news. A former VOA director, Sanford Ungar, commented recently that before 9/11, the VOA had evolved into a highly effective and credible player in the worldwide flow of information across borders. In many hot spots around the world, its correspondents are among the best and most courageous. Its two-source rule prevents it from making mistakes common to some other international news services. It reflects the daily experience of American democracy, warts and all. "Now more than ever, the Voice of America has important work to do. It must be able to interview anyone anywhere at any time, without fear of rebuke or reprisal, in order to provide honest and full coverage of momentous events. The State Department should keep its hands – and editing pencils – off the news."[14]

New Broadcasting Board of Governors

Since 2010 a new bipartisan Broadcasting Board of Governors (BBG) led by Walter Isaacson, a prominent journalist and biographer, is supervising the Voice of America, Radio Free Europe/Radio Liberty, Radio Free Asia, the Arabic-language services Radio Sawa and Al Hurra TV, and finally Radio and TV Marti which broadcast to Cuba.

America's strongest competition has long been the BBC, which produces radio services in thirty-two languages and, as mentioned, TV programs in Arabic and Persian, and has a weekly global audience of 180 million people, which is about 10 million more than the combined audiences of the US international stations. The BBC keeps its global audience listening in on an annual budget of $420 million. America spends almost twice as much – $750 million annually – to reach a smaller audience. There were hopes that the new BBG would make the US efforts more cost effective. In any case the BBG indicates that US foreign policy is still committed to international radio in order to pursue foreign policy goals.

The Propaganda War in the Middle East

As the Pentagon geared up for war in late 2010, the White House began to mobilize its resources for political warfare. Although the 9/11 attacks had evoked sympathetic responses from Western nations, terrorism was applauded and hailed throughout the Arab and Muslim nations. Subsequent television statements by Osama bin Laden made it clear that a war of words had begun, and the United States and its allies were at best playing catchup or even losing.

World opinion, including NATO allies such as France and Germany, was overwhelmingly against the US invasion of Iraq. American popularity was at an all-time low throughout this period. America's long-time support for Israel had been an important contributor to anti-American feelings. There was a broad chasm between the way Americans saw themselves and the way they were seen by other peoples. Traditional cultures have long been troubled by the invasion of powerful outside interests, which have featured social mobility and cosmopolitan thinking and thus undermined the traditional ways of clans, religious elders – and dictators. And, of course, just the presence of over 150,000 Western soldiers in Iraq created animosity in neighboring Arab nations and subsequent problems for US public diplomacy.

These factors represented a great and perhaps insurmountable challenge to the Voice of America and subsequent satellite television efforts. The first efforts to reach Islamic audiences were ineffective. A major effort was Al Hurra ("The Free One" in Arabic), a satellite news station that began broadcasting from outside Washington, DC, with a $62 million first-year budget, to provide an alternative to pan-Arab news stations such as Al Jazeera and Al Arabia. The purpose, according to President Bush, was to cut through the barriers of hateful propaganda and provide reliable news across the region. But Al Hurra earned little praise from its target audience. Many Arab commentators were quick to condemn the new station. The consensus was that the station was an abysmal failure, and it was beset with poor ratings.

The next US entry in the propaganda war was Radio Sawa, an Arab-language pop music and news station, which was touted as a success in reaching out to the Arab world. But a State Department report on the station charged that Radio Sawa was so interested in building its audience for music that it failed to measure whether it was influencing minds.

New Battle Lines

The Internet has become a new battleground of international political communication. Although China's efforts to control the Internet and its progeny – Google, Facebook, Twitter, etc. – have been the most publicized, across Southeast Asia Malaysia, Thailand, and Vietnam have turned to coercion and intimidation to rein in online criticism. These nations have been arresting bloggers and individuals posting contentious views online. In Saudi Arabia, where 29 percent of people use the Internet, considerable filtering of political and pornographic websites takes place. In Iran, where 32 percent are online, the government operates one of the most extensive filtering systems. Internet-freedom advocates worry that more governments beyond Southeast Asia and the Middle East will follow suit and tighten Internet controls.[15]

To exploit the Internet potential to open closed societies, the Obama administration is permitting technology companies to expand online services such as instant messaging, chat, and photo-sharing to Iran, Cuba, and Sudan. The more people who have access to the range of Internet technology, the harder it is for any autocratic government to crack down on speech and free expression, one official said. And former Secretary of State Hillary Clinton stressed the importance of Internet freedom, saying that "viral videos and blog posts are becoming the Samizdats of our day," referring to censored publications passed around clandestinely in Soviet-era Russia. Other targets of closed societies are Cuba and Sudan, plus North Korea and Syria.

A new unit in the State Department is trying to counter militant propaganda in Afghanistan and Pakistan, engaging in the war of words that always goes with a war. One plan would provide $150 million for local FM radio stations to counter militant broadcasting. The project would also step up the training of local journalists and help produce audio and video programming as well as pamphlets, posters, and CDs countering Taliban messages. US officials concede they have been losing the information war in Afghanistan and Pakistan.

The US criticism of Internet censorship annoyed the Chinese leaders, who accused Secretary of State Clinton of jeopardizing relations between the two countries. The day after her speech in January 2010, a spokesman for China's Foreign Ministry called on the United States to stop using the "so-called Internet freedom question to level baseless accusations." He also insisted the Chinese Internet is open. China has the most Internet users of any nation – 384 millions officially, but also the most sophisticated system of Internet censorship, called the "Great Wall."

Editorially the *New York Times* supported Mrs. Clinton's speech, writing that she picked the right battle by calling for censorship's end and naming governments that suppress the free flow of information, including China, Russia, Iran, Egypt, Saudi Arabia, Vietnam, Tunisia, and Uzbekistan. The speech "had pointed echoes of the cold war, including a warning that 'a new information curtain is descending across much of the world."[16] Foreign governments and international organizations will continue to influence the flow of news and we can expect that the news media and the expanding millions of "netizens" and their digital gadgets will influence those nations as well.

Classic Cold War behavior reappeared during the extended 2014 confrontation between Russian President Vladimir Putin and the United States and the NATO nations. Russian journalists were suppressed (and a dozen killed); Russia blocked dissident Internet sites, and Russian television was flooded with propaganda supporting Putin's actions while distorting news from abroad. Putin's aggressive return to Cold War propaganda encouraged the US Congress to overhaul the Voice of America system. But it insisted that VOA maintain a balance between a fair presentation of the news and promoting the United States broad foreign policy goals. At the same time it said that the standards of professional journalism and for unbiased news must not be sacrificed for simplistic propaganda.

Finally the future of global freedom of expression will depend on the ability of the Internet to reject efforts in various countries to control it. As mentioned before, over the next decade another 5 billion people will become connected to the Internet. The biggest increases will come in societies that are severely censored today.

Notes

1. Mark Landler, "Clinton Making Case for Internet Freedom," *The New York Times*, January 20, 2010, 6.
2. "Candor Becoming a Staple of Shortwave," *The New York Times*, March 13, 1989, 18.
3. Daya Kishan Thussu, *International Communication* (London: Arnold, 2000), 161.
4. "Candor Becoming a Staple of Shortwave."
5. "Candor Becoming a Staple of Shortwave."
6. Deborah Stead, "BBC is Expanding its Arabic Radio Broadcasts," *The New York Times*, February 18, 1991, 27.
7. Eric Pfanner, "BBC to Begin New TV Service for Middle East," *The New York Times*, March 4, 2008, A15.
8. Carolyn Weaver, "When the Voice of America Ignores its Charter," *Columbia Journalism Review*, November/December 1988, 36–43.

9. Morton Kondracke, "Fine Tuning," *New Republic*, May 28, 1990, 8.

10. Michael Nelson, *War of the Black Heavens: The Battles of Western Broadcasting in the Cold War* (Syracuse, NY: Syracuse University Press, 1997).

11. Mark Hopkins, "A Babel of Broadcasts," *Columbia Journalism Review*, July/August 1999, 44.

12. Stephen Kinzer, "Why They Don't Know Us," *The New York Times*, November 11, 2001, A5.

13. Walter Laqueur, "Save Public Diplomacy," *Foreign Affairs*, September/October 1994, 19.

14. Sanford J. Ungar, "Afghanistan's Fans of American Radio," *The New York Times*, October 5, 2001, A23.

15. James Hookway, "Web Censoring Across Southeast Asia," *Wall Street Journal*, September 14, 2009, A10.

16. "A Good Fight" (editorial), *The New York Times*, January 23, 2010, A16.

15

Conclusions and Outlook

Modern mass communications – computers and cellphones but still including television sets and newspapers – are among the many devices and cultural artifacts of Western society that have so inexorably spread throughout the world in the last half-century. Words on paper, recordings, electronic impulses, and images on tape and film have penetrated the minds and cultures of non-Western peoples with tremendous impact. Along with pop and classical music, Hollywood movies, television programs, and youthful lifestyles have come ideas and ideology: equality, human rights, democracy, freedom of expression, individual autonomy, and free enterprise. John Locke, Thomas Jefferson, John Stuart Mill, Abraham Lincoln, and Adam Smith were Westerners, as was Karl Marx.

International communication, travel, industrialization, commerce, and trade have all participated in this Westernizing process, an aspect of globalization which perhaps should be termed the *modernization* of the world because so many non-Western societies now contribute to the process. The practices of Western mass communication have been so widely dispersed and accepted by people everywhere that the adjective *Western* perhaps should be reserved for historians, as Professor John Roberts has suggested.[1]

The 9/11 events and the 2011 and 2014 upheavals in the Arab world, as well as the tsunamis, hurricanes, and other natural disasters, showed the crucial role that professional journalism, free of government controls, plays at a time of crisis by supplying reliable and verifiable news to the world. In many nations, the familiar anchors of network television have not only reported the news but have also reassured, steadied, and consoled millions

The World News Prism: Digital, Social and Interactive, Ninth Edition.
William A. Hachten and James F. Scotton.
© 2016 John Wiley & Sons, Inc. Published 2016 by John Wiley & Sons, Inc.

of viewers. When national security is endangered or great natural calamities threaten, people everywhere are reminded how important it is to know and understand the greater world.

Checklist of Global News Impacts

To summarize some main points of this book, we list ways that the new global journalism has influenced and, yes, even changed our world, for high-speed, international news communication is something new and different – in matters of degree if not in kind. Some of these effects have been global or geopolitical, others have directly influenced the media themselves, and some effects have been felt mostly by individuals.

- *Glorious digital disruption.* For over ten years, disarray among the traditional global news media has been accompanied by a greatly increased digital flow of news and information, mainly through the Internet, that also threatens the survival of the major ink-on-paper journals and magazines as well as broadcast television and radio news. Great media companies are taking severe revenue losses through drops in circulation and advertising. But, more importantly, social media, which enable one to send brief messages anywhere at any time, have greatly changed and expanded the exchange of information (and news) throughout the world. And most of the social media are just a few years old. The Internet itself only recently had its twenty-fifth birthday. And, like the social media, it was not foreseen. Further, most social media messages are exchanged by iPhones, iPads, and computers – not by radio or television sets.

- *The triumph of Western journalism.* Since the fall of the communist "second" world, the Western concept of journalism and mass communication (really the US/UK model) has become the dominant model throughout the world and is widely emulated. In journalism, many non-Western nations have adopted not only the equipment and gadgets of the Western press and broadcasting but also their practices, norms, ethical standards, and ideology. Throughout the developing and former communist nations, print and broadcast journalists today increasingly seek editorial autonomy and freedom from government interference. These journalists understand and aspire to the professional values of fairness, objectivity, and responsibility as well as the "checking effect" – the role of the press as a watchdog of government and authority. They want to report the news as they see it – not some government's version of events. But, of course, many autocratic nations still have controlled media.

- *Globalization of media.* The internationalization of mass communication has grown hand in hand with the globalization of the world's economy. In fact, the expanding international business media play a key role in "servicing" the world economy by supplying rapid, reliable economic and financial news. Globalization has its other traits, and independent news media provide forums for dissent and complaints. The media spread has been a dynamic process and has provided more diversity and variety to the global mix, particularly in China and its neighbors.

- *Mass culture accepted.* For better or worse, Western mass media also have conditioned much of the world to use the media for entertainment and leisure. (Political indoctrination by the media has been rejected by many people.) But with the war on terrorism, political persuasion – that is, propaganda – has increased on global media. Ever-growing audiences accept and enjoy the movies, television, pop music, and even the ever-present commercials. Today, the most traditional of parents find it almost impossible to prevent the influence on their children of that most powerful engine of mass education the West has yet produced, commercial advertising. Parents and others over 30 years old almost everywhere must be offended and repelled by the noisy, brassy music videos, but there is no doubting their appeal to teenagers literally everywhere. Yet in lands under the sway of religious fundamentalism, opposition to Western mass culture remains strong, though modern and traditional cultures increasingly tend to meld and combine.

- *Global audiences growing.* Each year, literally millions more people are being drawn into the global audience, mainly through competing satellite and cable services, computers, and short-wave radio. With satellite dishes and antennas sprouting everywhere, the lands of Asia, particularly China and India, are flocking to join the global village. Experts at Google predict that with the rapid increase of cellphones another 5 billion people will join the global audience of communicators in a few years. Recent terrorism events and environmental disasters saw a tremendous surge of interest in global television news. Some Asian nations welcome global television, but others see it as a threat to their cultural identity and political stability. Across the former Third World, governments have had only limited success in blocking satellite services. Governments are finding it nearly impossible to prevent people from getting news and entertainment from the skies. Satellite dishes, which are growing smaller, cheaper, and more powerful, are easily put together from imported kits.

- *Vast audiences for global events.* Great events – the terror attack on the World Trade Center and Pentagon, or the quadrennial Olympic Games – can attract significant parts of the global audience. About 3.5 billion people watched the 1996 Olympics in Atlanta. The biggest share of that audience was in China, because more than 900 million Chinese had access to television sets, and three channels broadcast events there all day long. And during the 2014 World Cup in Brazil a vast global audience watched the matches on television.

- *History speeded up.* Nations and people today react faster to important events because information moves so quickly and widely. A bomb explodes in an airliner and security measures tighten up in airports everywhere. War breaks out in the Middle East and the price of gas at the pump goes up everywhere. Actions that would have been taken later are now taken sooner, thus accelerating the pace of change.

- *"The whole world is watching."* The reality that many millions can watch on television as tanks rumble across borders, troops storm ashore in a distant land, or police fire on peaceful protesters gives much greater import and consequences to news reports. A camcorder's report of Los Angeles police beating a man named Rodney King set off repercussions lasting for years. Video taken by camcorders in the hands of European tourists and broadcast on television showed the horror of the Asian tsunami. A discarded "home videocassette" showing Osama bin Laden rejoicing over the New York City terror attacks provided what many considered the "smoking gun" that proved his complicity in the attacks. Americans are often surprised to discover that the world often learns full details about shootings and massacres, and all about a famed golfer's marital troubles, from online sources. News that Americans consider to be local can be gossip or sensation to global publics.

- *Diplomacy changed.* Foreign relations and the ways that nations react to each other are clearly influenced by public (and world) opinion formed by global communication. Television viewers seeing starving children in Somalia can use their iPhones to exert pressure on their government to intervene with military force, although they may later regret doing so. Media discussions and debate between diplomats and leaders can clarify policy and influence nations or alliances to act. Nonstop coverage by CNN and the BBC provides the opportunity to monitor news events constantly and disseminate timely diplomatic information. But some politicians are more concerned than elated by global, real-time broadcasting, fearing a loss of control and the absence of quiet time to make deliberate choices, reach private agreements, and mold the public's understanding of events.

- *Autocrats' loss of control.* Authoritarian regimes can no longer maintain a monopoly over news and censor what their people know. They cannot stop news from coming into their nation or getting out. Short-wave radio, fax, the Internet, cellphones and videophones, and communication satellites have changed all that and blunted the power of state censorship. Throughout the Middle East, the growing impact of the Internet and Al Jazeera has meant that millions of Arabs have access to news and information not sanctioned by their governments. This is a step toward open government. During times of crisis, dictators can no longer seal their borders and control information. The news will get out. And the social media – Twitter, Facebook, etc. – are making the censors' task even more difficult.

- *"Revolution" by personalized media.* Internet blogging, desktop publishing, camcorders, and cellphones have turned individuals into communicators who can reach out to their own audiences. Even photocopiers and audiocassettes have been shown to facilitate political upheavals or revolution. So-called "citizen journalists" have become an important adjunct to professional journalism, but it's too early to say how significant and lasting this phenomenon is. Few now doubt that the Internet and social media played a crucial role in the political upheavals that shook Egypt, Iraq, Syria, and the rest of the Arab world from Morocco to Yemen.

- *Surrogate media for fettered people.* Independent media from outside now provide news and information for people who are captives of their own governments. By publicizing human rights violations, torture, and political imprisonment, independent media help those victims to survive. It has been argued that a famine never occurs in a nation with a free press because the press, by reporting incipient food shortages, will bring pressure on its government to act before people begin dying. Western reporting of the harsh and brutal life of Afghans living under the Taliban augmented the argument for US intervention. The Committee to Protect Journalists (CPJ) and Amnesty International have proved helpful in aiding imprisoned journalists.

- *Reporting pariah states.* The foreign press's persistent reporting about pariah states, such as South Africa under apartheid or the Philippines under Marcos, can apparently help to facilitate political change by forming world public opinion, which in turn can lead to actions by governments. Persistent American and European press reporting of the civil war in Bosnia and growing evidence of genocide by Bosnian Serbs undoubtedly pushed the Clinton administration and NATO to intervene and impose a ceasefire.

- *The "copycat" effect.* With global news so pervasive and widely available, sometimes imitative acts occur that have unexpected consequences. A terrorist's car bombing in one country, widely shown on television, is replicated 3,000 miles away. Somali clansmen defy US soldiers in Mogadishu, and a few days later, Haitian thugs are encouraged to stage a near-riot as US troops try to land at Port-au-Prince, causing the US forces to withdraw. Like a newly published book, an important news story can have a life of its own – extending its influence far beyond expectations.

- *Profit-driven media.* The international communication system has grown and expanded so rapidly because there was money to be made by globalization of the world economy. The profit motive is, of course, a powerful force for technological change. The INTELSAT system, a crucial early component in expanding the reach of global news, expanded so rapidly and effectively because there were real profits from a more efficient and cost-effective way to make international telephone calls. A partial exception is the "public media" as exemplified by the BBC in the UK and the NPR and Public Television in the US, which are supported by public contributions. These are major contributors to world news flow. Business journalism has flourished because a globalized economy requires reliable and unbiased information to function effectively.

Whatever their faults, the "media barons" – Rupert Murdoch and Ted Turner, among others – are entrepreneurs who will take risks and are willing to innovate. When Turner proposed a twenty-four-hour global news channel, many thought he was crazy.

Now a kind word for the much-criticized media conglomerates. Commenting on the global activities of News Corporation, Time Warner, the Walt Disney Company, Bertelsmann AG, Sony, and CNN, John Keane said, "These global media linkages have helped to achieve something much more persuasively than the maps of Gerardus Mercator ever did: to deepen the visceral feelings among millions of people (somewhere between 5 and 25 percent of the world's population) that our world is 'one world' and that this worldly interdependence requires humans to share some responsibility for its fate."[2]

- *Globalization of advertising and public relations.* The two persuasive arms of Western mass communications, advertising and public relations, have become globalized as well. Here again, the Anglo-American model, speaking English, is the world standard. Though often criticized, advertising and public relations are necessary and inevitable components of market economies and open societies. Moreover, advertising and public relations often make news and are, in fact, an aspect of news. Peoples with diverse and impenetrable languages are increasingly conversing in English or its hydra-headed variations dubbed Globish.

The Downside of Global Media Effects

Rapid change causes dislocations and inequities, and global communication certainly has its negative impacts as well.

- *Decline of printed daily US newspapers.* Despite all the attractions of digital news media, a void exists in American communication with the sharp decline of numerous daily newspapers that report local and regional news in many US communities. The three surviving major dailies that reach national audiences – the *New York Times*, *Washington Post*, and *Wall Street Journal* – are still publishing, but they are not substitutes for the daily regional newspapers that monitor local news. Our democracy and freedom of expression have been weakened.
- *The fragility of democracy and open societies.* The worldwide surge of the late 1980s toward democracy and market economies – from eastern Europe to tropical Africa and South Asia – provided the promise and possibility of press freedom and independent media in nations long under one-party or military rule. Recently, more than half, or 99 out of 191, countries held competitive elections with varying but promising guarantees of political and individual rights. Yet most efforts to move from authoritarianism to democracy have failed more often than not after most revolutions, according to Seymour Martin Lipset. He wrote that cultural factors appear more important than economic ones. Some of the factors that have promoted democracy in the past are capitalism, economic growth, a moderate opposition, British influences, and Protestantism.[3] As a result of ethnic and nationalistic clashes, the democratic outlook for some nations in eastern Europe, the Middle East, and Africa today is not promising. The "failed states" of the Arab world,

which have been unable to modernize economically or to acquire democratic rule, have been a major breeding ground for terrorists.

The failure to relieve economic misery in the newly democratic governments in Africa has led to disillusionment with democracy, and this may lead to new military or civilian dictators. L. Gray Cowan said, "In most of the African countries where they have had elected democratic governments, the fundamental problem is that they are left with precisely the same economic and social problems they had before."[4]

The rise of democracy and a free press has been associated with market economies, but market economies do not guarantee democratic societies. Currently, the capitalist nations of Indonesia, Thailand, and Malaysia have modern media systems and rising standards of living, but are not yet fully democratic and are facing financial difficulties as well. Even the robust and successful Western nations have proved vulnerable to sneak terrorist attacks. The chief characteristics of globalization – open borders, lenient immigration policies, individual freedoms including privacy protection, and ample free trade – have made the United States and Europe particularly vulnerable to terrorist attacks. Terrorism has been rightly called the dark side of globalization. And when thousands of civilians are killed or endangered, national security becomes a dominant imperative and government controls are tightened.

- *Poor nations lag in the information age.* Optimism about the trends in global communication is based mainly on what is happening in the prosperous societies of the United States, Europe, and Japan, and in the modernized sectors of China and India. Among the poorer nations of the southern hemisphere, especially in Africa, development and growth of the media and their audiences have been painfully slow, in large part because the stubborn problems of poverty, overpopulation, poor health, illiteracy, and economic underdevelopment still defy solution. African countries and some other nations are not acquiring the technology and infrastructure needed to travel on the information superhighway. In absolute terms, the poorer nations are falling further behind and becoming further marginalized. In addition, the onrush of rapid technological change is further widening the gap between rich and poor nations. The lack of skilled workers, an industrial base (including investment capital), and a literate and educated middle class precludes the poor nations from participating fully in the information revolution, particularly the Internet. When most of a country's population still lives as illiterate peasants on subsistence agriculture, as in much of Africa, Asia, and parts of Latin America, terms such as "transnational data flows," "free flow of information," or "logging on" have little practical meaning. Further, deep political and cultural differences still contribute to hatred, envy, and animosities among many millions toward affluent Westerners. The communication revolution has been coming about through education, communications, technology, and dynamic free-market economies – regrettably all in short supply in too many developing countries.

- *Declining standards.* Some critics ask, where in this commercial scramble for profits and power is the concern for serious journalism and quality entertainment? Europeans, for example, lament the decline of public service broadcasting and of quality drama and entertainment. Serious international news is often pushed aside for stories that are more sensational and celebrity-oriented. Entertainment values are degrading news values.
- *Shortcomings of audiences.* In the affluent West, the majority of people attending to mass media have only a superficial interest in and knowledge of world affairs. They may know that Russia is having economic problems, but they do not understand the reasons. Most Americans were deeply shocked by the 9/11 attacks, in part because the news media, as well as the government, had paid scant attention earlier to the possibility of surprise terror attacks on America. In less affluent nations, most people lack the education and standard of living to pay attention to world events. In many cases, their own inadequate media are incapable of providing significant foreign news.

Indications of Improvement

The expanding capacity to communicate information rapidly around a world that has become ever more interdependent has begun to erase some differences and perhaps improve understanding among diverse societies. The better-educated and more affluent people of most nations – the media users – know more about the outside world and have access to more information than ever before. The educated elites of the developing nations, though small in number, travel more and are more conversant with world affairs than were their predecessors under colonialism. However, the euphoric reaction of some in the Islamic world to the 9/11 attacks was a sobering reminder to Westerners of the widespread hatred and anti-Americanism and anti-Westernism found abroad. Americans, who like to be liked, were shocked that so many do not like them.

The international news system, despite its inadequacies, moves a great deal of information, data, and pictures much faster than ever before, and there is every indication that this flow will expand in the years ahead. Walter Goodman, a frequent critic of television, had some good things to say about the little box: "Television, that product of the West, is by its nature on the West's side when it comes to freedom of information. Censors may hedge it in and manipulate it, but they cannot contain it; the content flows across boundaries and over the globe. When Communism fell, television, which every East bloc country boss thought was his to run for purposes of celebrating himself and suppressing his critics, was among the forces that gave it a shove.... Television's natural impulse is to reveal, not conceal."[5] The same can be said about the Internet and its proliferating progeny. History seems to be on the side of openness and the free exchange of information.

These are some of the reasons why the West's version of world news and events, largely gathered and disseminated by American and west European journalists, often antagonizes and annoys non-Western governments and peoples, despite their reliance on these sources of information.

To assist governments in dealing with their formidable problems of poverty, massive debt, environmental degradation, disease, and sometimes famine, some leaders would harness mass communications – a clear invocation of the developmental concept of the press. But under the Western concept, the press must be free of government to maintain liberty, to make democracy possible, and to provide reliable and objective news. Liberty is not the same as social justice or economic equality. History shows that when press freedom is sacrificed for some "greater good," political liberty and human rights usually disappear.

To the Western journalist, the press must be independent of authority, not an instrument of government, so that it can report the news and expose the abuses of governments at home and abroad. Now more than ever, because of their global reach, governments (and corporations) need watching. But whether democratic or authoritarian, only governments – not multinational corporations or media conglomerates – have the power to start wars, nuclear or conventional; to conscript soldiers and send them off to dubious wars; to punish dissidents; to establish gulags; to "ethnically cleanse" people with a different religion – or to deal with terrorists. Media in both North and South must contend with governments that try to control, manipulate, and suppress what the news media wish to report – and often succeed. Democratic government and private ownership give the press a better chance of resisting government control and serving the public interest, but they are no guarantee of independence. (But also it should be remembered that when national security is threatened, as after 9/11, people quickly turn to government for help to counter subversive terrorism.)

Modern history is replete with regimes marred by incompetence, venality, corruption, and brutality. Some journalists believe that the world's free press has done far too little, rather than too much, critical reporting about economic failures and political abuses, especially among developing nations. This basic impasse over the proper purpose of international news communication and the relations between the press and government will continue. But the greater the threat from abroad, the greater will be the interest in and need for foreign news.

What Can Be Done

Improvements in international news communication must come from several quarters. Western journalists and mass communicators can do much to improve their own effectiveness. And governments and journalists of the communications-poor developing nations can do more to involve themselves in transnational news, both as senders and receivers. Much can be accomplished as well by nations and journalists working together through international organizations to arrive at some consensus on policy questions and proposals for improved news communication. But it should be remembered that most journalism is essentially local and parochial – it serves the interests and needs of its own audiences. Therefore, the front pages of the leading papers in Japan, Turkey, Norway, and Nigeria will always feature quite different stories. And yet high-quality foreign news is still essential and does bring diverse peoples closer together.

A central argument in journalism today is about journalistic authority – who has it and what it is worth. One view is that the democratizing power of the Internet has rendered traditional forms of journalism obsolete and implies that the public should not pay for the news. This is a new world in which readers want to have the ability to make their own judgments and express their own priorities and learn from their peers as much as from traditional sources of authority. Reliance on professional journalists is seen as elitist and stifling.[6]

Opposing their view is a conviction that a significant number of serious readers feel the need for someone with training, experience, and standards – reporters and editors – to help them learn and understand the news. This view does not preclude the use of "citizen journalists" who add to the news flow. But the authority of professional journalists is both an aid for readers too busy to sort out the news for themselves as well as a civic good for a democracy to have trustworthy information upon which to base its decisions.[7]

But, as discussed earlier in this book, a central concern for the news business today is to find ways to pay for news gathering in today's digital environment. A new business model to improve the profitability of news media is essential for their survival. Proposals and suggestions for revised business models are frequent and useful. The *New York Times*, the flagship of global news coverage began to charge fees for access for certain news stories in 2011. Online users of *The Times* have free access to a certain number of stories a month and then have to pay once they have exceeded a cap. Think of it as an article cap similar to a salary cap in sports. *The Times* says the model provides a second revenue stream to support the advertising model and also fund its journalism. Print subscribers to *The Times* have full access without an article cap. The most prominent newspaper to date with a similar plan is the *Financial Times* of London, which allows readers ten articles a month for free and charges $4.25 for unlimited access. Other publications are considering similar plans. Mobile devices offer hope as well for print media. The fact that consumers pay fees for their various iPhones, iPads, and other mobile devices offers a way for journalism to back away from its earlier mistake of offering its digital news free of charge.

In conclusion, what has happened to international news communication in the past quarter-century is, of course, only one aspect of the broad trend of the revolution in information processing and diffusion that has been transforming the modern world and its economy.

For the foreseeable future, the current system of international communication will probably retain its present basic structure, with the flow of information and news steadily expanding and audiences steadily increasing. Modifications will come mainly from the adoption of more technological and economic innovations in the media themselves. In recent decades, communication technology and economic forces have proved powerful agents of change. The future of global journalism is tied to the future of political democracies where a free press can flourish. More open societies mean greater flow and exchange of news across borders, whereas autocracies try to block or distort the flow of news.

But more than that, a reliable flow of global news and other essential information is an absolute necessity for our interdependent world, and the "closed" nations that try to block out that flow will find themselves unable to compete and prosper. Global politics and wars influence and shape international communication, and in this uncertain and danger-fraught era, the world's news media will play a central role in helping people everywhere better understand the world beyond their borders. As the media remind us, the world faces unprecedented challenges – global warning, water and food shortages, widespread poverty, and growing populations – which international organizations and nation-states seem unable to cope with. An enhanced and improved system of global news media appears essential for the world to survive.

Notes

1. John M. Roberts, *The Triumph of the West* (Boston: Little, Brown, 1985), 290–295.
2. John Keane, "Journalism and Democracy Across Borders" in *The Press*, Geneva Overholzer and Kathleen Hall Jamieson, eds. (New York: Oxford University Press, 2005), 94.
3. "New Democracies Face Long Odds for Survival," *Stanford Alumni Review*, September 1993, 5.
4. Howard French, "African Democracies Fear Aid Will Dry Up," *The New York Times*, March 19, 1995, A1.
5. Walter Goodman, "Even If Used as a Weapon, Television Is True to Its Nature," *The New York Times*, January 20, 1998, B3.
6. Bill Keller, "Editor in Chief," *New York Times Book Review*, April 25, 2010, 1.
7. Keller, "Editor in Chief."

Selected Bibliography

Abdulla, Rasha. "The Changing Middle East Media over the Past 20 Years: Opportunities and Challenges," in *The Changing Middle East*, B. Korany, ed. Cairo: The American University in Cairo Press, 2010.

Abdulla, Rasha. *The Internet in the Arab World: Egypt and Beyond*. New York: Peter Lang, 2007.

Anderson, Stewart and Melissa Chakras (eds.). *Modernization, Nation-Building, and Television History*. New York: Routledge, 2014.

Anokwa, Kwadro, Carolyn Lin and Michael Salwen (eds.). *International Communication: Concepts and Cases*. Belmont, CA: Wadsworth, 2003.

Auletta, Ken. *Googled: The End of the World as We Know It*. New York: Penguin, 2009.

Baoguo, Cui (ed.). *Report on Development of China's Media Industry*. Beijing: Social Sciences Academic Press. 2007.

Boyd, Douglas A. *Broadcasting in the Arab World*, 2nd edn. Ames: Iowa State University Press, 1993.

Chadwick, Andrew. *Internet Politics: States, Citizens, and New Communication Technologies*. New York: Oxford University Press, 2006.

Chang, T. K. *China's Window on the Window on the World: TV News, Social Knowledge, and International Spectacle*. Cressfield, NJ: Hampton Press, 2009.

Chang, Won Ho. *Mass Media in China: The History and the Future*. Ames: Iowa State University Press, 1989.

Christians, Clifford, et al. *Normative Theories of the Media in Democratic Societies*. Urbana: University of Illinois Press, 2006.

Couldry, Nick and James Curran (eds.). *Contesting Media Power*. New York: Rowman & Littlefield, 2003.

The World News Prism: Digital, Social and Interactive, Ninth Edition.
William A. Hachten and James F. Scotton.
© 2016 John Wiley & Sons, Inc. Published 2016 by John Wiley & Sons, Inc.

Curtin, Michael. *Playing to the World's Largest Audience: The Globalization of Chinese Film and TV.* Berkeley: University of California Press, 2007.

Demers, David. *Global Media: Menace or Messiah?* Cresshill, NJ: Hampton Press, 1999.

Downie, Leonard and Robert Kaiser. *The News About the News.* New York: Vintage, 2003.

Enikolopov, Reben, Maria Petrova and Konstantin Sonin. *Do Political Blogs Matter? Corruption in State-Controlled Companies, Blog Postings and DDoS Attacks.* Moscow: Center for New Media and Society, 2012.

Fengler, Susanne et al. (eds.). *Journalists and Media Accountability: An International Study of News People in the Digital Age.* New York: Peter Lang, 2014.

Fenton, Natalie. *New Media, Old News: Journalism and Democracy in the Digital Age.* London: Sage, 2009.

Fenton, Tom. *Bad News: The Decline of Reporting, the Business of News and the Danger to Us All.* New York: HarperCollins, 2005.

Friedman, Thomas L. *The Lexus and the Olive Tree: Understanding Globalization.* New York: Anchor Books, 2000.

Friedman, Thomas L. *The World Is Flat: A Brief History of the 21st Century.* New York: Farrar, Straus & Giroux, 2005.

Friedman, Thomas L. *Hot, Flat and Crowded.* New York: Farrar, Straus & Giroux, 2008.

Geyer, Georgie Anne. *Buying the Night Flight.* Washington, DC: Brassey's, 1996.

Gwertzman, Bernard and Michael T. Kaufman (eds.). *The Collapse of Communism.* New York: St. Martin's Press, 1990.

Ha, Louisa and Richard Ganahl. *Webcasting World Wide.* Mahwah, NJ: Lawrence Erlbaum, 2007.

Hachten, William A. *Growth of Media in the Third World: African Failures, Asian Successes.* Ames: Iowa State University Press, 1991.

Hachten, William A. *The Troubles of Journalism: A Critical Look at What's Right and Wrong with the Press,* 3rd edn. Mahwah, NJ: Lawrence Erlbaum, 2005.

Hachten, William A. and C. A. Giffard. *The Press and Apartheid.* Madison: University of Wisconsin Press, 1984.

Hallin, Daniel C. and Paolo Mancini. *Comparing Media Systems: Three Modes of Media and Politics.* New York: Cambridge University Press, 2004.

Hawk, Beverly G. *Africa's Media Image.* New York: Praeger, 1992.

Heisey, D. Ray and WenxiangGong (eds.). *Communication and Culture: China and the World Entering the 21st Century.* Amsterdam: Rodopi, 1994.

Herman, Edward S. and Robert W. McChesney. *The Global Media: The New Missionaries of Corporate Capitalism.* London: Cassell, 1997.

Herscovitz, Heloiza G. "The Brazilian Journalist in the 21st Century," in *The Global Journalist in the 21st Century,* David Weaver and Lars Willnat, eds. New York: Routledge, 2012.

Hess, Stephen. *International News & Foreign Correspondents*. Washington, DC: Brookings Institution, 1996.

Hoyt, Mike, John Palettella et al. *Reporting Iraq*. New York: Mellville Howe, 2010.

Isaacson, Walter. *The Innovators*. New York: Simon & Schuster, 2014.

Jones, Alex. S. *Losing the News*. New York: Oxford University Press, 2009.

Kaplan, Robert D. *The Ends of the Earth*. New York: Vintage, 1996.

Kovach, Bill and Tom Rosenstiel. *The Elements of Journalism*. New York: Three Rivers, 2007.

Lynch, Mark. *Voices of the New Arab Public*. New York: Columbia University Press, 2006.

Makunike, Ezekiel. "Out of Africa: Western Media Stereotypes Shape Images." Malibu, CA: Center for Media Literacy, 2012.

McChesney, Robert and John Nichols. *The Life and Death of American Journalism*. Philadelphia: First Nation Books, 2010.

McCrum, Robert. *Globish: How English Became the World's Language*. New York: Norton, 2010.

McKensie, *Comparing Media Around the World*. New York: Pearson, 2006.

McPhail, Thomas L. *Global Communication: Theories, Stakeholders, and Trends*. Boston: Blackwell, 2006.

McQuail, Denis. *Mass Communication Theory*, 3rd edn. Newbury Park, CA: Sage, 1994.

Merrill, John C. *Global Journalism: Survey of International Communication*, 3rd edn. New York: Longman, 1995.

Meyer, Philip. *The Vanishing Newspaper: Saving Journalism in an Information Age*, 2nd edn. Columbia: University of Missouri Press, 2009.

Mickiewicz, Ellen. *Changing Channels: Television and the Struggle for Power in Russia*. New York: Oxford University Press, 1997.

Miles, Hugh. *Al-Jazeera: The Inside Story of the Arab News Channel That Is Challenging the West*. New York: Grove Press, 2005.

Morozov, Evgeny. *To Save Everything, Click Here*. New York: Public Affairs Press, 2014.

Mueller, Barbara. *International Advertising: Communicating Across Cultures*. Belmont, CA: Wadsworth, 1996.

Nacos, Brigitte L. *Mass-Mediated Terrorism: Central Role of the Media in Terrorism and Counter Terrorism*. New York: Rowman & Littlefield, 2002.

Naisbitt, John and Patricia Aburdene. *Megatrends 2000*. New York: Avon, 1990.

Nelson, Michael. *War of the Black Heavens: The Battle of Western Broadcasting in the Cold War*. Syracuse, NY: Syracuse University Press, 1997.

Overholzer, Geneva and Kathleen Hall Jamieson (eds.). *The Press*. New York: Oxford University Press, 2005.

Pan, Philip. *Out of Mao's Shadow*. New York: Simon & Schuster, 2008.

Parks, Lisa and Shanti Kumar (eds.). *Planet TV: A Global Television Reader.* New York: New York University Press, 2003.

Paterson, Chris and Annabelle Sreberny (eds.). *International News in the 21st Century.* Eastleigh, UK: John Libbey/Luton Press, 2004.

Pavlik, John V. *Journalism and New Media.* New York: Columbia University Press, 2000.

Roberts, John M. *The Triumph of the West.* Boston: Little, Brown, 1985.

Rugh, William. *Arab Mass Media: Newspapers, Radio, and Television in Arab Politics.* New York: Praeger, 2004.

Schmidt, Eric and Jared Cohen. *The New Digital Age.* New York: Alfred Knopf, 2014.

Scotton, James and William Hachten. *New Media for a New China.* Oxford: Wiley-Blackwell, 2010.

Seib, Philip. *Headline Diplomacy: How News Coverage Affects Foreign Policy.* Westport, CT: Praeger, 1997

Semati, Mehdi (ed.). *New Frontiers in International Communication Theory.* Lanham, MD: Rowman & Littlefield, 2004.

Shenk, David. *Data Smog: Surviving the Information Glut.* New York: Harper Edge / HarperCollins, 1997.

Silvia, Tony. *Global News: Perspectives on the Information Age.* Ames: Iowa State University Press, 2001.

Singhal, Arvind and Everette Rogers. *India's Communication Revolution: From Bullock Carts to Cyber Marts.* New Delhi: Sage, 2001.

Stevenson, Robert L. *Global Communication in the Twenty-First Century.* New York: Longman, 1994.

Strobel, Warren. *Late-Breaking Foreign Policy: The News Media's Influence on Peace Operations.* Washington, DC: US Institute of Peace Press, 1997.

Thussu, Daya Kishan. *International Communication: Continuity and Change.* London: Hodder Arnold, 2000.

Tumber, Howard and Jerry Palmer. *Media at War: The Iraq Crisis.* Newbury Park, CA: Sage, 2004.

Van Ginneken, Jaap. *Understanding Global News.* Thousand Oaks, CA: Sage, 1998.

Walker, Andrew. *A Skyful of Freedom: Sixty Years of the BBC World Service.* London: Broadside, 1992.

Zayani, Mohamed (ed.) *The Al-Jazeera Phenomenon.* Boulder, CO: Paradigm Press, 2005.

Index

The World News Prism: Digital, Social and Interactive, Ninth Edition.
William A. Hachten and James F. Scotton.
© 2016 John Wiley & Sons, Inc. Published 2016 by John Wiley & Sons, Inc.

CPSIA information can be obtained
at www.ICGtesting.com
Printed in the USA
BVHW041815081118
532476BV00016BA/137/P